Princess of Wales

DULCIE M. ASHDOWN

Princess of Wales

JOHN MURRAY

Printed in Great Britain by
Fletcher & Son Ltd, Norwich

0 7195 3485 2

Contents

ACKNOWLEDGEMENTS

Extracts from J. Pope-Hennessy's book *Queen Mary* (George Allen & Unwin, 1959), from archive material in the Royal Library, Windsor, are reproduced here by gracious permission of Her Majesty The Queen. Permission to reproduce quotations from published sources in copyright has been obtained from the following:

B. T. Batsford Ltd: H. Walpole, *Memoirs and Portraits*, ed. M. Hodgart (1963).

The Bodley Head: *The Diary of a Lady-in-Waiting* . . ., ed. A. F. Steuart (1908).

Constable & Co Ltd: J. Brooke, *King George III* (1972); G. Battiscombe, *Queen Alexandra* (1969); F. A. Mumby, *The Youth of Henry VIII* (1913).

Evans Brothers Ltd: *Dearest Child* and *Your Dear Letter*, ed. R. Fulford (1964 and 1971).

Eyre & Spottiswoode: Lord Hervey, *Some Materials towards Memoirs of the Reign of George II*, vol. I, ed. R. Sedgwick (1931).

Faber & Faber Ltd: M. Collis, *The Hurling Time* (1958).

William Kimber & Co Ltd: *Lord Hervey's Memoirs*, ed. R. Sedgwick (1952).

Macmillan: *Letters of George III to Lord Bute*, ed. R. Sedgwick (1939).

Oxford University Press: *The Life of the Black Prince by the Herald of Sir John Chandos*, ed. and trans. M. K. Pope and E. C. Lodge (1910); R. L. Arkell, *Caroline of Anspach* (1939).

SOURCES OF PICTURES

CHAPTERHEAD CAMEOS

THE PRINCESSES OF WALES
IN THE ROYAL LINE

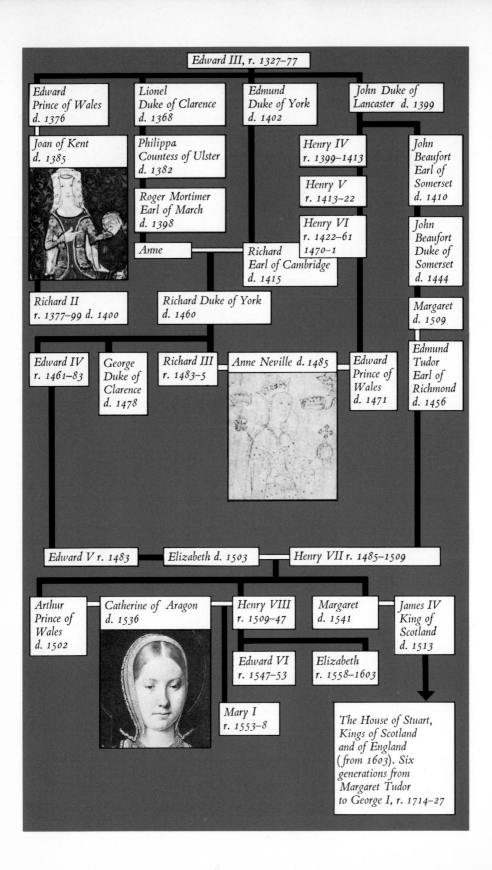

Edward III, r. 1327–77

Edward Prince of Wales d. 1376 | Lionel Duke of Clarence d. 1368 | Edmund Duke of York d. 1402 | John Duke of Lancaster d. 1399

Joan of Kent d. 1385

Philippa Countess of Ulster d. 1382

Roger Mortimer Earl of March d. 1398

Anne

Henry IV r. 1399–1413

Henry V r. 1413–22

Henry VI r. 1422–61 1470–1

Richard Earl of Cambridge d. 1415

John Beaufort Earl of Somerset d. 1410

John Beaufort Duke of Somerset d. 1444

Richard II r. 1377–99 d. 1400

Richard Duke of York d. 1460

Margaret d. 1509

Edward IV r. 1461–83 | George Duke of Clarence d. 1478 | Richard III r. 1483–5 | Anne Neville d. 1485 | Edward Prince of Wales d. 1471

Edmund Tudor Earl of Richmond d. 1456

Edward V r. 1483 — Elizabeth d. 1503 — Henry VII r. 1485–1509

Arthur Prince of Wales d. 1502 | Catherine of Aragon d. 1536 | Henry VIII r. 1509–47 | Margaret d. 1541 | James IV King of Scotland d. 1513

Edward VI r. 1547–53 | Elizabeth r. 1558–1603

Mary I r. 1553–8

The House of Stuart, Kings of Scotland and of England (from 1603). Six generations from Margaret Tudor to George I, r. 1714–27

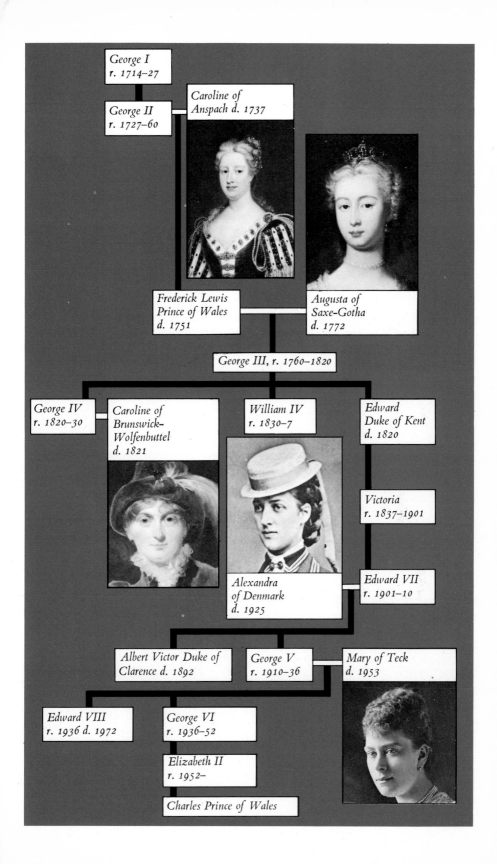

George I
r. 1714–27

George II
r. 1727–60

Caroline of
Anspach d. 1737

Frederick Lewis
Prince of Wales
d. 1751

Augusta of
Saxe-Gotha
d. 1772

George III, r. 1760–1820

George IV
r. 1820–30

Caroline of
Brunswick-
Wolfenbuttel
d. 1821

William IV
r. 1830–7

Edward
Duke of Kent
d. 1820

Victoria
r. 1837–1901

Alexandra
of Denmark
d. 1925

Edward VII
r. 1901–10

Albert Victor Duke of
Clarence d. 1892

George V
r. 1910–36

Mary of Teck
d. 1953

Edward VIII
r. 1936 d. 1972

George VI
r. 1936–52

Elizabeth II
r. 1952–

Charles Prince of Wales

Introduction

Legend has it that King Edward I created the title of Prince of Wales when his son Edward was born at Caernarvon in Wales in 1284. It is said that the King did so there and then, to appease the Welsh people whose rebellion against English rule he was repressing and whose native princes he had deprived of power. The King is reputed to have held the child up to the populace and declared, 'Here is a native-born Prince of Wales who can speak no word of English!' A colourful story, but one totally devoid of truth: the future Edward II was in his teens when he became Prince of Wales in 1301.

Since then the title has been borne by the eldest sons of monarchs, as 'heirs apparent' to the throne. When a king or queen regnant had no son, the title went into abeyance: a daughter, brother or cousin of a monarch was only 'heir presumptive', because each could be displaced in the line of succession by the birth of a son to the monarch. Thus the late King George VI was never Prince of Wales, because he succeeded his brother on the throne, and, before her accession in 1952, Queen Elizabeth II was 'Princess Elizabeth', not 'Elizabeth, Princess of Wales', and became Duchess of Edinburgh at her marriage.

Thus the title 'Princess of Wales' has never been held by a woman in her own right, only by marriage to the royal heir.★ And strangely, though there have been some twenty Princes of Wales, some died un-married, others married only after they became king: only eight of them married while they were Prince of Wales.

The first Princess of Wales was Joan of Kent, wife of the 14th-century Edward, 'the Black Prince' (grandson of the first Prince of Wales): he died before his father, Edward III. The next was Anne Neville, the wife

---

★ The future Queen Mary I was sometimes hailed as Princess of Wales in her early childhood, but she was never formally accorded the title. Sophia of Hanover, cousin and temporarily heiress of Queen Anne, occasionally signed herself 'Sophia, Princess of Wales', but with no shred of right and without royal approbation.

of Edward, son of Henry VI; Edward died in battle in his father's lifetime, but Anne later married the future King Richard III and became queen. A somewhat similar situation occurred a few years later, with Catherine of Aragon who married Arthur, Prince of Wales, the eldest son of Henry VII, and as a widow married Arthur's brother Henry VIII.

Thus the first Princess of Wales whose husband succeeded to the throne by the natural course of events was Caroline of Anspach, consort of George II – four centuries after the creation of the title of Prince of Wales. Caroline and George's son Frederick, Prince of Wales, predeceased his father, leaving a widow, Augusta of Saxe-Gotha. Two generations later, the future King George IV was Prince of Wales for nearly sixty years before he succeeded to the throne, and for twenty-five of those years he had a princess, Caroline of Brunswick-Wolfenbuttel (though since she loathed him as much as he detested her, the British public never saw the Prince and Princess of Wales together after the first year or so of their marriage).

In the last century, Albert Edward, Prince of Wales, made the title peculiarly his own: a flamboyant man aptly complemented by a beautiful wife, Alexandra of Denmark. The son of Queen Victoria, he was in his sixtieth year when he became king (as Edward VII), and so loath was he to confuse the public mind by bestowing his long-held title on his heir, the future George V, that he did so only reluctantly, a year after his accession. Until that time George was still known as Duke of York, the title he had held since infancy, though he did automatically become Duke of Cornwall, another traditional title held by the heir apparent but one not needing the specific sanction of the monarch as does that of Prince of Wales. George's wife was Mary of Teck, one of the last of the Victorian *grandes dames* in her dignity and splendour, a woman of great character still remembered with respect today, a quarter of a century after her death.

In the periods of history when there has been a Princess of Wales, that name has inspired various reactions: sometimes a princess was respected, even loved by the nation, sometimes her name evoked derision and anger. The eight Princesses of Wales have been women of widely diverse talents and ambitions, manners and morals. Their one point in common was their expectation of being the wife of a king and the mother of a king. The ways in which these women prepared themselves for their vocation, and the ways in which they fulfilled their destiny, are the subject of this book.

The Royal Succession

★ denotes a Prince of Wales

WILLIAM 'the Conqueror' reigned 1066–87. He had married Matilda of
Flanders in 1052 and was succeeded on the throne by their son

WILLIAM II, who died, unmarried, in 1100 and was succeeded by his
brother

HENRY I, who married, that same year, Matilda of Scotland, and after her
death, Adelicia of Louvain in 1120. At the King's death in 1135 the
crown was disputed by his daughter Matilda and her cousin

STEPHEN, who was generally accepted as king throughout the civil war
which ensued. He was married to Matilda of Boulogne, by whom he
had several sons who might have succeeded him, but in 1153 he was
induced to name his cousin Matilda's son Henry as his heir. A year
later Stephen died, and the crown reverted to

HENRY II, who reigned from 1154 until 1189. In 1152 Henry had married
Eleanor, Duchess of Aquitaine (divorced wife of Louis VII of France),
who gave him nine children. The eldest surviving son, another Henry,
was designated his father's heir in his lifetime (and entitled 'the young
king') but predeceased Henry II, so that the latter was succeeded by his
son

RICHARD I, who reigned some ten years, dying in 1199. Richard's queen,
Berengaria of Navarre, whom he married in 1191, was childless, so that
the crown devolved upon his brother

JOHN. Shortly after he came to the throne John divorced his wife Hawisa,
heiress of the earldom of Gloucester (by whom he had no children)
and married Isabelle of Angoulême. The King died in 1216, leaving the
throne to his infant son

HENRY III. In 1236 Henry married Eleanor of Provence, mother of his
successor

EDWARD I, who reigned from 1272 until 1307. In 1254 Edward had
married Eleanor of Castile, who died in 1290; his second wife was
Margaret of France. By Eleanor, Edward's eldest surviving son was
Edward, the first Prince of Wales, who succeeded him as

EDWARD II.* Soon after his accession, the King married Isabelle of France who, in 1327, engineered his deposition (and subsequently his murder) in favour of their son

EDWARD III,* who reigned until 1377. This king's eldest son, by Philippa of Hainault (whom he married in 1308), was Edward 'the Black Prince',* but the latter died before his father, his own son (by Joan of Kent) succeeding to the throne as

RICHARD II.* Richard married first, in 1382, Anne of Bohemia, and then, in 1396, Isabelle of France. Both were childless, and the King's successor by law was the chief descendant of his uncle Lionel, Duke of Clarence, but in 1399 his throne was usurped by another cousin, the Duke of Lancaster, and he was murdered in the following year.

HENRY IV, the usurper, first king of the House of Lancaster, reigned until 1413 and was succeeded by his son (by his first wife, Mary de Bohun)

HENRY V,* who married Catherine of France in 1420 and died two years later, to be succeeded by his ten-month-old son

HENRY VI.* This king's right to the throne was challenged by his cousin Richard, of the House of York, and in 1461 he was deposed by Richard's son

EDWARD IV, who reigned until 1470, when he was routed by the forces of Henry VI's wife, Margaret of Anjou. Henry VI was briefly reenthroned, but in the following year the Yorkists won great victories at the battles of Barnet and Tewkesbury (where Henry's only son Edward, Prince of Wales,* was killed), and Edward IV was restored. Henry was murdered in captivity.

The first monarch of the House of York, Edward IV, lived until 1483 when he was succeeded by his elder son (by Elizabeth Woodville)

EDWARD V.* In the power-struggle for possession of the boy-king, the Woodvilles were defeated and Edward's uncle, the Duke of Gloucester, gained the upper hand and possession of the King and his brother the Duke of York. Subsequently Gloucester seized the throne, becoming

RICHARD III, the boys were held in the Tower of London, to disappear from view and probably murdered by order of Richard. The King had married, in 1473, Anne Neville, widow of Henry VI's son, and by her he had one son, Edward, Prince of Wales,* who died in 1484. In 1485 Richard's tenure of the crown was challenged by a Lancastrian claimant, Henry Tudor, who defeated him at the battle of Bosworth, and became king as

HENRY VII, first monarch of the House of Tudor. Soon afterwards, Henry married Elizabeth, daughter of King Edward IV. Their eldest son was Arthur, Prince of Wales,★ who married Catherine of Aragon in 1501 and died a few months later. Thus Henry was succeeded, at his death in 1509, by his second son,

HENRY VIII,★ who married his brother's widow and fathered by her one surviving child, Mary. In 1533, Henry obtained a divorce from Catherine and married Anne Boleyn, mother of his daughter Elizabeth. Three years later, Anne was beheaded for treasonable adultery, and in 1537 the King married Jane Seymour, who gave him a son. Henry VIII married three times more, but had no more children. When he died in 1547, he was succeeded by Jane Seymour's son

EDWARD VI,★ then still a child, who died before reaching maturity (and unmarried) in 1553, whereupon the throne was seized by the Duke of Northumberland on behalf of Edward's cousin

LADY JANE GREY, but she reigned for only a few days before Henry VIII's daughter by his first marriage,

MARY I, overthrew the usurpation. Mary married Philip II, King of Spain, whom she created King Consort, but died childless in 1558. Her successor was her half-sister (daughter of Henry VIII by Anne Boleyn),

ELIZABETH I, who never married and died in 1603, leaving her crown to her cousin King James VI of Scotland (a great-great-grandson of Henry VII) who also became

JAMES I of England. James had married Anne of Denmark in 1589 and their eldest son Henry became Prince of Wales★ at his father's accession to the English crown. But Henry died in 1612 and James's successor, at his death in 1625, was his son

CHARLES I.★ Soon after his accession, Charles married Henrietta Maria of France. In 1649 the King was tried by his Parliamentarian enemies for alleged crimes against Church and State, and executed.

After an interregnum of some eleven years (during part of which the Protectorate of Oliver Cromwell was established), the nation invited Charles I's son

CHARLES II★ to return from exile and take the throne. Charles subsequently married Catherine of Braganza but had no children by her and was succeeded in 1685 by his brother

JAMES II. James had married Anne Hyde in 1660, and had two daughters,

Mary and Anne. By his second wife, Mary of Modena, he had a son, James Francis Edward, Prince of Wales,★ born in 1687. The following year the King was deposed by his son-in-law, Mary's husband, William of Orange, and sent into exile with his second family.

In 1689 the crown of England was offered jointly to the Prince and Princess of Orange, who reigned as

WILLIAM III and MARY II. Mary died in 1694, her husband in 1702, and since they were childless, the crown devolved upon the second daughter of James II,

ANNE. The queen had married George of Denmark in 1683 and had several children by him, but none survived. Rather than have the crown return to the exiled, Catholic Stuarts, it was decided to offer it to Anne's German, Protestant cousins, descendants of James VI and I. Thus it was that

GEORGE I, of the House of Hanover, came to be King when Anne died in 1714. By his (divorced) wife Sophia Dorothea of Celle, George had one son, who succeeded him in 1727 as

GEORGE II.★ George had married Caroline of Anspach in 1705, and at his accession to the throne their eldest son, Frederick Lewis, became Prince of Wales.★ But the latter (who married Augusta of Saxe-Gotha) pre-deceased his father, and George II, who died in 1760, was succeeded by Frederick's son

GEORGE III.★ Soon after his accession, George married Charlotte of Mecklenburg-Strelitz. This king reigned for some sixty years (though a regency was latterly exercised on his behalf when he was declared mad), but in 1820 he was succeeded by his son

GEORGE IV.★ George had married Caroline of Brunswick-Wolfenbuttel in 1785, and had one daughter by her, Charlotte, who would have succeeded him on the throne had she not died in 1817. Thus, at George's death in 1830, he was succeeded by his brother

WILLIAM IV. William had no surviving children by his wife, Adelaide of Saxe-Meiningen, and was succeeded in 1837 by his niece (daughter of his late brother Edward, Duke of Kent)

VICTORIA. Queen Victoria's eldest son (by Albert of Saxe-Coburg-Gotha, Prince Consort) was Albert Edward, Prince of Wales, who had lived some sixty years before succeeding his mother, as

EDWARD VII,★ in 1901. In 1863 he had married Alexandra of Denmark, and their surviving son came to the throne at his father's death in 1910 as

GEORGE V.* George had married Mary of Teck in 1893, and the eldest of their sons succeeded him as

EDWARD VIII* in 1936. But before the year was out the King had abdicated (becoming Edward, Duke of Windsor), and his brother Albert, taking the name

GEORGE VI, became King. By his wife Elizabeth Bowes-Lyon, George VI had two daughters, the elder of whom succeeded him as

ELIZABETH II in 1952. By her husband Philip, Duke of Edinburgh, Her Majesty has four children, the eldest of whom, CHARLES, Prince of Wales,* is her heir.

MEDIEVAL ENGLAND

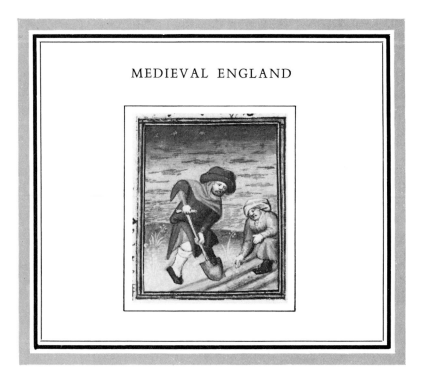

A time-traveller flying over medieval England would sight few man-made landmarks to direct his course. Rivers and ranges of hills would be his main guide-lines, with here and there a town – London, York, Coventry, Bristol and Norwich, but as yet no Birmingham or Manchester or any of the great conurbations of the midlands and north. For the rest, there were vast tracts of forest and heath, gradually being cleared as the centuries of the Middle Ages passed.

The population of England south of the Tees in the period 1100 to 1500 has been estimated at some million and a half at the earlier date increasing to twice that figure by 1500. London was England's capital, but its inhabitants still numbered only some 50,000; York's 10,000, with 5,000 for the then leading trade-centres of Bristol, Coventry and Norwich; maybe half that number, or as little as a thousand, for the county towns and boroughs. Between 5 and 7 per cent of the population lived in towns; the rest were scattered over the land in villages, which were often little more than a few huts in forest clearings.

If our time-traveller ignored the natural contours and sought major roads to guide his flight, he would soon become lost. Hoof-trodden, wheel-rutted tracks (with the occasional vestige of a stone-based Roman road, survival of a thousand years) were the arteries of English trade and news. There was little need for more, for most of the population was stationary, providing for their needs from local resources: even large towns were provisioned mainly from suburban fields. News permeated slowly through medieval England: if a would-be traveller lacked a horse, he must rely on his own feet or a passing cart to take him to his destination, trusting to local information to direct his way.

There was gradual social and economic change in the Middle Ages, but it was slow and haphazard, far less easily charted than political developments.

At the beginning of the period, England had only recently suffered an invasion – by the Normans under William 'the Conqueror', who overran the land, replacing the Anglo-Saxon kings and lords. In the centuries that followed, the Norman-French families maintained their rule over the 'occupied' country, a recognisable and resented caste of aristocracy. In many respects they bore a marked resemblance to the Victorian administrators in India, who kept their own language and customs in their adopted land, speaking the native tongue only to underlings of the oppressed race, their loyalties always reserved. Until the loss of the English empire in France (which, at its greatest extent, stretched down the west coast, and far inland, from Channel to Mediterranean), many lords had estates on both sides of the Channel, and England's policies were frequently dictated by Continental interests.

The visible legacy of this period are the great structures, military and ecclesiastical, on which so much effort and expense were lavished by the Normans. Their massive castles still dominate many hills, reminders that England was occupied territory; their cathedrals still soar heavenward, witnessing to a confident 'age of faith'. But while stone endures, wood and plaster, the building materials of farm and cottage, soon disintegrate: little is left today to show how the 'average' Englishman lived.

Who was the 'average' Englishman? Certainly not one of the Norman élite, privileged in status and usually in wealth, only very gradually absorbed into the population. Already by 1100 the English were a diverse people, their local dialects far more prevalent and bewildering to strangers than they are today. But then, England had been invaded and colonised so many times that there was a mixture of races in amazing variety: Britons, Celts, Romans, Angles and Saxons, Norse – and then Normans, gradually mingling by intermarriage: even so, there remained (and would for hundreds of years) pockets of recognisable 'racial types'.

Nor was the average Englishman a townsman, as we have seen. Most of the population not only lived on the land but were tied to it. Serfs, or 'villeins', were characterised by their obligation to remain on the manor on which they were born, forbidden to leave it without express orders or permission. In return for the small parcels of land which they cultivated to meet their families' needs, these serfs owed their lord specified labour on his own land, especially at ploughing and harvest-times, with their specialised skills (such as smithing or coopering) always at his service; they were liable to 'fines' at marriage or to receive an inheritance, and all their misdemeanours and disputes were settled locally, in the manorial court. Serfdom continued in England (in varying degrees according to locality) to the end of the Middle Ages; though it had almost disappeared by 1500, some vestiges of the system remained in the customary dues owed by a peasant to his landlord, usually, by then, commuted into a money payment and becoming indistinguishable from the rents paid by freemen. In fact, the serf had always existed alongside the freeman, their life-style and possessions often in parity; a serf could also, with permission, hold land by rent instead of labour-dues, an anomalous situation which upsets the neatness of the so-called 'feudal system'.

But, slave or free, Englishmen knew who their masters were, and it was centuries before the Norman nobility truly identified with England.

Medieval English society has often been described as a pyramid, with the King at the apex, under him the great magnates who held their land from him directly in return for service in government and war, and below them the barons and knights who tenanted their estates – with their own tenants, free and servile, at the base. All were bound together by mutual obligations, ideological, legal and personal. Also inside this system was the Church, whose higher clergy often held land of the King on terms comparable with those of the lay nobility (English bishops still sit in the Parliamentary House of Lords along with lay peers, in direct line from their medieval predecessors). Outside the system were the towns, slowly growing in importance as the centuries passed. Townsmen were freemen, accountable (under the King) only to their own rulers – the mayor, aldermen and councillors whom we still know – and their own courts.

The King and the various degrees of landowners, lay and clerical, wielded the real power in the kingdom in the first centuries of the Middle Ages. Even before the Norman conquest, it was a recognised principle that the King must govern in consultation with his lords. King John, early in the 13th century, was forced to give his barons their 'Magna Carta' as a guarantee that their rights in government would not be overridden by royal high-handedness. But gradually the royal council broadened its composition to take on recognisable characteristics of our modern Parliament. The early Norman assemblies were aristocratic in complexion, but from the mid-13th century the 'Commons' – knights of the shires and representatives of the boroughs – were regularly called out to take their place with the peers. Their prime function and obligation was to vote taxes for the use of the executive, but in the 14th century they began to take an ever-more vociferous share in legislative business too. In 1348 a landmark was reached when the Commons asserted that redress of grievances must precede their vote to taxes to the King. Such temerity was not firmly maintained: the power and ambition of the Commons fluctuated throughout the Middle Ages and beyond; but the Commons always remained a force to be reckoned with, a force for change and – after many centuries – for democracy.

Nevertheless, the King was still the fount of power and honour, title and wealth, through to the end of the period. Kings might temporarily be forced into submission to a group of magnates, but they had time on their side: a dynasty of strong men (such as the Norman and Plantagenet kings of England certainly were, with but few exceptions) endured beyond transitory political conditions.

In the Middle Ages, royal power was not bounded by the sea: the Norman duchy and the vast lands of Gascony made English kings a vital factor in Continental affairs, continually brought into rivalry with their neighbour France, even before King Edward III laid claim to the French crown itself in the early 14th century. Kings and their armies were the main travellers of the Middle Ages; cumbrous and slow-moving as royal armies were, they could fight one year in southern France, another in rebellious Wales, another against the neighbouring kingdom of Scotland. Land was the basis of power in the Middle Ages, and any number of lives were expendable to win or keep it. In the 15th century Henry V won the kingdom of France to his great glory, but only by far over-extending his resources. It could never be held. In the next reign not only the French kingdom but also the great bulk of English territory abroad were lost: it was shaming at the time, but out of such defeat came the growing 'national consciousness' of England, restored almost to its natural frontiers.

Many men died in war in England and across the Channel, but in a society with only the most primitive medical knowlege, many more were carried off by disease and accident. The great plague known as the 'Black Death' which swept through the country in the 1340s was disaster and catastrophe with its immense toll of lives (some 25 per cent of the population is the usual estimate), but even without such an unusual episode, the death-rate was always high. Infant mortality rates cannot even be guessed at, so usual was death at or soon after birth, while women's death in childbirth was a continual hazard. Few men or women lived to be old in the modern sense.

And what of the women of medieval England? It was the men who went to war and to Parliament, who held the vast majority of the offices of the Church; in the whole of national life, spiritual and temporal, it was the men who made the rules and wielded the power. No medieval man would criticise the system; no woman denounced it. To the medieval mind, male dominance seemed a natural as well as (by contemporary inter-pretation) a God-given law.

In theory, women were cruelly dominated by men, the possessions of fathers and husbands from the cradle to the grave, to be given and taken in marriage at male whim, denied the right to own property, barred from public office, shut out from higher education. In fact, then, as for many centuries, a clever woman could occasionally circumvent convention, could make her opinions well known in her family and through a com-plaisant husband influence her community; marital love did exist – even under the system of arranged marriages – and shared interests in family and estate or business were a great bond where it did not. In the lowest classes, a woman was no mere ornament, no housebound housewife, but shared the bread-winning by toiling in the fields with her husband; hundreds of entries in town and guild records show women working alongside their husbands in shops and businesses; the great lady was ex-pected to supervise armies of servants, and, in time of war, occasionally to have direction of more serious armies in defence of castle and estate in the absence of her husband. Lip-service might everywhere be paid to the theory of female insignificance and subservience, but in practice, women were an essential labour-force and, when circumstances permitted, well able to hold their own.

Very, very few women were literate. In fact, literacy of any degree was largely the preserve of the clergy, who were the only beneficiaries of higher education and who made up the bulk of the learned professions. No serf would need literacy in his daily drudgery, few knights would find a use for penmanship; for tradesmen and artisans, counting and a good memory would serve well in place of reading and writing; not every king in the Middle Ages could write – King John did not sign Magna Carta but set his seal to it. Until the very end of the 15th century, every book was hand-written – by monks, in the main – and books were costly

and rare. Only the very rich, the devoutly pious or the very highly educated would aspire to possession of books (which were, almost invariably,
written in Latin or French anyway). If a man could write his own name,
he could do more than most; if he could read a book, he would be
accounted a scholar: few women shared the distinction.

This, then, was the England of the Middle Ages: strange, it seems to us
now, accustomed as we are to overcrowding and intensive cultivation of
the land, to democracy and mass literacy, to notions of the equality of the
sexes. But the change most noticeable of all is surely the difference between
medieval living-standards and our own: while the poor lived in huts
with earth floors and smoke-holes in the roof, even the richest noble was
accustomed to the bitter chill of stone-built castles, devoid of running
water, without adequate sanitation. Life was full of pain, from birth to
death, with barbaric punishments for crime vying with barbaric surgery
to make life miserable.

And yet, against such a background, almost unimaginable today, men
and women not only survived but could be happy, could laugh and love
and sing just as we do. At the end of the 14th century the poet Geoffrey
Chaucer wrote his verses about pilgrims making merry on their way to
Canterbury – verses which are still fresh and lively today, and in which
we can find men and women little different from ourselves in their love
of life.

Those pilgrims were the contemporaries of Joan of Kent, the first
Princess of Wales, a woman of the Middle Ages.

Facing: *A miniature of Joan of Kent in a contemporary manuscript written at
the Abbey of St Albans, of which she and her husband were patrons*

THE FIRST PRINCESS

Joan of Kent

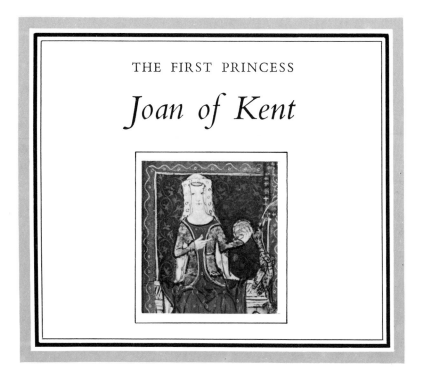

The first Princess of Wales was Joan, 'the Fair Maid of Kent', wife of Edward, 'the Black Prince', who was the grandson of the first Prince of Wales (subsequently King Edward II) and son of King Edward III. As the Black Prince predeceased his father, however, Joan never became Queen.

She was herself of royal blood, through her father, Edmund, Earl of Kent, one of the sons of Edward I by his second wife and thus half-brother of Edward II. Joan's mother was Margaret Wake, daughter of Lord Wake of Liddell, who had married Edmund after the death of her first husband, John Comyn of Badenoch, a kinsman of the Scottish royal House.

The exact date of Joan's birth is not known, but it is thought to have been in the year 1328. It was a troubled time for England, for only a year earlier King Edward II had been dethroned by his wife, Isabelle of France, and her lover, Roger Mortimer, who now controlled the government. The Earl of Kent had assisted in his half-brother's overthrow, but he was appalled when he learned that Isabelle had subsequently had her husband murdered. When he heard rumours that the King was not dead but in hiding, Edmund gladly pledged his sword to restoring his half-brother.

In fact, Edward II *was* dead, and the rumours were mere fabrications by men who had cause to hate or fear the Isabelle/Mortimer regime and who wished to draw to their cause this Earl who was so influential throughout the country. But their conspiracy failed. In March 1330, Edmund, Earl of Kent, was arrested. On the 16th, at Winchester, he confessed his complicity in the plot against the Queen. Three days later he was beheaded.

When Edmund was condemned as a traitor, his estates were confiscated and his family were imprisoned. His children, Edmund, Joan and Margaret, and his wife, who was in advanced pregnancy, were sent first to Salisbury Castle, then, soon after the Earl's execution, to the great fortress of Arundel. There, on 7 April, his posthumous son was born.

However, the unpopular rule of Isabelle and Mortimer could not long survive, for there was much discontent in England. The Queen's son, the adolescent puppet-king Edward III, himself headed another conspiracy against her and seized power. Isabelle was put into safe custody – Mortimer was murdered. By January 1331 the verdict on the King's uncle had been reversed and his possessions restored to his wife and elder son.

The child Joan, who can have understood little of her family's troubles apart from their sudden moves from castle to castle, had by then already been provided with a permanent home by Edward III's young wife, Philippa of Hainault. The Queen had one child already, her son Edward (the future Black Prince), born in June 1330, and he and his cousin Joan, some two years his senior, were sent to the palace of Woodstock in Oxfordshire where the royal nursery was to be housed. As the years passed, they were joined by several more baby princes and princesses.

The Court was always on the move, settling at Westminster or Windsor or one of the royal manors in the shires as the business of government demanded. Edward III was often abroad too, for scarcely had he come to the throne before he embarked on a long-drawn-out war with France. Such an itinerant life was not deemed conducive to a healthy childhood, and Woodstock was a safe, comfortable home for the royal children during their first years. Sir William and Lady Catherine Montague (from 1337 Earl and Countess of Salisbury) took the place of parents to Joan and her cousins, and their own children, William, born in the same year as Joan, and John, two years their junior, joined them.

Joan of Kent was probably not educated to any high degree. Like most noblewomen of the age, she was taught to read and write in French, the lingua franca of international court-life and the language of contemporary courtly literature. (It was to be several years before the poet Chaucer popularised English as a language fit for poetry and romance – until then

Facing: *The tomb-effigy of King Edward III in Westminster Abbey*

it was regarded as the language only of the common people, unfit to express profound ideas and fanciful images.) Joan would also have learned to cast accounts, to sing and dance and probably to play on a stringed instrument. She would learn enough Latin to understand the Mass, but it is unlikely that she would have been able to do more than pick her way through the Latin documents in which royal clerks detailed her property at the time of her approaching marriage.

Girls of noble and royal birth were married young in the 14th century. As granddaughter of Edward I and sister of the Earl of Kent, Joan was a very eligible *partie*, and even before she entered her adolescence, there were plans afoot to marry her to William Montague, a suitable match in terms of their families' titles and estates.

However, Joan had a mind of her own. In 1340, at the age of twelve, she fell in love with, and secretly married, the Salisburys' steward, Thomas Holland. It is not surprising that she was afraid to ask permission to marry him openly. First, it was unheard-of for a young noblewoman to choose her own husband, for by all the *mores* of contemporary society, a girl was bound to accept her parents' choice, especially if a great fortune were at stake. Sometimes a girl might even be expected to marry a man she had not seen before her wedding-day; sometimes she might already know and dislike her bridegroom; only the fortunate few might marry men they cared for, and then that was only a happy adjunct to more material considerations. Among the nobility there were very few love matches though occasionally a widow, in possession of her own fortune, might be so independent as to choose her own mate. Only the poor – the most fortunate class, perhaps, in this instance – might marry for love with impunity. In Joan's case, the son of a mere knight, employed as a steward, would never be considered a fit match. There was no chance that her mother could be persuaded to deem him worthy of her hand.

Thomas Holland, twenty years old to Joan's twelve, must have been attractive indeed to warrant her defiance, albeit secret, of social conventions. But marry him she did. Perhaps the form the wedding took was merely that of a solemn betrothal *per verba de praesenti* – that is, a vow in front of witnesses rather than a ceremony performed by a priest. But such a betrothal by adult consenting parties was equally binding in the Middle Ages. Nevertheless, even after the wedding, Joan and Thomas dared not confess what they had done: some way might be found to part them.

No sooner were the couple married than Holland went away to the wars, hopeful, most likely, of returning with battle-honours and rich

Philippa of Hainault, wife of Edward III: her tomb-effigy in Westminster Abbey

King Edward III presides over a tournament held in honour of the Countess of Salisbury. For centuries historians have debated whether it was Joan or her mother-in-law who, as Lady Salisbury, was the object of the King's attentions. (Illumination in a 15th-century Flemish edition of Froissart's Chronicles.)

booty to claim his bride. There were great fortunes to be made and high titles to be won by fearless knights who also had luck on their side.

Thus Joan, left alone in England, was in a difficult position when, about a year later, her wedding to William Montague was at last arranged. She must have had qualms of conscience, as well as heartache, when she made the decision to obey her mother and marry William. Without much hope of ever being allowed to live with Holland – who might, after all, be killed in battle at any moment – and, as she later asserted, not daring to go against the wishes of her family, Joan gave in. She probably realised that she could petition (as she later did) for a divorce from Montague on the grounds of her pre-contract with Holland.

As wife of the Earl of Salisbury (William's father died in 1344 and he inherited the title), Joan was one of the leading ladies at Court. Her youth was no bar to her position, for an adolescent girl was considered already sufficiently mature to supervise the great household maintained in her husband's castles and to hold her own in sophisticated Court society. And it was a splendid era for young women fond of dress and entertainment for Edward III was staging the most exciting and colourful series of tournaments ever seen in England. While knights displayed their prowess in jousts and mock battles, ladies too played their part: they would lead out their chosen knights to the tournament-ground in gay processions and sit in decorated *loges* to watch the fray.

A contemporary chronicler was shocked by the extravagance and immodesty of these Court ladies, and he wrote:

In those days arose a great rumour and clamour among the people that whenever there was a tournament, there came a great concourse of ladies of the most costly and beautiful but not of the best in the kingdom, sometimes forty or fifty in number, as if they were part of the tournament, in diverse and wonderful male apparel, in divided tunics, one part of one colour and one of another, with short caps and bands in the manner of cords wound round the head and cones well bound with gold and silver, and in pouches across their bodies, knives called daggers; and thus they proceeded on chosen coursers or other well-groomed horses to the place of their tournament, and so expended and devastated their goods and vexed their bodies with scurrilous wantonness that the rumour of the people sounded everywhere; and thus they neither feared God nor blushed at the chaste voice of the people.[1]

In later years there were many 'chaste' mutterings against Joan's love of immodest dress, so probably she was one of the sinners in this case also.

Still, she had good reason to deck herself out, for she had beauty that could only be enhanced by finery. Queen Philippa's secretary, the chronicler Froissart, described Joan as 'the most beautiful and lovable woman in the kingdom of England in her time'[2] and a French chronicler wrote that she was 'one of the loveliest women in the world'.[3] From contemporary pen-portraits it seems that Joan was of medium height, with a good figure; she had an oval face with a bright complexion, which flushed and paled when she became excited; she had expressive dark eyes and waist-length, bright auburn hair. Nor, it seems, did she discourage admiration.

The 14th century saw the height of the convention known as *fine amour*, courtly love. Marriage was a uniting of great names, fortunes and political interests, not an affair of the heart, and a wife was expected to be totally submissive to her husband's will; but in 'courtly love' she might choose a knight (not her husband) who would offer her the admiration and devoted service of a lover, while she could be as capricious as she chose with her 'servant'. The knight might, or might not, share her bed depending on the lady's fidelity to her husband, or on their opportunities. That the sighings and oglings of courtly love might be a mask for adultery was widely recognised, but few husbands would risk humiliation by revealing their suspicions unless the lady was so indiscreet as to arouse whispers and nudges among their friends. Most of the young married people of the Court played the game of *fine amour* – the unmarried girl did not, for she must wait until safely protected by matrimony to display her talents and graces to men in general.

There is no evidence that Joan chose a knight according to these conventions while she was Salisbury's wife, but some sources claim that she was openly admired by no less a person than her cousin the King himself. She has been identified, though with no certainty, as the lady who dropped her garter in the midst of a Court ball: the King picked it up, exclaiming *'Honi soit qui mal y pense'* ('Evil to him who evil thinks') with true chivalric courtesy, when courtiers sniggered. Later – the exact date is not known – Edward III founded the Order of the Garter, to this day the highest order of English knighthood, with the garter itself as its symbol.

It is also said that Joan was Edward's mistress at one time, or, alternatively, that he once raped her. For years historians have written learned essays arguing whether it was Joan or her mother-in-law (only a couple of years older than Edward) or some other lady who was so honoured by the King. In view of Edward III's later opposition to Joan's marriage to his eldest son, it may well have been she.

Joan lived with the Earl of Salisbury (though she had no children by him) until Holland's return and his demand for his wife in 1347. Until then he had been rarely in England, making only brief visits in 1341 and 1342 when he was still in no position to claim Joan. Late in 1343 he went on crusade against the Moors in Spain before joining Edward III in his war in France. It was from that time that Holland began to accumulate a vast fortune from the ransoms of prisoners taken in battle. In 1347, with sufficient resources behind him to pay the costs of a divorce, he petitioned the Pope to recognise his marriage to Joan and declare null that with the Earl of Salisbury. Inevitably, the wronged husband was furious; he even imprisoned Joan for a time in one of his castles. However, strangely, all three parties in the dispute were together for Christmas 1348, at the royal gathering at Otford. It must have been embarrassing for them all.

Then, in November 1349, the Pope declared in favour of Thomas Holland, and at last Joan was free to go to the man she loved. Surprisingly, Salisbury seems to have shown no resentment. He married again and had children, and many years later, when Joan was the widowed Princess of Wales, he figured high in the list of her political counsellors. He must have been in daily conference with his former wife, and he seems always to have been loyal to her interests.

Sir Thomas and Lady Holland could not afford to live in the high state to which Joan was accustomed. The divorce had been expensive, and Holland's remaining booty money was not sufficient to provide the same luxuries as the rents and tributes which a landed earl enjoyed. In fact, in August 1352, Holland was awarded a royal pension of a hundred marks a year, 'for the better support of his wife' (another mark of Edward III's favour to his former mistress?). But in 1353 all such problems were solved when Joan's brother died and she inherited his earldom of Kent and the lordship of Wake, which had come to the family through her mother who had died in 1349. Thomas Holland was called, 'by courtesy', Earl of Kent.

By that time Joan and Thomas were rearing a young family. Their first son, Thomas, was born in 1350, John in 1352. There was another boy, Edmund, who died in childhood, as well as two daughters, Joan and Maud.

In 1358 Joan went abroad with her husband when he became governor of an English-held fortress in northern France. He was later appointed to supervise the execution of the terms of the Treaty of Bretigny, by which England and France made peace in 1360. But only a few months later, on 28 December 1360, he died. In the new year Joan returned to England, a widow in her early thirties.

It was not to be expected that she would long remain unmarried. After all, she was a peeress in her own right, with fortune enough to tempt any man, besides having abundant personal charms. Soon, several lords and knights were vying for her favour.

One of her suitors, Sir Denis de Brocas, begged Joan's cousin the Prince of Wales to use his influence with her on his behalf. When Prince Edward approached Joan, however, she would have none of the hopeful young man, saying that she would never marry again. A contemporary chronicler recorded the scene:

The Prince was enchanted with her.

'Ah, my dear cousin, is it the case that you refuse to marry any of my friends in spite of your great beauty? Although you and I are of the same lineage, there is no lady under heaven that I hold so dear as you.'

Thereupon the Prince became greatly enamoured of the Countess. And the Countess commenced to weep like a subtle and far-seeing woman. And then the Prince began to comfort her and kiss her passion- ately, grievously distressed at her tears, and said to her,

'I have spoken to you on behalf of one of the most chivalrous men in England and one of the most honourable of men.'

Madame the Countess replied in tears to the Prince,

'Ah, sir, before God, do not talk to me thus, for I have given myself to the most chivalrous knight under heaven, and for love of him it is that, before God, I will never marry again as long as I live. For it is impossible that I should have him as my husband, and my love for him parts me from all men: it is my intention never to marry.'

When the Prince begged Joan to tell him who it was that she loved, she refused to divulge his name at first. But when the Prince swore that he would always be her enemy if she would not tell him, Joan said:

'My dear and indomitable lord, it is you, and for love of you that I will never have any other knight by my side.'

As they fell into each other's arms, Prince Edward declared:

'My lady, I also vow to God that as long as you live, never will I have any other woman save you to be my wife.'[4]

Thus, within nine months of becoming a widow, Joan of Kent married the Prince of Wales.

The Black Prince, as Edward later became known (probably from the colour of the armour worn by his effigy over his tomb in Canterbury Cathedral, for he was not so named until two centuries after his death), was already an internationally famed war-hero. At the age of sixteen he had played no mean part in his father's victory over the French at Crécy. He was awarded no command in that battle, no control over tactics, for he was totally inexperienced, but this was a good opportunity for him to display personal prowess and courage, which he did in no small measure. Thereby he also won the prestige necessary to command the respect of the knights who would later take his orders. At the later battle of Poitiers Edward was in full command of an army and won an overwhelming victory over the French against tremendous odds. He thus became one of the most admired military commanders of his day.

Tall, robust and good-looking, two years Joan's junior, the heir to the throne of England was a fine catch as a husband. Joan may indeed have been 'a subtle and far-seeing woman' to win such a prize. However, from the evidence of their years of harmonious marriage, there is no reason to believe that Joan was not fond, at least, of the man who seems always to have been faithful to her. (The Prince had three bastard sons, it is true, but they were all born before his marriage to Joan.)

Edward III was not pleased with his son's choice. It may have been that he resented the Prince's marrying his own former mistress, though the King never brought such a charge against Joan to prohibit the marriage. More likely, he was angry at losing to an English countess such a prize as his son would be on the marriage market, an intrinsic part of international alliances between monarchs. A foreign princess as his son's bride would have been both more prestigious and more useful diplomatically than a mere Countess of Kent, for all her wealth and beauty. But then, Edward III had singularly failed in his attempts to mate his son with a foreign princess: when the Prince was only one year old, there had been negotiations on his behalf for the hand of the baby Princess Jeanne of France, which were repeated, unsuccessfully, in 1337; later, Margaret of Brabant and daughters of the Count of Flanders and the King of Portugal were named as prospective Princesses of Wales, but without result. At thirty, the Black Prince was comparatively old, by contemporary standards, to be marrying for the first time.

Whatever his reasons for opposing the match in principle, the King made no decisive move to prevent the wedding. The Pope was duly petitioned for a dispensation to allow the marriage – for Joan and Edward were related 'within the prohibited degrees' of kinship, and besides, he was godfather to one of her Holland sons, which was a relationship which generally precluded marriage under Canon Law. Though the Pope gave them his blessing, in later years doubts were still cast on the validity of the marriage and on the legitimacy of Joan and Edward's son Richard, the

The Black Prince kneels in the traditional ritual of homage, receiving the principality of Aquitaine from his father in 1362

then King Richard II, because Joan's 'first husband', the Earl of Salisbury, was still living at the time of Richard's birth. (Divorce, even when sanctioned by a Pope, could often be revoked if policy required.) When Richard was dethroned in 1399, there were many men willing to please the usurper Henry IV by shouting 'Bastard!' at the former King.

Edward III did not attend the wedding, celebrated in October 1361, but his wife Queen Philippa was there, accompanied by her daughter

Isabella and by her sister-in-law Queen Joan of Scotland. Archbishop Simon Islip of Canterbury performed the ceremony.

The Prince and new Princess of Wales lived quietly in England for nearly two years after the wedding – in England, not in Wales, for the Prince showed little interest in his principality beyond his frequent demands for its support in manpower and money in time of war. By Christmas 1362 the King must have become reconciled to his son's marriage, for he was among the royal family's party at the Waleses' manor of Berkhamsted.

Then, the following February, Joan and Edward embarked for Aquitaine, the English-held province of south-western France, which needed constant supervision. Created Prince of Aquitaine by his father, the Black Prince was provided with a prime opportunity to practise in government for his future role as King of England.

Bordeaux Cathedral, in which the future King Richard II was baptised on 9 January 1367

Edward held magnificent court at Bordeaux. His retinue was swelled by the lords and knights of the province who came to pay him homage. Joan was treated as a queen, and her household became a byword for luxury. Again, of course, there were puritans ready to criticise. A certain Breton lord, in Bordeaux on business, was appalled at the unrestrained extravagance and lax morals of the Court and refused to allow his own wife to imitate the flamboyant fashions of Joan and her ladies. He declared: 'I do not want my wife abandoning the dress of an honest woman and adopting the fashions of the mistresses of the English or the Free Companies [the Prince's mercenary soldiers]; for it is they who have introduced this fashion for luxurious trimmings and low-cut bodices. As to copying these creatures, I am disgusted by those women who follow such a bad example, particularly the Princess of Wales.'5

In August 1365 Joan gave birth to her first son by the Black Prince, whom they named Edward for his father and grandfather. By the time she was pregnant with her second child, in 1366, the Prince was tiring of life in Aquitaine, with so little scope for his military talents. He was looking south, to the kingdom of Castile, where there was a disputed succession to the throne. Never averse to a military adventure, Edward took up the cause of Don Pedro of Castile, against the latter's usurping half-brother, Henry of Trastamara. He prepared a large army to go to fight in Spain, on Pedro's promise of a great reward if his throne should be restored by the English.

Joan was sick and worried at the thought of her husband's going into danger.

> 'Alas! [she said], what should I do, God and love, if I were to lose the very flower of nobleness, the loftiest flower of grandeur, him who has no peer in the world in valour? Death then would be at hand. Now I have neither heart nor blood nor vein, but every member fails me, when I call to mind his departure, for all the world says this, that never did any man adventure himself on so perilous an expedition. Oh very sweet and glorious Father [God], comfort me of your pity.'6

The Prince stayed with his wife until, on 6 January 1367, she was safely delivered of a second son, whom they named Richard, but then he set off for Spain.

The army's march through the snowy Pyrenees was hazardous, and a large army faced them in northern Spain, but at last the Black Prince and Don Pedro won a decisive victory, at the battle of Nájera (Navarette). 'My dearest sweetheart and much loved companion,' Edward wrote to

Joan after the battle, 'all of us send you our warmest good wishes.'[7] He told her of the battle and gave the good news that he would soon be on his way home.

Unfortunately, he was delayed. Don Pedro did not honour his obligations, and the army was forced to wait, unemployed, while the Black Prince and his former ally wrangled over the payment due to the English and Gascons. Added to this, the defeated but still bellicose Henry of Trastamara now formed an alliance with France and, even as the Black Prince reached Bordeaux, unpaid and angry, Henry was raiding on the borders of Aquitaine. The Prince's men were furious at having gone so far, ventured their lives and won so great a victory without receiving their due reward (Edward had relied on Pedro's money to pay them off), and the lords of Aquitaine were soon in revolt against the high taxes which Edward imposed to clear up his debts and provide for future war against France.

The Prince's governorship of Aquitaine, which had begun with such high promise, disintegrated into a farce of mismanagement and resentment not all his own fault. At the same time, he was ill (of dropsy, his doctors said), which did not improve his already choleric temper. Edward was bedridden at Angoulême when he heard that the French army was approaching but roused himself sufficiently to take and cruelly sack the enemy town of Limoges, in 1370.

The Black Prince was always cited by contemporaries as the epitome of chivalric virtues, a paragon of mercy and generosity to fallen enemies. When he defeated and captured King John II of France at the battle of Poitiers, he insisted on serving the King at a banquet with his own hands, deferring to the unhappy monarch and providing him with servants and lodgings suited to his rank. However, it was well understood that peasants and burghers were outside the convention of chivalric conduct, and the massacre of the townspeople of Limoges, men, women and children, though shocking in modern terms, was an inevitable part of medieval warfare and not at all damaging to the Prince's reputation in the eyes of contemporaries.

In January 1371, with the Prince becoming increasingly enfeebled, he and Joan were preparing their return to England, when their elder son, Edward, died, at the age of five. In sorrow, they left France, taking their only surviving child, Richard, to the homeland he had never seen.

In August 1372 Edward III and the Black Prince made an attempt to cross the Channel to make a new war in France, but long gales turned them back. Soon the Black Prince was too ill to think of active service.

In October 1372 he formally ceded Aquitaine to his father before an assembled Parliament.

Queen Philippa had died in 1369, during her eldest son's absence. Now Joan was the first-ranking lady in England, seated at her father-in-law's right hand at state banquets. Immense retinues of knights and ladies followed the Prince and Princess of Wales on their journeys, and their castles, palaces and manors overflowed with servants. Berkhamsted was the Black Prince's favourite residence, however: a small, homely place compared with the grim fortresses which dominated the countryside and with the gilded palaces in London and Westminster, but far more comfortable for the ailing Prince, ill and unused to the cold English winters after years in southern France.

Nevertheless, as Edward sank deeper into lethargy, he could not wholly ignore the fact that England was in a bad state. At its head, the King, his father, was in premature dotage, infatuated with one Alice Perrers, a young woman who had been lady-in-waiting to the late Queen and who was now flaunting herself as the King's mistress in regal state. Not content with garnering the contents of the royal jewel-case, she was avidly collecting bribes for the use of her influence in the law-courts.

Parliament was in uproar over royal misgovernment, both at home and abroad, and with the Black Prince too ill to play the leading role which his position demanded, it fell to his less experienced brother John of Gaunt, Duke of Lancaster, to take the lead on behalf of the royal family. Not only was John unable to hold in check the Commons' demands for reform, vehemently expressed in the 'Good Parliament' of 1376, but he himself became a prime target for criticism.

All Edward, Prince of Wales, could accomplish before his death was to persuade Parliament to recognise his son Richard as heir to the throne, and then, in June 1376, the Black Prince died.

In 1360, when the Pope had granted the dispensation necessary for Edward and Joan's marriage, the Prince had vowed money to build a chapel in the crypt of Canterbury Cathedral in thanksgiving. Before his death, he asked that he should be buried there when the time came. However, the 'Undercroft' chapel was not considered sufficiently grand a resting-place for the body of so eminent a prince, and Edward's remains were consigned to a tomb in the Cathedral proper, with a fine effigy, in full armour, lying on the casket under an ornate canopy.

Before the interment Joan and her son Richard came up-river from Kennington Palace and prayed together before the embalmed corpse lying in state at Westminster. Then she led the future King into the

The tomb-effigy of the Black Prince in Canterbury Cathedral. Until cleaning brought the gleaming metal to light, the figure was black – which may explain why Prince Edward became known as 'the Black Prince', though that may be a sobriquet devised by the French after his infamous massacre of the citizens of Limoges in 1370

Great Hall of Westminster Palace and presented him to the assembled Members of Parliament.

In June the following year, King Edward III died. With no dissenting voice, Richard II was proclaimed King.

He was only ten years old, too young to rule, and a Council of State was set up to govern in his name. However, he was old enough to endure the rigours of a coronation, and on 16 July the small boy, weighed down in robes and jewels, was taken to Westminster Abbey. After the ceremony, there was a state banquet, which Joan watched from a gallery. Like many others present, she may have been seriously disturbed to see the child complain of the weight of the crown: his cousin the Earl of March had to hold it above Richard's head as he dined. When the little King also kicked off one of the precious slippers of St Edward, which he had worn at the coronation, and it was lost, there were many superstitious men ready to read an unhappy future for Richard II in the two omens.

After this excursion into public life, Richard retired with his mother to Kennington Palace, and it was not until 1381 that he next appeared. Then, it was as a man and a king, although he was still only fourteen years old.

In 1381 the peasants of the southern and eastern counties arose in simultaneous revolt against their overlords and the clergy, with numerous grievances which leaders such as Wat Tyler aimed to put before the King for redress. The south of England swarmed with peasants on the march, aggressive and threatening.

Princess Joan was at Canterbury, at the heart of peasant unrest, when the rebellion broke out – she was probably visiting the newly erected tomb of the Black Prince, as well as the famous shrine of St Thomas. She set off for London but, inevitably, was waylaid by violent men. It says much for the respect in which her late husband was held, and for her own popularity, that Joan went unharmed. However, she escaped only after submitting to being kissed by the men who surrounded her retinue. Perhaps her famous beauty had endured, though she was reputedly very fat and was by then in her early fifties, an old woman in those times of rare longevity.

Once in London and reunited with her son, the Princess's troubles were by no means over. The City was full of peasants gathering to present their petitions. In his finest hour, King Richard rode out to treat with them at Mile End, while Joan took refuge in the Tower of London. However, the reputedly impregnable stronghold was unable to hold out long against the insurgents, and they came bursting into Joan's bedchamber, arrogant and glowing with their unexpected victory. Again there were kisses – and

The fourteen-year-old Richard II lands at Rotherhithe, on his way to quell the rebellious peasants who had flocked into London to demand social reforms (1381)

apparently some horseplay, for Joan's bed was overturned in the mêlée. Fainting and tearful, she was borne off by her servants to the royal Wardrobe, an important department of the royal household (whose officials' duties consisted of far more than care of royal apparel), which was housed in Carter Lane, by St Paul's.

It was there that King Richard found his mother when he returned, flushed with triumph, from his encounter, with the peasants.

'Ah, dear son, you can imagine how anxious I have been,' cried Joan.

'Indeed I can, madam,' replied Richard, 'but now, thank God, I may be happy, for today I have recovered the crown I had lost.'[8]

It was to be some time, however, before Richard II took into his own hands the reins of government and began that ill-fated career which led to his deposition in 1399 and death in 1400. Foremost in English politics in the years of his minority was his uncle John of Gaunt (the most feasible alternative as King of England in Richard's place but a man constant and loyal to his nephew). Like many of Joan's friends and supporters, the Duke of Lancaster was a patron of John Wyclif, the Oxford don and churchman who was stirring up the Church with his controversial criticisms and demands for an English bible to replace the Latin version which had so long been in use. At the height of the ensuing troubles, with Wyclif on trial before a Church tribunal in London and Lancaster at the throat of the Bishop of London, the citizens of the capital rose against the Duke, and he was forced to take to a boat on the Thames to escape with his life. His refuge was with Joan at Kennington, and it was to her that he turned at this time of trouble, begging her to use her influence with the Londoners to come to terms.

Joan and the citizens had always enjoyed a good relationship. When Richard was a young child, a deputation had come out to the palace from the City with musicians and mummers to amuse him; kindly citizens played dice with the boy, letting him win and awarding him a gold cup and ball as prize. Now, the Londoners proved more than amenable to the emissaries the Princess sent to them, and though their suspicions of Lancaster's motives were not allayed, peace was restored.

Joan settled down into a comfortable old age. In 1382 Richard had married Anne of Bohemia, daughter of the Emperor Charles V, whose rank was supposed to make up for her lack of dowry. Princess Joan presided over the married children, though the new Queen took on many of her mother-in-law's ceremonial duties. Sadly, Anne failed to give Richard a child.

Of course, Joan was by then a grandmother, through her Holland children. Her eldest son, Thomas, was a great warrior (probably held up to his young half-brother as a paragon of military virtue – Richard was always overshadowed by Thomas, as well as by his famous father the Black Prince, but he never measured up to their standards). The younger Holland, John, had also been at the wars: he had been knighted by the Black Prince himself and was married to Elizabeth of Lancaster, a daughter of John of Gaunt. Joan Holland married John de Montfort, Duke of Brittany (widower of one of the Black Prince's sisters), and Maud became the wife of Hugh Courtenay, Earl of Devon. The Holland family had come a long way since Joan's illicit wedding to a mere steward.

It was one of the Hollands and Richard II himself who hastened their mother's death.

In July 1385 King Richard embarked on his only military venture, to

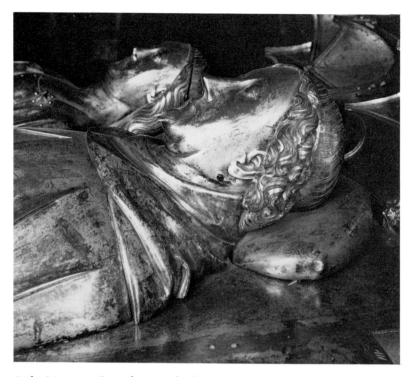

Richard II and his first wife, Anne of Bohemia: their tomb-effigies in Westminster Abbey

meet the Scots who had been raiding the Borders. While the royal army was encamped at Beverley Minster in Yorkshire, a favourite squire of John Holland's was killed by a son of the Earl of Stafford in a brawl. In vengeance John killed the Stafford boy. When the grieving and angry father claimed justice against the murderer from Richard II, the King saw it as his duty to punish his half-brother. He banished him and confiscated his goods.

Joan, who had long since proved her power as a mediatrix, was now unable to gain mercy for John, though there had never been any apparent ill feeling between Richard and the Hollands to give reason to the King's recalcitrance. In her haste to reach Richard and plead in person, Joan tried too severely her already frail health. She died on 7 August 1385.

The troublesome reign and sad end of Richard II are well known through the biographical play by Shakespeare. Having alienated the most powerful magnates of his kingdom, Richard was hounded, caught, imprisoned, dethroned and killed.

Throughout the last years of his reign, his Holland half-brothers employed, and themselves were used as, pawns against Richard's power. They reached their zenith when John was created Duke of Exeter and Thomas's son became Duke of Surrey in 1397 (Thomas himself had died earlier in the year). Then came the virtual civil war among the nobility, Richard's 'abdication' and the usurpation of John of Gaunt's son Henry. In January 1400 the Holland uncle and nephew joined in a revolt against Henry IV, and both died in battle.

Though Joan's son Richard II lost his throne, which passed, for more than half a century, to the House of Lancaster, in 1461 another of her descendants became King: Edward IV of the House of York, whose paternal great-grandmother, Joan Holland, was a daughter of Joan of Kent's son Thomas. The younger Joan's sister Margaret married John Beaufort, Earl of Somerset, and became the great-grandmother of Henry Tudor, who took the throne in 1485. Thus, 'the Fair Maid of Kent' who never herself became Queen, was the ancestress of generations of kings and queens of England to this day.

A possible likeness of Joan of Kent on a boss in the chantry-chapel in Canterbury Cathedral. Since the Black Prince endowed this chapel, it is certainly feasible that it is Joan, as the benefactor's wife, who is portrayed here

THE WARS OF THE ROSES

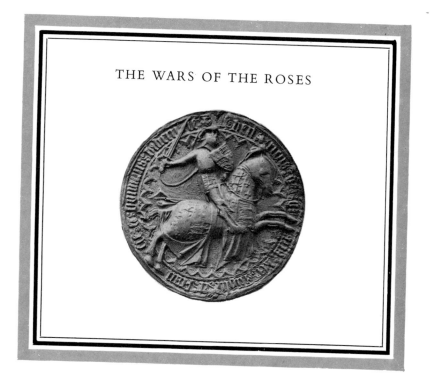

The Wars of the Roses were a strange phenomenon in English history. Primarily they were fought for possession of the crown: princes of the House of Lancaster trying to keep the crown they had earlier won by force, those of York denying that 'might was better than right' and asserting that superior lineage, not tenure, was the main point of justice. Today such a war would be laughable, irrelevant to modern issues – since English monarchs have been gradually stripped of their powers in government; in the Middle Ages, the crown was still a glittering prize, bestowing the ultimate in power over millions of subjects.

The origins of the Wars lay in the last year of the 14th century, when Richard II (son of the Black Prince and Joan of Kent) had so alienated his nobles by his arbitrary government that the majority banded together under the leadership of his cousin Henry of Bolingbroke (son of John of Gaunt, Duke of Lancaster) to overthrow him. Richard was captured, forced to abdicate and sent to his death in prison. Bolingbroke took the throne, as Henry IV, first king from the House of Lancaster, and, after some initial resistance, held the kingdom's loyalty.

His son, Henry V, succeeded peacefully to the throne and subsequently seemed to justify his crown by leading armies to victory in war against France. But Henry died young, before succeeding to the French crown which had been promised him and before he had consolidated his position on the Continent. His heir was a mere baby, Henry VI. Inevitably the French took advantage of the weakness of the protectorate organised for the child's minority, and, under the inspired leadership of Joan of Arc, beat the English back until, in 1453, they were forced to come to terms and withdraw from all but a minute portion of their former Continental empire.

During Henry VI's minority, the English nobility had entered on a power-struggle for control of the government, a situation which continued even after the King had gained his majority. Henry was a different man from his father and grandfather: intensely devout and 'other-worldly' he was totally inadequate and uninterested in regaining for the monarchy the powers which the nobility had usurped; later, the King was undoubtedly mad, and once again a regency had to be set up to rule in his name. The 'Lord Protector' of 1454 was Henry's cousin Richard, Duke of York (his heir-presumptive until the birth of a son to the Queen, Margaret of Anjou, in 1452).

However, Richard's power was everywhere challenged by Edmund, Earl of Somerset, and his partisans, a rivalry which led, after one political manœuvre and another, to the two factions closing in battle in 1455. Somerset was removed from the scene by York's victory, but the struggle did not abate. In 1460, York found that he could no longer control the government against increasing Lancastrian opposition and made a bid for the crown on his own account, asserting that he had a better title to the throne than any of the House of Lancaster, since he was descended from the second son of Edward III, while the Lancastrians derived their claim from only the third son.

Richard of York died in battle in the last days of 1460, but his son Edward maintained the attack on the Lancastrians and in the following year dealt them so strong a blow that he was able to seize the throne. He ruled for almost a decade before Henry VI's supporters were able to re-gather for another round of the battle.

That they could do so was partly Edward IV's fault, for he had alienated several of his formerly loyal friends. The royal cousins' quarrel was only part of the cause of the Wars of the Roses: they were also the result of the ambitions of the nobility. The key man in this respect was Richard Neville, Earl of Warwick, whose faction and army had been the main factor in the Yorkist victory of 1461. When Warwick was disaffected from Edward IV, unable to maintain his lead in the royal Council against the King's favoured associates, he turned traitor and offered his sword to Henry VI. Briefly, in 1470–1, Warwick and the Lancastrians triumphed, and Henry VI was re-enthroned, but Warwick's many rivals would not tolerate his return to power, and when Edward of York again faced his enemy with an army, his fortune turned. Warwick died in battle, Henry VI was captured and later murdered, and Edward IV reigned secure until his death in 1483.

Two women had played major roles in the drama of the civil war. The first was Margaret of Anjou, the wife of Henry VI, whose force of character had been a foil to her husband's weakness. It was her alliance with Somerset which Richard of York had so resented, her energy and bravado which had gone furthest towards mounting a defence of the Lancastrian cause in 1460. Margaret was temporarily defeated, but she was not the woman to bow meekly to fate: she vowed revenge, and in the end, she almost achieved it.

The second woman was Elizabeth Woodville, whose blonde beauty lured the womanising bachelor Edward IV into marriage. She herself had no political influence, but she had a large and rapacious family, whose spectacular rise to wealth and title, along with their inducement from Edward of key posts in government, enraged Warwick and resulted in his defection from the Yorkists.

When Warwick abandoned Edward IV, he went not to Henry VI (then a prisoner) but to the exiled Queen Margaret. Though she had good reason to hate the Earl, she saw in him the only means of restoration of the Lancastrian dynasty on the throne. She cared little for the 'weak' Henry but passionately doted on her only son, and it was for him that she abased her pride and came to terms with Warwick. But, having entrusted her cause to him, there was little more that she could do. When Warwick was defeated and killed by Edward's army in 1471, the Queen made a last stand with her troops at Tewkesbury before, suffering defeat, she was once more sent off into exile – this time permanent.

There was a third woman on the stage, but hers was a silent role. Unlike Elizabeth Woodville and Margaret of Anjou, she did nothing to influence events. She was, rather, the victim of events, helpless in the toils of her father, Warwick, and of Queen Margaret, to whose son she was married to cement the alliance of 1470. This was Anne Neville, who, by Warwick's machinations, became Princess of Wales.

THE SECOND PRINCESS

Anne Neville

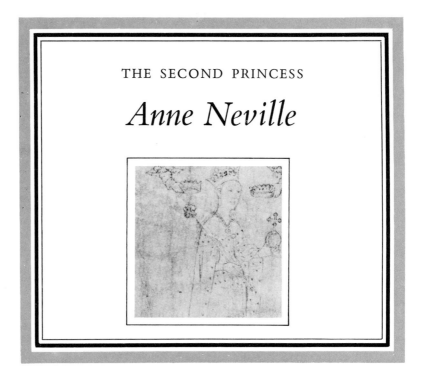

The personality of Anne Neville is one of the minor enigmas of 15th-century English history. She, almost alone among the consorts of England's kings, has not had her character analysed and her personality delineated by historians.

Such work can be done only on the basis of evidence, from the subject's deeds and the comments of contemporaries who observed them. On the first count, Anne Neville is not known to have performed any one independent act which affected her own life. On the other, there is only one reliable source, a contemporary who described Anne as 'seemly, amiable and beauteous, and in condition full commendable and right virtuous and according to the interpretation of her name "Anne" full gracious'.[1] But then that writer, John Rous, was the biographer of Anne's family, sparing with any criticism of its members. She might have been ugly and un-gainly, malicious and crude, but he would not have admitted it.

She might have been so – but more likely she was not, for such faults would certainly have been noted by less biased chroniclers (like modern 'columnists', more ready to note blemishes than purity). Contemporary chroniclers were not slow to describe Anne's first mother-in-law, Margaret of Anjou, as passionate and vindictive, or to lable her sister-in-law, Elizabeth Woodville, haughty and arrogant. The singular dearth of evidence on Anne Neville's character surely suggests that she was so colourless than no one could say anything interesting of her.

It seems strange that one who led such an eventful and strange life as Anne should have made no mark on her times. Though events of national importance involved her closely, she played a completely passive role.

The medieval nobility expected total obedience from their daughters. A girl's main duty was to serve her family by accepting a husband advantageous to the policy of her father and to bring to her husband fortune and useful connections. Anne obediently married Edward, Prince of Wales, to strengthen her father's alliance with Edward's parents and their cause; later, she obeyed King Edward IV in marrying his brother Richard, Duke of Gloucester (the future King Richard III), to provide him with her inheritance of estates and wealth. She was obedient to those who had power over her, no more.

Margaret of Anjou, riding with armies and manipulating politicians, was certainly worthy of comment; Elizabeth Woodville, a penniless widow whose guile and beauty won her a king as her husband, was by no means of the ordinary run of medieval women. Anne Neville merely played the role allotted to her, with docile submission to male authority.

On the face of it, she was fortunate. Not for Anne the never-ceasing toil in winter cold and summer heat of contemporary peasant women or the continual busyness and worry of the housewife. She was born to high rank, brought up in the luxury of her class and destined from birth to comfort and ease. Her obedience to authority gave her yet higher rank and more material comforts. But pawns are expected to be useful: their happiness is immaterial to the controllers who move them at will for their own gain. If one certain statement can be made about Anne Neville's life, it is that she had little happiness.

The Nevilles had long been established among the aristocracy of England by the time of Anne's birth in 1456. For generations they had been lords of Raby in the north country, and her great-grandfather, Ralph, became Earl of Westmorland. Ralph fathered twenty-three children, by two marriages, and Anne could count several earls and three duchesses among her great-uncles and aunts, through the family's judicious mating with titles and fortunes. Her paternal grandfather, Ralph's son Richard, became Earl of Salisbury by marriage, and her father, another Richard, married Anne Beauchamp, heiress of the earldom of Warwick. Born in

Anne Neville, her (second) husband Richard III and her son Edward, Prince of Wales: a herald's sketch on a roll of arms. Apart from such sketches in contemporary manuscripts, there is no other picture of Anne in existence

1428, this younger Richard was one of the most powerful and wealthy men in England by mid-century. Unlike Ralph, he had only two children, both daughters: Isabel, born on 5 September 1451, and Anne, born on 11 June 1456.

The whole of Anne's infancy, of which no personal detail is known, was coloured by civil war in England. The Nevilles were distant cousins of King Henry VI and were for years staunch supporters of his House of Lancaster. In 1452 they proved their loyalty by putting down the pretensions to power of Richard, Duke of York (the Earl of Warwick's uncle by marriage). It was the family's unrelenting acquisitiveness which changed their allegiance: in 1453 began their long, acrimonious dispute with Edmund, Duke of Somerset, over possession of valuable land in Wales. Since Somerset was Henry VI's chief counsellor, virtual ruler of the

Anne Neville's parents: the famous 'King-maker', Earl of Warwick, and his wife Anne Beauchamp

kingdom, the Nevilles were effectively alienating themselves from the Crown. May 1455 found the Earls of Salisbury and Warwick allied with the Duke of York against the Duke of Somerset at the battle of St Albans. Their victory replaced Somerset's political hegemony by that of York and gave Warwick the prize of the Captaincy of Calais, the foremost military command under the Crown.

Then, in 1459, when Anne was only three years old, her father had to flee England as a traitor, when the Yorkist faction fell from power. Warwick's countess and their two daughters had to make a hurried journey to the safety of the Earl's stronghold of Calais. But the convoluted twists of politics and war brought the Yorkists back by the spring of 1461 – with King Henry himself in flight and York's son Edward becoming King of England. The new King was, of course, the first cousin of the

Earl of Warwick, through his mother, Cecily Neville, Duchess of York, the beautiful 'Rose of Raby'.

In the years that followed, Warwick gave Edward IV sterling service. He put down the pro-Lancastrian rebellions, repulsed the Scots from the Borders and settled the north country – his own sphere of influence – into obedience to the King. However, the Earl expected recompense for his efforts: he gathered in all the estates and titles and offices which he could wring from a grateful Edward, not only for himself but also for his kinsmen. An uncle became Earl of Kent, one brother Earl of Westmorland, another, George, already Chancellor of England, became Archbishop of York in 1465.

It is at the installation of George Neville that we catch the first glimpse of Anne. At the great celebratory banquet at Cawood Castle, near York, she sat at the ladies' table with her sister. Only eight years old, Anne had already been trained sufficiently to behave well among the greatest nobles of the realm, in obedience to the father who was already planning her golden future. The only male among the ladies was a small, dark, sallow boy, some four years Anne's senior – a boy who, many years hence, was to play a vital part in her career: he was Richard, Duke of Gloucester, the youngest brother of the King. Edward IV had made Warwick Richard's guardian, and the boy was growing up in the Earl's household, training in swordsmanship and horsemanship under one of the most experienced and famed military commanders in England.

Despite the splendour of the Neville family's position in 1465, the Earl of Warwick was uneasy. Edward IV had not proved as pliable as Warwick had expected: where the Earl had planned an alliance with France and the King's marriage to a French princess, Edward had chosen to ally the kingdom with France's enemy Burgundy and had married an English lady of far more beauty than fortune or political significance. The new Queen, Elizabeth Woodville, came of a family no less rapacious than the Nevilles, and her brothers and sisters were receiving from the King all the titles, lands and marriages which Warwick sought for his own family and supporters.

By 1468 the Earl was seething with discontent, and he soon found fellow-feeling in Edward IV's brother George, Duke of Clarence. Drawing on all the Neville connections, they formed a conspiracy to put Clarence on his brother's throne. In July 1469 the Neville ladies were shipped across the Channel to Calais, and there, on 11 July 1469, George of Clarence married Isabel Neville to seal his pact with Warwick. There was no honeymoon: within the week Clarence and Warwick were back in

England, joining their armies to those of the Nevilles who were already in open rebellion in the north. On 26 July they fought and won the battle of Edgecote.

Soon after, Warwick made the King himself his prisoner and for a few weeks attempted to rule in his name. But the nobility – always mistrustful of one of their number amassing such power – refused to support the Earl; even his own family warned him against going too far. In August Warwick was forced to give up his prisoner. With amazing magnanimity, Edward IV harboured no rancour against Warwick and Clarence. However, when another rebellion broke out, the following February, even the King could not turn a blind eye. The Earl and the Duke were proclaimed traitors.

Warwick Castle, one of the most important of the Neville strongholds

Again the Countess of Warwick was forced to flee her home. She and Anne made a rapid journey to the coast, meeting Isabel at Exeter in mid-March. On 3 April Warwick and Clarence joined them, and together the whole family embarked for Calais.

Warwick had expected a welcome and firm support from the English garrison at Calais, over which he had ruled for so many years, but when his fleet approached, it was warned off by cannon fire: Calais was loyal to the King. While Warwick parleyed with Lord Wenlock, Keeper of Calais, the pregnant Duchess Isabel went into labour. It was her first, and it was difficult. Even now Wenlock would not allow any of the party to land at Calais, but he relented so far as to send two casks of wine on board the Earl's ship.

Fortunately, since there was no other help at hand, the Countess of Warwick was a skilled midwife, 'glad to be at and with women that travailed of child, full comfortable and plenteous then of all things that should be helping to them'.[2] However, even with the Countess's ministrations, the child was born dead. The small corpse was committed to the sea.

Warwick had one last hope. He had proved over the past decade that he was a loyal friend to France and to the alliance between the two kingdoms which Edward IV had refused. Using all the fighting power at his fleet's command, he swept through the Channel, preying on all the Burgundian shipping he could find and at last anchoring at Honfleur, at the mouth of the river Seine, ready to present to King Louis XI of France, sworn enemy of Burgundy, proof of his willingness to ally to mutual advantage.

On about 1 May, after weeks at sea, the Neville ladies came to safe harbour. They disembarked and were lodged in a convent near by. Soon afterwards, Warwick and Clarence rode off to treat with King Louis, leaving their wives and Anne behind. The King himself, however, was not so neglectful: he feared their proximity to the coast, where Burgundian ships and troops were daily reported.

> You enrage me by allowing the ladies to stay so near the Seine and that area [wrote the King to his agents there], I beg you, make sure they go deeper into lower Normandy; even if it doubles the expense, I will gladly pay. . . . Those abbeys are not strongly walled, and a night attack could defeat those who guard the ladies, which would be to me the greatest annoyance in the world.[3]

The French King was at his chateau of Amboise on the Loire, and it was from thence that he sent out his lords to welcome Warwick and Clarence.

Already Louis had formulated a plan of alliance which was as brilliant as it was outrageous.

Though the Lancastrian King Henry VI had been a prisoner of King Edward IV since 1465, his wife, Margaret of Anjou, and their son, Edward, Prince of Wales, had escaped to France. They had been living for the past eight years at the castle of St Mihiel in the duchy of Bar. A passionate, vindictive woman, Margaret hated the Earl of Warwick who had played so great a part in her husband's overthrow and her own misfortunes. Yet it was Louis's plan to reconcile Warwick with Margaret, to have Warwick espouse the Lancastrian cause and to send him to England to head a Lancastrian army in the name of Henry VI. In return, Warwick was to be guaranteed a pardon and future, unspecified, honours. Louis, who would assist in the financing of the venture, would gain an English alliance against Burgundy once Henry was back on the throne.

But his major card was his proposal to marry Warwick's daughter Anne to the Prince of Wales. Louis knew that the Earl would give a good deal to see his blood flowing with that of Plantagenet in generations of future kings of England. Once, the Earl had thought to see his Isabel Queen of England, when he had sought to dethrone Edward IV in favour of George of Clarence. With that hope gone – for now no Yorkist lord would desert Edward to put Clarence on the throne, with so obvious a puppet-master as Warwick behind him – Warwick's only hope for regaining the power he had lost and for future advancement was to revert to his Lancastrian loyalty. Warwick was readily brought round to Louis's thinking. Without compunction he jettisoned the Duke of Clarence (though later it was proposed to appease him by making him heir to the kingdom if the Prince of Wales and Anne should fail to provide an heir themselves).

Nevertheless when the Earl heard that Margaret's arrival was imminent, he retired into Vendôme: he was not so sure that the Queen would be amenable to a reconciliation with her old enemy, and he had good cause to fear her right royal rages.

When Louis and Margaret met at Angers, the French King unrolled to her his plan. At first she was appalled and as angry as Warwick had feared. To suggest that she should entrust the Lancastrian cause to the very man most responsible for ruining it! To marry her only child to the daughter of her worst enemy!

> . . . the Queen would not in any wise assent thereunto for offer showing, or any manner request that the King of France might make her [wrote a contemporary]. Some times she said that she saw neither honour nor

profit for her, nor for her son the Prince. In other she alleged that if she would, she should find a more profitable party and of more advantage with the King of England. And indeed, she showed unto the King of France a letter which she said was sent to her out of England the last week, by the which was offered to her son my lady the Princess [Elizabeth, Edward IV's eldest daughter]; and so the Queen persevered fifteen days ere she would anything intend to the said treaty of marriage, the which finally, by the mean and conduct of the King of France and the counsellors of the King of Sicily [Margaret's father], being at Angers, the said marriage was agreed and promised. . . .[4]

On 22 July Warwick and Margaret met in the town of Angers, closely superintended by Louis XI. On his knees the Earl begged forgiveness of the Queen. Margaret, however anxious she had by then become to make use of this man, could not resist prolonging his humiliation: she kept him kneeling a quarter of an hour before consenting to receive his homage. Warwick had also to promise to repeat the performance in England later, before his peers.

The next three days were occupied with negotiations. For all the weakness of her position, Margaret drove a hard bargain: she would not allow her precious son to accompany Warwick and Clarence on the invasion of England – he should follow when the country was made safe; nor was he to marry Anne until her father had proved his loyalty in battle against Edward IV. Anne was to be put into the 'hands and keeping' of the Queen, a hostage for the Earl of Warwick's good behaviour.

On 25 July Edward and Anne were betrothed in Angers Cathedral – but only Edward was present. After all, it was not necessary for the couple to meet before they were united: the Prince of Wales was marrying Warwick's daughter for her father's alliance not for her own beauty, virtues or abilities. She was totally insignificant in herself, as far as the alliance was concerned.

Once Margaret and Warwick had sworn to their treaty on a fragment of the 'True Cross' at Angers, the Earl hastened away to set in motion his invasion of England. Envoys were dispatched to Rome to beg the dispensation for Edward and Anne's marriage (necessary since the couple shared a great-great-grandfather in John of Gaunt).

Louis XI's queen, Charlotte of Savoy, issued an invitation for Anne, her mother and her sister to visit her at Amboise, where Margaret and her son would join them. This was the fourteen-year-old Anne's first chance to see her fiancé. Perhaps she thought it a great and splendid thing to be Princess of Wales and future Queen, or perhaps she feared that such a position would only involve her in war and political intrigue as it had Queen Margaret. Probably her father had impressed on her the awful risks he was taking to give her so great a title.

If Queen Margaret was wary of committing her son to a bride whose father had harried and threatened the royal family for years, surely Anne must have been frightened at being put into the hands of a woman whom she had been taught to fear since childhood and at being married to a man who had always been spoken of as an enemy. But, as to whether she smiled or wept at the prospect, we have no clue.

Certainly, the Prince of Wales seems not to have been an attractive boy – but then, he had had little chance to live a normal life and to develop attractive traits. He was born in October 1453, during one of his father's bouts of madness. (There were scandalmongers in plenty at Court to whisper that Edward was the son not of the King but of one of the Queen's lovers, but when Henry VI recovered his senses, he did not demur at accepting the child.) From 1460 onwards the Prince was almost always on the move, travelling with his mother and her army as far afield as Wales and Scotland. At the age of seven, after witnessing the (second) battle of St Albans, he was knighted by his father and put in charge of proceedings against captured Yorkists. The boy himself was given the power of life and death over the fallen enemy: he ordered death. A few years later the Milanese ambassador to England wrote home:

> This boy, though only thirteen years of age, already talks of nothing else but of cutting off heads or making war, as if he had everything in his hands, or was the god of battle, or was seated on the throne.[5]

Of course he could talk of nothing else! For almost all the years in England which he could remember, Edward had lived in fortresses and army camps, where victory in battle was the only goal for which to strive. And then, for half his life, he had lived in bitter exile, daily hearing his mother revile her enemies, planning their miserable fate. Margaret, who despised her weak husband and had long been unfaithful to him, pinned all her hopes on her son, urging Edward to prepare to fight and describing his future once he became King. Of course this boy, nineteen years old when he was betrothed to Anne Neville, was a freak!

No chronicler saw fit to describe the meeting between the Prince of Wales and his prospective bride.

Meanwhile, the Duke of Clarence had been sulking and skulking at Calais, bitterly regretting ever throwing in his lot with perfidious

Warwick. Then he received a message from his brother Edward IV which raised his spirits. The messenger sent by the King was one of that noble female army of 'undercover agents' so frequently found in English history. Unnamed by the chroniclers, she is described as 'a woman well advised and of few words' and proved herself 'the only contriver of the enterprise whereby the Earl of Warwick and his whole faction were utterly destroyed'.[6] On the pretence of travelling to become a lady-in-waiting to Duchess Isabel, the woman was allowed to cross the Channel without hindrance. But, once arrived, it was to the Duke not to the Duchess that she went. By her, Edward IV had sent a promise to his brother that he would be forgiven and reinstated if he would forsake Warwick. It was a tempting offer to George, who had as little fidelity to his friends as any man in his time and certainly sufficient provocation to treachery.

Nevertheless, for the time being he made no open break with his father-in-law but joined him in his invasion schemes. In September 1470 the two men landed in Devon, and from all over England Lancastrians flocked to join their army. Edward, on the other hand, could muster little support: his regime had become increasingly unpopular over the past months, and his support had melted away. The Yorkist King was forced to take ship for Burgundy.

On 6 October Warwick entered London and made obeisance to the pitiful Henry VI, who was bewildered at his new freedom. A week later the King was re-crowned.

On 13 December Margaret of Anjou fulfilled her part of the bargain: at Amboise Anne and Edward were married. (In fact, the Queen may have made a very clever, and devious, move by her apparent good faith. The papal dispensation had not arrived from Rome, and Edward and Anne were married under a temporary dispensation granted by the visiting Patriarch of Jerusalem. Should Margaret deem it wise, at any later date, to have the marriage dissolved, she could use this lack of the proper dispensation to gain a divorce for her son.)

Had Margaret sailed for England immediately, all might have gone well. Her open support for Warwick – and for the French alliance – was vital to ensure support from Parliament and the nobility. As it was, such an alliance with England's age-old enemy, championed by a man so mistrusted as Warwick still was, was a handicap to the re-establishment of the Lancastrian King.

In March 1471, while Margaret was still hesitating to leave France, Edward IV and his brother-in-law Charles of Burgundy mustered ships and men for the Yorkist invasion of England. Claiming at first that he had come only to regain his duchy of York, Edward marched unchallenged into the Midlands. Then, at Warwick Castle itself, he proclaimed himself King.

It was at this point that 'false, fleeting, perjur'd Clarence' turned his coat. He met his brother near Banbury on 3 April and made his submission. On the 11th Edward's supporters entered London and took Henry VI. Warwick, who had been at Coventry, was on his way south. On Easter Sunday, 14 April 1471, the two armies met in battle at Barnet just as dawn broke. By 8 a.m. the battle was over. The Lancastrians were defeated, and Warwick was dead.

That very day, Margaret of Anjou, her son and daughter-in-law landed at Weymouth. There were still Lancastrians in plenty to form a new army, and (perhaps not too sorry to learn of the death of Warwick, who could only have caused her trouble in the future) the Queen rode forth on a successful recruiting drive in the south-west. *En route* for Wales, however, she met the army of Edward IV. At Tewkesbury, on Saturday, 4 May, battle was joined.

Edward IV himself was there, supported by his always-faithful youngest brother Richard, Duke of Gloucester. Against them, Edmund Beaufort, Duke of Somerset, commanded the Lancastrian army; Edward, Prince of Wales, was nominally commander of the middle guard, but Lord Wenlock had the real authority. In fact, it was Wenlock who was mainly responsible for the Lancastrian defeat. His loyalty had always been dubious, for he had changed sides twice already, and now, by holding back his division, he let Somerset's perish. Furious at Wenlock's inactivity, Somerset himself killed the man. Without his mentor, the Prince of Wales was almost helpless. He was directly attacked by Edward IV and put to flight. The last that was seen of him, he was calling on his brother-in-law Clarence to help him. But Clarence was not there. Edward, Prince of Wales, fell.

When the battle had begun, Margaret and Anne had crossed the river Severn and taken shelter for a while at Payne's Place, a house on the Tewkesbury–Bushley road. By the time news reached them of the defeat and the death of the Prince, they were at a 'poor religious place', probably Little Malvern Priory. Soon the Queen and the Princess of Wales were taken prisoner. They were sent to King Edward, who had taken up headquarters at Coventry.

On the night of 21 May, in the Tower of London, King Henry VI was murdered. Margaret of Anjou lived on, first as a prisoner in England, then in ignominious exile in France. She had more than ten years, before her death, to reflect on her defeat and her sins.

The Countess of Warwick had not crossed the Channel with her daughter and the Queen. She had landed some miles along the coast, at Portsmouth, and was riding to join Margaret when, at Southampton, she heard that her husband had died at Barnet. The Countess begged church sanctuary at Beaulieu and went unmolested in the days that followed the collapse of the Lancastrian enterprise.

Where was Anne? She is not named among the prisoners sent to London with Margaret. In effect, the widowed Princess of Wales disappears from the scene for the next few months.

Her mother, the Countess, may have inquired for her daughter. Certainly, Richard, Duke of Gloucester did. Suddenly he evinced a great desire to marry the Princess.

Nineteenth-century sentimentalist historians and even modern devotees of Richard claim that the young man was in love with Anne and had been in love with her ever since those distant days of their childhood. Now, they say, was the first time that he could claim her as his bride. It is only to his credit, they say, that he sought out the girl whose father had been so disgraced and whose future looked so bleak. Unfortunately, there is no evidence to support that hypothesis, and it seems more likely that Gloucester wanted Anne's fortune, not herself. Since Warwick's death, she was joint heiress, with her sister Isabel, of his lands; there were also those broad acres and well-filled coffers which made up the estate of her mother. But Clarence, as Isabel's husband, was the obvious claimant to the joint Neville–Beauchamp fortune, and Clarence was high in Edward IV's favour since his reneging. If Richard were to have a share in the spoils, he must marry Anne as quickly as possible, before George of Clarence could intervene.

Whether Anne wished to marry Richard is not known. Perhaps she did have some *tendresse* for him, warmed in childhood. But perhaps she hated and feared him as an enemy. If the latter was the case, perhaps it was Anne herself who begged Clarence to hide her from Richard when he was seeking her out in the summer of 1471. But then, Clarence would not have needed much persuasion to do something so much to his advantage: if Anne remained unwed – perhaps she might take the veil – all the fortune would come to him through Isabel. So perhaps Anne had no such fear of Richard until Clarence put it into her head and persuaded her to hide. Or perhaps he forced her into hiding against her will. This is the historian's typical dilemma of ignorance in the story of Anne Neville: there is an appalling dearth of evidence as to motive.

The battle of Tewkesbury, May 1471: a Lancastrian defeat which ended the attempt to restore King Henry VI. During, or soon after, the battle, Anne Neville's first husband, Edward, Prince of Wales, was killed

Nevertheless, Anne reappeared before long. Richard 'discovered the young lady in the City of London, disguised in the habit of a cookmaid'[7]: contemporaries noted that the owner of the house in which she was found was a friend of the Duke of Clarence.

Richard could not marry Anne without the King's permission. To keep her out of Clarence's clutches meantime, he put her into sanctuary at St Martin's. However, the end of the year came, and the couple were still unmarried: Clarence was obstinate in his refusal to share the inheritance. But Richard had Edward IV on his side, and by the King's mediation the two dukes came to an agreement: Richard should take Anne, and with her the great fortress of Middleham and some of her father's Yorkshire estates, but he must yield to his brother the earldoms of Salisbury and Warwick. Effectively, the brothers were carving up not only the Earl of Warwick's lands but those of his wife also. The widowed Countess, who was nominally mistress of her inheritance and only by whose death could it be passed on to her daughters, was now reduced to such a cipher as Anne had been.

Without waiting for the dispensation under canon law (needed since Richard's grandfather was Anne's great-grandfather), the couple were married in the spring of 1472. Anne Neville, Princess of Wales, became Duchess of Gloucester.

It was not a 'happy ever after' story, though at first it may have seemed to Anne that she had found security, even affection, at last.

For the next ten years the main centre of the Gloucesters' life was to be Middleham Castle in Yorkshire, which both had known in childhood. There, in 1473, her only child, a son, was born and named Edward. Perhaps Richard did love Anne when he married her, or came to love her afterwards, for in the year after their wedding, he begged the King to release the Countess of Warwick from her virtual imprisonment at Beaulieu and brought her home. In 1474 Anne's uncle George, the Archbishop, was freed through Richard's agency.

But even before Anne's real troubles began, with her husband's usurpation of the throne in 1483, there were tribulations to be borne.

Isabel Neville, too, seemed to have found peace at last. As wife of the King's brother George, Duke of Clarence, she had her castles and London mansions, her jewels and gowns and numerous servants, as did her sister Anne. Having lost her first child in that nightmare sea-voyage, Isabel gave birth to a daughter, Margaret, in 1473, and a son, Edward, in 1475. In October 1476 she produced another son, named Richard (perhaps for his paternal uncle rather than for his ill-famed maternal grandfather), but

RICARDVS · III · ANG · REX ·

King Richard III (artist unknown)

she was never completely well after the birth. On 12 December of the same year Duchess Isabel died. Her baby followed her to the grave just over a fortnight later.

A strange sequence of events followed Isabel Neville's death. On Saturday, 12 April 1477, a gang of Clarence's men fell on the village of Cayford in Somerset and made off with one Ankarette Twynhoe, a former lady-in-waiting to the Duchess. Imprisoned at Warwick Castle, she was charged with having caused the death of the Duchess by poisoning her over the weeks before she died. Inevitably, despite her plea of innocence, she was found guilty and hanged, sharing the gallows with a certain John Thuresby of Warwick who, it was said, had poisoned the baby Richard. It was implied, though never stated, that Twynhoe and Thuresby were merely agents for some malevolent power. In fact, Clarence was suggesting (probably by the fabrication of the whole affair) that Edward, his own brother, hated and feared him so much that he would even murder a woman and child.

In the months that followed, the already strained relations between the brothers finally came to breaking point. More and more evidence was piled up against Clarence, amounting to virtual proof of his treason. Accused by Edward IV in public, the Duke was sent to the Tower. He emerged for his trial before Parliament in January 1478 and was condemned to death. On 18 February he was privately executed – rumour had it that he was drowned in a butt of malmsey wine.

Never once had Richard, Duke of Gloucester, given Edward IV cause to doubt his loyalty. '*Loyauté me lie*' ('Loyalty binds me') was in fact his motto. Never, to the moment of his brother's death, did the actions of Richard of Gloucester so much as hint at an ambition to be king. In his own north country the Duke was popular and respected, but he took good care to make it clear that he ruled there only on behalf of his brother.

Then, in April 1483, Edward IV died, after having ruled England for nearly a quarter of a century. His eldest son became King Edward V. But the new King was only twelve years old and was surrounded by his Woodville relations, the most hated men in the kingdom. To many of the nobles it seemed the duty, the natural responsibility, of Richard to 'release' his nephew from these evil counsellors and himself rule for the boy's minority. In a sudden *coup* at Stony Stratford, Gloucester took possession of the King, sending the Woodvilles scurrying for cover. Edward V was taken to London and lodged in the Tower; soon his only brother, Richard, Duke of York, joined him.

During the last week in June, London was agog with rumour, first spread by a preacher patronised by Richard of Gloucester, that the marriage between Edward IV and Elizabeth Woodville was null and void, since the King was precontracted to another woman at the time of his wedding. Thus his children, including Edward V himself, were illegitimate and ineligible to inherit the crown. Since Clarence's children had lost all rights by his conviction for treason, the only true heir of Edward IV was Richard of Gloucester.

On 26 June King Richard III was enthroned and proclaimed.

Anne had come south to join her husband by then, arriving on 5 June. On 6 July Richard III and Queen Anne walked barefoot from Westminster Hall to the Abbey, to their coronation. It was a strange turn of fortune, of which the late Earl of Warwick would surely have approved.

There has been no reign in English history so controversial as that of Richard III. Some chroniclers claimed that Richard was a good and merciful king, and a wise ruler; others wrote that the reign was harsh and bloody, with heads rolling in public and innocent children murdered in secret (that is, Edward V and his brother Richard, who were seen no more). At this distance of time, it is hard to assess the truth. Certain it is that many of the adverse chronicles were written in the reign of Richard's successor, the Lancastrian Henry VII, who wished to discredit the last Yorkist king to give respectability to his own usurpation. More than that, it is hard to say with any conviction.

Anne's life-style changed immediately. Formerly she lived as her mother had lived in previous years, as the châtelaine of her husband's castles, receiving visitors, issuing orders to bailiffs and stewards, presiding at the high table, spending hours with her ladies at their embroidery and gossip. Now, she had command over innumerable palaces and castles, moving from one to another amid an enormous retinue of guards and servants; her guests now were foreign ambassadors not Yorkshire squires.

At York, in August 1483, Richard and Anne were crowned again, and their son, ten years old, was invested as Prince of Wales. The King and Queen walked through the city streets, Anne leading her son by her right hand.

Then, on the last day of March 1484, the boy died at Middleham – of what illness no chronicler mentions. Richard and Anne were not with him; they were at Nottingham. 'You might have seen his father and mother in a state bordering on madness, by reason of their sudden grief,'[8] wrote the Croyland chronicler.

A medieval king without a son was an unhappy man. Richard III was more desperate than most. His accession to the throne had barred the children of his brothers Edward and George from succeeding him, but so hard-pressed was Richard, fearing a Lancastrian challenge for the throne should he die without an heir, that he took the dubiously wise step of instating Clarence's son Edward, Earl of Warwick, as heir to the throne.

However, there were rumours that Richard would prefer to replace his dead son with a new one – not by Anne, since it was obvious that she would give him no more children, but by a new wife. Some sources hinted at a proposed divorce, others at a more sinister means by which the King might rid himself of a now useless wife. Since Anne was known to be in low health since the death of her son, report of her death would cause no surprise.

It is hard to sort out what is truth and what is the fabrication of anti-Richard reporters. It is especially difficult when the 'other woman' is introduced.

She was Elizabeth of York, the eldest child of the late King Edward IV. Soon after her father's death, Elizabeth, her mother and her sisters had taken sanctuary for fear of Richard, and they did not emerge until Christmas 1484. Then they came to Court, where Elizabeth was treated 'as a sister' by Queen Anne. Perhaps Richard did not treat the Princess quite as a niece: certainly, the chroniclers assert that he had designs to marry her. After all, since the presumed death, never confirmed, of her brothers, she was the heiress to the throne in the eyes of Richard's Yorkist enemies. At the same time, she had been sought in marriage by the King's Lancastrian enemy, Henry Tudor, then in exile abroad. By marrying Elizabeth himself, Richard would be rid of her actual and potential danger to his throne and would have a good chance of fathering more children. Eighteen years old, with the robust good health of her Plantagenet blood, Elizabeth had a far better chance of motherhood than Anne, approaching thirty, who had shown no sign of pregnancy for more than ten years.

> During this feast of the Nativity [wrote a contemporary in 1484], far too much attention was given to dancing and gaiety, and vain changes of apparel presented to Queen Anne and the Lady Elizabeth, . . . being of similar colour and shape; a thing that caused the people to murmur and the nobles and prelates greatly to wonder thereat; while it was said by many that the King was bent either on the anticipated death of the Queen taking place, or else, by means of a divorce, for which he supposed he had quite sufficient grounds [probably because of a lack of a dispensation at the time of their wedding], on contracting a marriage with the said Elizabeth. For it seemed that in no other way could his kingly power be established. . . .[9]

Less than three months after that Christmas, on 16 March 1485, Anne Neville died at Westminster. There were not a few hints, especially in later years when everything was being done to blacken the name of Richard III, that foul means had been used to hasten Anne's end. Had Richard made any attempt to marry his niece, suspicion would certainly have been warranted. However, the King did not only *not* marry Elizabeth but publicly proclaimed that he had no intention of doing so.

Five months later, on 22 August 1485, Richard III faced the Lancastrian pretender Henry Tudor on Bosworth Field. There, Richard's army was defeated, and he was killed. Henry Tudor became King, as Henry VII, and later married Elizabeth of York. After more than 300 years on the throne of England, the line of royal Plantagenets was replaced.

Anne Neville had lived less than thirty years. Her life-span coincided almost exactly with the period in English history known as the Wars of the Roses. Those wars and the politics behind them coloured the whole of her life. Amid that brilliant array of kings, queens, statesmen and warriors whose ambitions and fears created the wars, the passive figure of Anne Neville moved quietly and unobtrusively, devoid of either sanctity or maleficence, even of ordinary human emotion, it now seems, through the lack of contemporary chroniclers' interest to provide us with a real insight into her character.

DAWN OF THE MODERN AGE

Historians have customarily chosen the date 1485 to mark the end of the Middle Ages in England, the beginning of the 'modern era'. It is an arbitrary choice, for, in social life, government and man's outlook on the world, there were modern elements before 1485 and medieval survival, after that date. But in 1485 Henry Tudor had defeated Richard III on Bosworth Field, ending the rule of the Plantagenet dynasty and establishing his own in its place: a convenient hiatus for historians, despite the fact that a simple exchange of kings does not, in itself, determine the character of an age.

The 'modern age' in England was characterised primarily by a growing assertion of national identity. When William Shakespeare wrote of

> This royal throne of kings, this sceptred isle,
> This earth of majesty, this seat of Mars,
> This other Eden, demi-paradise, . . .
> This blessed plot, this earth, this realm, this England . . .

with such passionate intensity, he was expressing what many of his fellow countrymen felt. Local loyalties were still strong, and Wales and the northern marches of England retained an independence which was a thorn in the side of monarchs for many years, but, at the same time, the nationwide government machine which the Tudors created went far towards welding the kingdom into one recognisable entity.

For centuries, the State had held only part of a subject's loyalty: the rest was accorded to the international Church under a mighty Papacy which, through its hierarchy, could exact money dues, impose pains and penalties in its own courts and command allegiance – in extremity – even above allegiance to the sovereign. But already, by 1485, the hold of the Church was loosening: when a Pope called European rulers to mount a defence of Christendom against the invading infidel Turk in 1453, there was no response to this appeal for a new crusade. In part, this decline of Church obedience and enthusiasm was due to the recent bad record of Popes and their higher clergy as spiritual and moral shepherds, in part to the abuses of a corrupt and decadent Church, but more to the increasing resentment of many European monarchs and their councils against the intrusion of papal authority into secular affairs. Another factor was the 'renaissance' of pre-Christian philosophy, which not only enthralled scholars but captured the interest of statesmen in national assemblies. No longer did the God-centred, hierarchical theories of St Augustine and St Thomas Aquinas dominate in political practice: Machiavelli and Marsiglio of Padua, humanists and realists, took their place, with far-reaching consequences for the government of the people of Europe.

The 15th-century revival of ancient learning and a change of emphasis in the arts from God- to man-centred themes were only part of the change of intellectual atmosphere. Another factor in the faster-moving development of attitude and outlook was the growth of mass literacy. There was the 'chicken and the egg' situation of the spread of learning and of the means to it, with the introduction of printed books (William Caxton had set up the first printing-press in England in the last years of Edward IV's reign) which made literature of all kinds available to an insatiable readership in the middle classes in the 16th century. At the same time, while men's minds were being led into wider spheres through education, their minds' eyes were being offered visions of a wider world too, by the discovery of new lands across the ocean. In 1492 Christopher Columbus landed on the outermost islands of the American Continent, and after him there sailed mariners who dared circumnavigate the world, with explorers, evangelists and freebooters in their wake, bringing home a bounty not only of gold but also of wonderful tales which fired the imagination of countless millions of Europeans.

The peasant might continue to toil, oblivious of such amazing revelations of intellect, invention and exploration but it could not be long before he, too, was affected by them indirectly, in the political, social and religious changes which ushered in the new age.

The political change in England's life was noticeable first, for the new King Henry VII speedily carried his realm into an era of internal peace, disciplined government and growing prosperity, free from the debilitating effect of civil war. Henry drew the teeth of the over-mighty nobles with shrewd inside-knowledge of their ambitions and ploys – though even he, shrewd statesman that he was, could not foresee that he was exchanging one royal bugbear for another: the Commons in Parliament. His son, Henry VIII, too, played a part in the process when he used his Parliaments to effect his reformation of the Church, awarding the Commons an unprecedented importance in national affairs which they would not afterwards allow to diminish. Only at the end of the 16th century did a third-generation Tudor monarch, Elizabeth I, begin to feel the effects, and drawbacks, of this development, with her Parliamentarians flexing their muscles to take on the Crown itself in a fight to the death, in the following century.

The 'modern age' in England, though not in some other parts of Europe, was the age of the free man: the last ties of bondage had been loosened not by revolution but by natural evolution, not by theories of human rights but by practicalities. Ever since the middle of the 14th century, the trend had been away from the feudal obligations of labour dues towards the payment of cash-rents to a landlord, and by the beginning of the 16th century the transformation was almost complete.

Another facet of this climb towards a more widespread money-based economy was the breakdown of the family system in agriculture and industry. Some yeoman farmers remained, increasingly proud of their status and independence, but there were thousands more wage-earning peasants, without land sufficient to provide for their families' needs. In the towns, craftsmen and artisans were evermore doomed to sell their labour for wages without hope of becoming masters on their own account, as the guild system lost its grip. And, where a man must go outside the home to work, his wife, who had shared his resources as an equal contributor to the home economy, lost both career and status. The yeoman farmer's wife could still utilise home and garden resources to best advantage, and the craftsman-shopkeeper's wife could continue to work in the family business, but the wife of a 'wage-slave' was forced to take in 'home-work' such as spinning or washing, badly paid and usually exploited. Men and women now no longer reaped the whole profit of their own labour but, for a wage, gave the cream of that profit to their employers.

This development was one aspect of the introduction of the system now known as capitalism. Another was the rise of the specialist in the national economy: the self-sufficient farmer was replaced in the main by the specialist crop-raiser or the sheep-farmer. Purchase, in every part of society, rather than production of the staple means of existence, came to be the norm. Usury, too, once forbidden by the Church, was now openly practised in raising the capital necessary for all sorts of ventures, from starting a small business to opening a coal-mine or sending a galleon across the ocean to bring home gold and silver – to make more money for usurer and borrower alike, with the creditor taking more profit from other men's labour. Once under way, these trends were hard to control, and 'inflation', in fact if not by name, was a well-known problem for the 16th-century national economy.

Whereas, in general, England was more united in the 16th century than ever before, in one sphere of life division was created in that period: in religion. The 'humanism' of the Renaissance made its greatest impact on scholars, as did the doctrines of the German Church-reformer Martin Luther in the first phase, but by the middle of the 16th century England had experienced a rapid and traumatic spread of new ideas which split the kingdom into religious factions. The medieval Church had always been harassed by doctrinal heresy: in England, in the 14th and early 15th centuries there had been the Wyclifite, or Lollard, heresy which had been put down firmly and harshly. Heresy alone could be combated by the Church courts, but when it was aligned with an attack on the Church structure itself, championed by all the powers of government, such a force could not easily be withstood. Henry VIII for a time attempted to stem the tide of religious controversy, but by the end of the 1520s even he, who had been named by the Pope 'Defender of the Faith', was exploiting the religious ferment in Europe and at home and denying papal authority within his realm. Through his Parliaments, he threw off obedience to the Papacy and deprived the Church in England of much of its power, offering his people what might have been a new factor in national unity but which came to be a major cause for division. Many Englishmen refused to withdraw their allegiance from the Papacy, many refused to accept the doctrinal changes which followed in the wake of Church reform. Now it was the orthodox Catholics who were the 'heretics', potential traitors to the monarch who was 'Supreme Head of the Church of

England'. And, at the opposite extreme, there was the growing band of Puritans, those who went further doctrinally than the Anglicans, and who sought freedom of worship outside the newly established Church. Again, it was Elizabeth I who reaped the bitter harvest of her predecessors' sowing, with the attacks on Church and State of determined non-conformists.

Nevertheless, despite religious persecution, political upheavals, price rises and the foreign wars into which increasing involvement in Continental affairs drew the nation, the 16th century was still a 'golden age' in English history. Europe's Renaissance of learning and the arts had bloomed in the 15th century, England's flowered in the 16th, with a generation of geniuses in literature and drama, and unprecedented advances in the visual arts and music. Castle-building for defence and the construction of great cathedrals to the glory of God gave way to the raising of fine palaces, sturdy country mansions and solid town-houses, with an emphasis on the comfort, not the protection, of man and on his, not God's, glorification through his works. If the Middle Ages had been 'an age of faith' in God, the 16th century brought in the modern era with 'an age of confidence' in man and his potential.

The third Princess of Wales, Catherine of Aragon, was born in the Middle Ages (using the year 1485 as the dividing line) and died in the 'modern age'. To her eventual doom, she remained a woman of the Middle Ages, clinging to her faith in the Church and to the old values of internationalism, unable to accept the new, rational but often hard-hearted realism in politics. Her inability to come to terms with the new world cost her her crown and her life.

Facing: *A youthful Catherine of Aragon (portrayed as St Catherine), by Michael Sittow*

THE THIRD PRINCESS
Catherine of Aragon

We learn at school that the Wars of the Roses ended in 1485 when Henry Tudor defeated and killed Richard III at the battle of Bosworth Field. But that is not quite true: for years afterwards there were Yorkist plots and rebellions against the new King Henry VII. Though in fact Henry would reign for nearly a quarter of a century and hand on his crown safely to his son, in the early years of the reign the throne seemed anything but secure. To the people of England, by then long accustomed to the 'alarums and excursions' of civil war, the accession of the Tudor King marked no watershed: their troubles continued.

Nevertheless, Henry did manage to overcome Yorkist opposition. By the end of the century he had the Yorkist pretenders firmly in his power: he had killed off the child Earl of Warwick who presented the main threat and had married Elizabeth of York, the heiress of Edward IV; the most important of his enemies among the nobility were either dead, in exile or in submission. At the same time Henry imposed a high degree of law and order upon his kingdom, based on strong central government and a wide network of administrators and judges in the shires. He made himself financially independent of his Parliaments and actively promoted

England's commerce with the Continent. By the turn of the century Henry VII ruled a kingdom of increasingly complacent subjects.

By the last years of the 15th century Henry VII could look forward, with no little certainty, to the continuance of his dynasty on the English throne. His heir was his eldest son Arthur, born in September 1486. Named for the British hero of legend and created Prince of Wales at an early age, blessed with good looks, intelligence and princely bearing, Arthur promised a bright future for the nation when he should succeed his father as king. But even in his boyhood Arthur could serve England: anxious to gain a recognised place among his peers in Europe, the King sought to win prestige by an advantageous marriage for his son. Even before Arthur had celebrated his second birthday, his father had opened negotiations with Spain for the child to marry a daughter of King Ferdinand and Queen Isabella. To have the Spanish monarchs' agreement to the match was one of the Tudor's most substantial triumphs in the early years of his reign, even though the wedding was not to take place until the Spanish bride and the English groom had reached their early teens.

The child selected to go to England was the Infanta Catalina, the youngest daughter of Ferdinand and Isabella. Born on 16 December 1485, she was some ten months older than her prospective bridegroom – but still only two years old when the negotiations for her future marriage were opened.

So Catalina (the Spanish form of the name Catherine) was brought up with the certainty of her destiny. It was no unusual matter for a princess to be betrothed in her cradle and wed in her early teens: in most cases girls accepted their fate unquestioningly, passing their childhood in full knowledge that they must soon leave home and family to go to a distant Court. They had no power to rebel – and, indeed, few would wish to do so, with such a prospect of glory.

However, Catalina had some happy years at home before she was sent north to her wedding in 1501. In her later, unhappy years she had the solace of memories of a sunny childhood in one of the greatest Courts of Europe and with one of the kindest royal mothers.

Her parents, King Ferdinand of Aragon and Queen Isabella of Castile, whose marriage united the long-disparate people of Spain, were famed and admired throughout the Continent for their crusade against the Moorish infidels in the south of the Iberian peninsula. In fact, much of Catalina's childhood was spent in their war-camp at Granada, with the enemy only a few miles away. Legend has it that in one sally of the Moors into the royal encampment, they set fire to the pavilion in which Catalina

The Alhambra of Granada: the Moorish citadel captured by Ferdinand and Isabella in 1492, in which Catherine spent part of her childhood

and her sisters were lodged. But when she was six years old, Ferdinand and Isabella rode in triumph into the Moors' citadel, Granada, and, though the Court was continually on the move in the summer months, much of the Princess's childhood was spent amid the beauties of the great palace of Alhambra, with its shady courts and sparkling fountains.

She was the youngest of the royal children: the eldest of the princesses, Isabella, fifteen years Catalina's senior, had left home in her teens to marry the King of Portugal – only to return, at twenty, a widow, prematurely endowed with patience and dignity; she begged to be allowed to become a nun, but international diplomacy demanded that she return to Portugal to marry her late husband's cousin, the new king. In 1498 she died in childbirth, and her sister Maria, little more than a child, was sent to take her place. Already Catalina had lost her adored only brother Juan, the heir to the thrones of Castile and Aragon, who had died in 1497, and her sister Juana, who had left home in 1496 to marry the Emperor's son and live in Burgundy. Then Catalina was left alone with her mother.

Queen Isabella was a great lady: not only had she ridden with her armies through years of battles and sieges but she had strengthened and united Castile after years of anarchy. It was she who had commissioned Christopher Columbus's exploration of the New World and she who opened dark, superstitious Spain to the bright light of Renaissance culture. Deeply pious, she lived only for her country and her family, a formidable influence and example for the young Catalina. The Princess's father, on the other hand, was in the more traditional mould of Spanish kings: a lover of warfare and international intrigue but without the charisma and dedication of his wife – very much the weaker partner in the royal marriage and government.

Like her mother, Catalina was well imbued with the religious tenets of the age, and, with the flowering of Spanish scholarship, she was taught and tutored in Latin and philosophy as well as the accomplishments necessary to one who was destined to rule a Court. Duty was the main principle instilled into her by her mother – duty to form herself into as great a lady as Isabella and to serve God and her country single-mindedly.

Thus, when Catalina set off for her wedding in England in 1501, she carried with her all the good intentions in the world. That is not to say, however, that she expected to have to make unbearable sacrifices as the pawn of her parents' policy, although she was fully aware that she might never see Spain or her family again. To one bred as she had been, queen-ship was the greatest career with which she could be entrusted. For years she had known that she must go to England; for years she had been complimented and flattered by English envoys who had laid before her the delights of her future home and the charms of her future husband.

Of course, Catalina had never seen Arthur, though she may have received his portrait. But the Prince had written to her frequently, in the elegant Latin which was still the lingua franca of international correspondence. For example, shortly after the young couple had been married by proxy in the summer of 1499, the Prince of Wales had written to her:

Most illustrious and most excellent lady, my dearest spouse, I wish you very much health, with my hearty commendation.

I have read the most sweet letters of your Highness lately given to me, from which I have easily perceived your most entire love to me. Truly, those your letters, traced by your own hand, have so delighted me, and have rendered me so cheerful and jocund, that I fancied I beheld your Highness and conversed with and embraced my dearest wife. I cannot tell you what an earnest desire I feel to see your Highness, and how vexatious to me is this procrastination about your coming. I owe

Queen Isabella of Castile: a detail from The Adoration of the Madonna *by a painter of the School of Castile*

Arthur, Prince of Wales, Catherine's first husband, who died at the age of fifteen

eternal thanks to your excellence that you so lovingly correspond to this my so ardent love. Let it continue, I entreat, as it has begun; and, like as I cherish your sweet remembrance night and day, so do you preserve my name ever fresh in your breast. And let your coming to me be hastened, that instead of being absent we may be present with each other, and the love conceived between us and the wished-for joys may reap their proper fruit.[1]

Such sentiments were, undoubtedly, the mere product of a courtly education, for Prince Arthur was only thirteen when he wrote them, but at that era an adolescent boy looked on marriage as a sign of manliness and would be willing to make the best of it; besides, he would have been assured by his family and their counsellors that only great good for the kingdom, and personal respect for himself, could accrue by this alliance with Spain.

On 21 May 1501 Catalina set off for England. Her retinue was enormous and splendid, composed of priests and diplomats, noble ladies and innumerable servants. As they journeyed across the plains and sierras, which Catalina now saw for the last time, they were a gay and colourful cavalcade, awe-inspiring to the peasants whom they passed. At Santiago, Catherine paused, spending the night in prayer in the great church there, before the shrine of Spain's beloved St James; then, on to Corunna, where her fleet was waiting.

However, it was to be some two months before the Princess saw the first of her new home, for scarcely had she set sail than violent storms sent her ships scurrying back into port, and there was a month of tedious waiting while the battered vessels were repaired before braving the seas again.

Then, on 2 October 1501, Catalina – now Catherine, to the English – landed at Plymouth.

It surely seemed as though the whole of England was coming out to greet her, for, as Catherine journeyed eastward, her retinue was swelled by parties of the aristocracy riding up to join her. 'The Princess could not have been received with greater joy had she been the Saviour of the world,'[2] wrote a Spaniard in a report to Queen Isabella. However, the receptions and feasts with which Catherine was regaled served only to delay her arrival at Court. When, in early November, news reached King Henry at Lambeth that his prospective daughter-in-law was only fifteen miles away, at Dogmersfield, he decided to forego the formal reception which was planned and to ride out to meet her.

Messengers rode ahead to warn the Spanish party – throwing them into a flurry of apprehension. Don Pedro de Ayala, the Spanish Ambassador, was horrified at the informality of the English monarch. Riding off to meet the King before he arrived at Dogmersfield, de Ayala declared to Henry that it was an outrageous breach of etiquette that the bride should be seen before her wedding, and he insisted that Catherine should remain veiled, Moorish-fashion, until the ceremony.

Henry was a suspicious man: could it be, he wondered, that Catherine was deformed or hideously ugly? What was Spain trying to hide from him with its gauze veil? Did the Spanish monarchs think to make a fool of him by foisting a sub-standard bride on his son?

Even more resolute, the King angrily spurred his horse and galloped towards Dogmersfield, leaving his son and their retinue far behind. Striding into Catherine's chambers, he demanded to see her immediately, declaring that she was now his subject, owing obedience to him and not to the rules imposed by her parents. The Princess was resting, quavered her servants. 'Tell the lords of Spain', thundered Henry, 'that the King will see the Princess even were she in her bed.'

When Catherine appeared, Henry's mind was set at rest. She was a healthy, well-formed young woman, with just such a clear complexion, auburn hair and grey eyes as suited English tastes. But since Henry's only foreign language was French, of which Catherine had only a few words, direct expression of his approval was impossible: when at last the royal entourage arrived, interpreters facilitated an exchange of compliments. Then and there the young couple were betrothed again, in the presence of English and Spanish witnesses.

Everyone relaxed. After supper there was dancing – not Arthur and Catherine together, though, but separately, performing before the King (and each other) the traditional dances of England and Spain.

If King Henry had over-awed Catherine, with his sudden appearance and resolute demands, there was nothing in Prince Arthur's manner to daunt her: ten months her junior, he was a slight, slim boy, a few inches shorter than herself. But a courtly education would not permit diffidence with strangers, and once the formalities were over, the Prince and Princess could exchange a few halting words in Latin.

London was decked with flags and bunting and ringing with cheers as Catherine entered the City. Even had the King not sent out orders for a festive reception of his son's bride, the citizens would have greeted her joyfully, for they knew well that their trade and commerce could only benefit by such an alliance with Spain. Besides, they were waiting for the moment when their conduits would begin to spout wine, at the King's expense.

Then, the next day, came the wedding. Early on the morning of Sunday, 14 November, Catherine arrived at St Paul's and was led to the altar by her bridegroom's younger brother, Prince Henry, aged only ten but already a fine specimen of health and beauty, especially in contrast to the willowy Arthur. Catherine wore a white dress, flowing over wide hoops – England's first sight of the farthingale – her lustrous hair covered with a large white silk veil embroidered at the edges with gold and set with precious stones. With the girth of her skirts and her own superior height, Catherine must have dwarfed her bridegroom.

Day after day brought ever more splendid festivities. There was a tournament at Westminster, pageants and masques, banquets and balls. Young Henry distinguished himself in the dancing, discarding his dignity with his jacket and cavorting in his glee. To Catherine, surrounded by the Tudor family – parents, two boys, two girls and their grandmother, it must surely have seemed that she had returned to the days of her child-hood – though here she was the eldest, not the youngest of the children.

Yet it was not a child who was put to bed each night beside Prince Arthur. Many girls of Catherine's generation were already mothers by the age of sixteen. It was the duty of every royal wife to provide heirs to the throne as soon as possible, and Catherine was given the chance to do her duty. But already there were disquieting signs that Arthur was ailing. Was he too exhausted, after long days of ceremonial and entertainment, to do his share? He said not: calling for ale the morning after his wedding night, he swore that he was thirsty, for he had 'been in Spain this night'. Perhaps it was a boy's boast, mere bravado, for Catherine went to her grave vowing that the marriage had never been consummated.

Scarcely had the wedding celebrations been concluded before the Prince and Princess of Wales were sent off to take up residence in their principality. On 2 December a new cavalcade was formed, an immense train of Spaniards and English, with wagons and pack-horses laden with their luggage, this time bound for the west.

Wales was important to Henry VII: not only was he endeared to the principality by his Welsh ancestry but, when he made his bid for the throne in 1485, it was the men of Wales who had been the first to rally to his colours. Now, by sending his son to be nominal head of the Welsh government, Henry could obviate the dangers of over-mighty lords and rustic discontent in Wales. Already Arthur had spent some months at Ludlow Castle, before his wedding, and his government had already made useful ordinances.

Ludlow Castle, deep in the marches, was to be Catherine's new home, and it was as unlike gay London as it was the sunny Alhambra. Built as a fortress rather than a palace, it was gaunt and bleak. When she arrived there, in the depths of winter, it must have seemed hostile and daunting to the Princess. Totally unused as she was to such cold and dreary weather

Ludlow Castle, Welsh Marches: Catherine and Arthur's home until his death in 1502

and scenery, the south of Spain must have seemed a world away. For Arthur there were long days of routine business, interspersed with hours of tuition: for Catherine, little occupation beyond presiding at the high table at communal meals. For the rest, she must endure tedious hours spent in drafty halls, beside open, smoky fires, her Spanish ladies huddling together against the cold. Perhaps, though we are not told so, Catherine began to learn English at Ludlow, though with so large a household of Spaniards to wait on her, few of whom would bother to learn a new language properly, it must have been hard to concentrate on her task.

The biting winds of March blew in, with sickness in their wake. An epidemic of the 'sweating-sickness', probably a virulent influenza, struck the castle. The Spaniards succumbed one after another, Catherine included. She was too ill to nurse her husband when he too fell a victim to the dreaded plague.

Catherine recovered, but on 4 April 1502 Arthur, Prince of Wales, died.

Too weak and shocked to shake off her fever, Catherine lay helpless while her husband's body was embalmed and shrouded and borne off, with the solemn pageantry of a funeral cortège, to Worcester Cathedral, and there buried. Meanwhile, the news had been carried to London. The King's confessor took upon himself the responsibility of telling Henry that his son, the heir to his throne, was dead. Henry VII is reputed to have been a dour, self-possessed man, but he broke down and wept. He clung to his wife, the now tired and faded former beauty Elizabeth of York. 'We are both young enough to have more children,' she comforted him. 'God has left you a fair Prince and two fair Princesses.'

When the sad news reached Spain, Ferdinand and Isabella, too, re-membered that there was still a 'fair Prince' in England, and one who was certainly sufficiently robust to survive to manhood. (Their eldest daughter Isabella had lost one husband, the King of Portugal, only to marry his cousin and heir. Why should not Catherine do the same?) By the time the Princess had returned to London, in May, there were already plans afoot for continuing the Anglo-Spanish alliance with a new wedding. King Henry had no objections. He was anxious to retain his links with the Spanish monarchs and the accruing international advantages.

However, there were problems. First and foremost, canon law pro-hibited the marriage of in-laws. A papal dispensation would be needed before Catherine and Prince Henry could wed. Secondly, Henry himself was only ten years old, and some years must elapse before he could be a husband. Finally, there was the problem of Catherine's dowry. She had brought only part of it to her marriage by the time of Arthur's death: a large moiety was still owing. But should she not have a new dowry before she could marry Henry? Or at least, should not the residue of the first be paid off?

The widowed, sixteen-year-old Princess of Wales was largely un-aware of the diplomatic entanglements in which she was being trapped. In the spring she was at Richmond, in the care of her mother-in-law, with two little sisters, Margaret and Mary, aged twelve and six, to cheer her. Then, in the summer, she moved to her own dower house, Durham House, on London's Strand – a massive, graceful building, with lawns stretching down to the Thames.

For the first few months of her widowhood, Catherine was watched very closely. Should it prove that she had become pregnant by Arthur, the whole diplomatic situation would change, for her child would become heir to the throne. The alliance would be intact, and there would be no need – and no possibility – of marrying Catherine to her late husband's brother. In fact, she had not conceived, for, as she herself averred, the marriage had never been consummated. Only Catherine's virginity would make the marriage with Henry possible under canon law. The Princess's duenna reinforced her mistress's assurances with her own testimony; on the other hand, Catherine's confessor, Don Alessandro

Geraldini, asserted that the Princess had certainly been Arthur's true wife.

The King of England chose to believe his daughter-in-law's word, and the English entourage said nothing to challenge it. Whatever Arthur had said to his friends, either in boast or with truth, they were too much aware of the importance of reforging Spanish links to voice their doubts.

Yet Henry VII, always devious, hesitated over the important decision he must make. At one moment he would seem anxious to ratify the Spanish alliance, at another he would seem to be taking seriously the offer of a French bride for his heir. He was also beginning to chafe at having to support his daughter-in-law: she had not brought her full dowry; she had not, it seemed, done her duty in giving England a new heir; even if he did decide to allow her to marry Henry, the boy was not yet in his teens, and it would be several years before he and Catherine could marry and cohabit: so why should she now enjoy the great jointure of lands and moneys which should support her and her large household?

One possible solution presented itself on the death of the Queen in February 1503. Henry was determined to marry again, partly to beget more sons to safeguard the succession, partly to mate with a prestigious princess. He saw no reason why, if Catherine could be granted a dispensation to marry his son, she could not be given one to become his own wife.

> This would be an evil thing [wrote Queen Isabella to her harassed ambassador in England, Dr de Puebla], one never before seen and the mere mention of which offends our ears. We would not for the world that it should take place. Therefore, if anything be said of it, speak of it as a thing not to be endured. [3]

Such a mating of May and December was *not* unknown in the royal dynasties of Europe, whatever Isabella might say – but she was well able to appreciate that Catherine – the wife of an old king, probably mother to children who would never inherit the throne, certainly doomed to years of widowhood without power or influence – was a very different prospect from Catherine the wife of a young king, the mother of a future king of England. If Catherine married the elder Henry, she might give Spain a few years of safe alliance with England, but who could tell if the younger Henry, on his father's death, would not reverse the whole system by marrying with Spain's enemy, France?

When the Spanish monarchs sent a ship to England to collect their daughter – and her dowry – to bring her home, Henry capitulated. He had no wish to offend Spain or to lose his 'bird in the hand'. On 23 June 1503 Catherine was formally betrothed to Prince Henry: Henry VII

King Henry VII, Catherine's father-in-law: a portrait by Michael Sittow (1505)

was well content that Spain agreed that Catherine should now relinquish her jointure, while at the same time promising to pay the outstanding amount of her dowry.

For Catherine herself, little seemed changed at first. She knew that she must wait three years until Prince Henry should reach his fifteenth birthday, before she could marry him, but until that time she might have pleasure without responsibility. She had the company of her young sisters-in-law (at least, until Princess Margaret, at fourteen, left to join her new husband, the King of Scotland, leaving only the child Mary in the royal nursery) and could broaden her knowledge of England, the English people and the English language during her frequent visits to Court. At eighteen she was nominally mistress of her own household and, though she had now no income as of right, she was provided with a pension of £100 per annum.

It was not long, however, before the Dowager Princess of Wales came to see that her future was not as rosy as she had hoped or as certain as she had once believed. Early in 1503 came news of the death of her mother, Queen Isabella – in itself a severe blow for, despite the many miles which separated them and the pressure of business which had kept Isabella from a close correspondence with her daughter, the Princess had always known the security of her mother's devoted interest; but more than that, the death of the Queen of Castile altered the diplomatic relations of England and Spain.

First, Catherine's father, King Ferdinand, had no rights in his late wife's kingdom and was overwhelmed with fear that Spain would be swamped by rule from the Empire, for Isabella's heir was her daughter Juana, the wife of the Emperor's son Philip. To Henry VII this meant that if he wanted a really useful Spanish alliance, it was to the Empire that he must now look, not to the weak kingdom of Aragon and Ferdinand's family. Secondly, a trade treaty, advantageous to the English, was revoked on Isabella's death, and hundreds of English merchants were bankrupted when they were forced to close their businesses in Castile.

The first sign to Catherine that her position was changed came when the King stopped her allowance. She did not know that at the same time Prince Henry had been guided to make a secret, but well-witnessed, protest against his engagement to Catherine, on the pretext that it had been contracted while he was a minor; no rumour of this leaked out. Ever more worried about her mounting debts, and without the prospect of English money to pay them off, the Princess wrote in desperation to her father: 'Your Highness shall know, as I have often written to you, that since I came to England, I have not had a single maravedi, except a certain sum which was given me for food, and this is such a sum that it did not suffice without my having many debts in London; and that which troubles me more is to see my servants and maidens so at a loss, and that they have not wherewith to get clothes.' She went on to pour out her resentment against the Spanish ambassador, Dr de Puebla, who, she asserted, was hindering rather than helping her, giving in to Henry to keep his favour. She wrote:

> I entreat your Highness *that you will consider that I am your daughter* and that you consent not that on account of the Doctor I should have such trouble, but that you will command some ambassador to come here who may be a true servant of your Highness, and for no interest will cease to do that which pertains to *your* service. . . . As for me, I may say . . . that in seeing this man do so many things not like a good servant of your Highness, I have had so much pain and annoyance that I have lost my health in a great measure. . . . 4

No comforting reply and no money answered Catherine's urgent requests. Ferdinand had more to worry about than an indigent daughter.

The Princess's anger against de Puebla was largely unfounded, for the ambassador was almost as powerless as she in the face of the overwhelming odds against the Spanish alliance and his own master's negligence. Catherine might have realised that fact were it not for the enmity between the ambassador and her own duenna, Doña Elvira Manuel, whom Catherine trusted implicitly. Queen Isabella herself had placed Doña Elvira in command of Catherine's household, and the domineering, self-seeking woman had taken full advantage of Catherine's obedience to her mother's will. Since the first bewildering days of her widowhood, the girl had clung to her as her mother's substitute and, as difficulties crowded in, it was to Doña Elvira that Catherine had always turned for counsel. In fact, her trust was misplaced. Doña Elvira was no friend to King Ferdinand. She had a brother, Don Juan Manuel, who was a trusted counsellor of the Archduke Philip, husband of the new Queen Juana of Castile, Catherine's elder sister, and Elvira was determined that through Catherine she should strengthen England's links with the Empire, to Don Juan's benefit. She persuaded Catherine to write to Juana, begging her help in the matter of her allowance and suggesting that the Queen should visit her in England. In doing so, Philip and Juana might well make an important treaty with Henry VII much to mutual advantage – but which would, of course, virtually put an end to Ferdinand's expectations of an alliance with England through Catherine.

By chance the Princess showed her letter to de Puebla, who at once opened Catherine's eyes to her duenna's deceit. It was totally against the interests of Spain, he told her, to summon aid from the Empire: such a move could only harm the grand design of Queen Isabella and could only mar Catherine's own prospects in England. Duty to her mother's policies was Catherine's guiding star and, for all the years of service which Doña Elvira had rendered, the Princess had no compunction in dismissing her. (Doña Elvira and her husband, Catherine's chamberlain, Don Pedro Manrique, left England for the Court of Philip and Juana, never to return.)

Nevertheless, Juana and her husband did visit England, in January 1506, and the alliance with the Empire and Castile was negotiated. Catherine had no chance to speak to her sister alone, no opportunity to present her grievances or to explain to Juana the harm that could accrue to them both from a policy of opposition to their father. In conclave at Windsor a whole new system of royal marriages was agreed – King Henry would marry Philip's sister Margaret, Prince Henry the Princess Eleanor, and the little Princess Mary would be betrothed to Juana's son Charles. This last match was the most dazzling of all, for Charles would one day inherit not only his mother's kingdom of Castile and his maternal grandfather's kingdom of Aragon, but his paternal grandparents' immense lands in the Netherlands, Burgundy, Germany and Austria – and it was probable that he would be elected Holy Roman Emperor. To the former Welsh pre-tender to the throne of England, who had known poverty and obscurity in his youth, who had had to fight both physically and intellectually to gain and secure his throne, this match was beyond even his ambitions.

Secretly, Henry and Philip inserted another clause into their agreement: should either party go to war, the other would support him. Only one interpretation would be put on this treaty, that Philip intended to make war on his father-in-law, who was disputing his and Juana's rights to rule Castile. In fact, the need never arose, for Philip was welcomed by the Castilians, and shortly after his arrival in Spain a reconciliation with Ferdinand was effected. Nevertheless, when Philip died, only three months later, there were several voices to whisper the rumour that the Archduke-King had been poisoned by agents of King Ferdinand. The widowed Juana, who had been obsessed by her love for the faithless Philip, was so distraught at her husband's death that she had to be held in restraint. So it was Ferdinand who ruled Castile for 'Juana the Mad' and her infant son Charles.

Catherine was now a mature woman. She could see more clearly than in past years the many currents which were flowing against her. But what she could not see, even after the incident with Doña Elvira, was that Dr de Puebla was her friend and not the pawn of Henry VII. Interspersed with her appeals to her father to send her dowry and some more money for her own use were numerous complaints against the inactivity of his ambassador. All that Ferdinand would do was to grant Catherine the power to treat with King Henry as an ambassador in her own right, a concession which in fact gave her no tangible advantage beyond opening to her the vast collection of documents which explained the causes of her plight.

Meanwhile, with Doña Elvira gone, Catherine had to face fresh difficulties in the ordering of her own affairs. Without any form of income, her debts mounted alarmingly. When King Henry declared that the Princess of Wales could not continue without the supervision of a duenna and that she should therefore reside at Court, Catherine had no power, or will, to refuse. She lived amid the splendour of the Tudor Court, but as a pauper, her clothes gradually becoming older and less fashionable, her servants continually complaining about their unpaid salaries.

> My lord [she wrote to her father], I am in the greatest trouble and anguish in the world, on the one part seeing all my people that they are ready to ask alms; on the other, the debts that I have in London. About my own person, I have nothing for chemises; wherefore, by your Highness's leave, I have now sold some bracelets to get a dress of black velvet, for I was all but naked; for since I departed thence [from Spain] I have had nothing but two new dresses, for till now those I brought from thence have lasted me, although now I have got nothing but dresses of brocade. On this account, I supplicate your Highness to command to remedy this, and that as quickly as may be; for certainly I shall not be able to live in this manner.[5]

Catherine, now desperate, did not stop at selling her bracelets; she had a large store of plate and jewels, which had formed part of her dowry and which the King had allowed her to keep in her possession at Arthur's death, though they now legally belonged to him, and at length she had to resort to selling or pawning them, to pay off the worst of her debts. Horrified, Ferdinand remonstrated, driving his daughter to write to him with open scorn:

> ... If your Highness had read attentively my former letters, you will remember that I informed you in them of the same as I write in this,

King Henry VIII as a young man: a portrait by Joost van Cleve

viz., that my necessities have been so great and have lasted so long a time, that I have been forced to sell my plate. A portion of this is therefore deficient and will be as long as your Highness does not provide me with money.[6]

Thus, when Ferdinand was finally induced to send bills of exchange for the monetary payment of her dowry (in the hands of his new ambassador, Don Gutierre Gomez de Fuensalida), Catherine was quite unable to produce her jewels and plate, a vital part of the dowry according to the original terms of the contract. Fuensalida managed to persuade Ferdinand to make up the deficit, but himself so offended Henry VII with his continual demands (couched in the most undiplomatic language) for the ratification of the marriage, that he undid all the good that the Spanish money had wrought. Henry instead confirmed his treaty with the Emperor and turned his back, seemingly once and for all, on Spain.

Catherine was ignored and slighted at Court. Entitled Princess of Wales, ranking as the first lady in the land, she was nothing but a beggar at her father-in-law's Court. At the same time, her Spanish attendants let her remain in no doubt as to their resentment at being so disdained: in particular, some of her ladies were outraged at having to waste their youth attending a penniless princess when they had come to England in the expectation of making grand matches with the English nobility or of being provided with good dowries to marry back in Spain. One of their number, Francesca de Carceres, so offended Catherine with her plaintive, often belligerent, reproaches and with her intrigues with the now odious Fuensalida, that the Princess turned on her in fury: Francesca decamped from Court and made a hasty marriage with a wealthy Italian merchant.

On 21 April 1509 King Henry VII died. All at once the Court was full of whispers: the new King, Henry VIII, would marry Catherine in obedience to his father's deathbed command, it was said.

After a few days of anxious waiting, Fuensalida was summoned to see the King. He was told that Henry would marry Catherine without delay. His policy demanded a grand alliance of England with both Spain and the Empire against France, for which Catherine was to be the pledge.

Many historians have sought to uncover the truth behind this sudden volte-face. Some claim that Henry VII was struck by remorse, as he lay dying, at the wrongs he had inflicted on the hapless Catherine and now sought to make amends to her. Some have pointed out that the match and the international *entente* which brought it about, were in keeping with currents in Tudor policy at the time. The more romantic suggest that

Henry VIII, seventeen years old at his accession, had long been in love with his sister-in-law; the more moderate say that he had long admired her beauty, learning and character.

Be that as it may, after seven years of uncertainty, Catherine had her reward. Not only was she to be queen at last but she was to be the wife of one of the most attractive men in Europe. In his late teens, Henry was a blond, athletic giant, without an ounce of that superfluous fat which so soon would mar his good looks. He was a true son of the Renaissance, well versed in politics, philosophy and theology, a prodigy in musical composition and performance, as faultless in the modern languages as he was in those of classical antiquity. To his subjects, long inured to respecting but not cherishing their formal, reserved late monarch, Henry VIII came as a god from the golden age. To Catherine he was a deliverer from penury and shame, the provider of honour, comfort and affection.

On 11 June Henry and Catherine were quietly married, but a fortnight later there was no such skimping of expense or dignity in their coronation. In white satin, crowned with the finest jewels, the new Queen of England came into her own.

Catherine now entered into some years of perfect happiness. Her loyal servants in the days of her adversity were well rewarded: her ladies Ines de Venegas and Maria de Salinas were married to great nobles, Lord Mountjoy and Lord Willoughby, and remained at Court, but Catherine was now able also to load with gifts those of her household who wished to return to Spain. Consequently, with more English servants around her in their place, her command of the language improved rapidly.

The early Court of Henry VIII was one of the jewels of Renaissance culture, full of scholars, painters, musicians and poets. With England under firm government by Cardinal Wolsey, Henry's Chancellor, and riding high on the wave of international prestige, it was a fine thing to be the nation's Queen. The perfect intellectual complement to her husband, even if she could not match him in high spirits, Catherine was all that her mother could have wished.

However, as the years passed, there were inevitably shadows to cloud her sunshine. For all his early devotion to his wife, Henry VIII did not prove a faithful husband. Even before the great upheavals at Court with the advent of the fascinating Anne Boleyn in 1532, Catherine had rivals for Henry's affections. And while his mistresses bore the King healthy children, Catherine could not. Of several babies, and apart from several miscarriages, Catherine could produce only one healthy child, a daughter, Mary.

Henry VIII displays his prowess at jousting before Queen Catherine, in a tournament held to celebrate the birth of their son Henry in February 1511. The Prince died a few weeks later

As early as 1522 Henry began to have thoughts that his marriage with Catherine was not blessed by God. True, he had received the papal dispensation, based on assurance of the non-consummation of Arthur and Catherine's union, but he, well versed in his Bible, could find texts which suggested that it was wrong for a man to marry his brother's widow. Though one verse actually bade him do so, to 'raise up seed' to his late brother, another, in Leviticus, declared that 'if a man shall take his brother's wife, it is an unclean thing . . . they shall be childless'. After all, reasoned Henry and his complaisant counsellors, having a daughter was as good as being childless when a male heir was so important to the kingdom. Henry was particularly vulnerable on this point: first, the Tudor dynasty owed its establishment to his father's former usurpation of the crown, and there were plenty of Plantagenets still living who would be only too ready to put in their own claims in the event of a disputed succession should he, Henry, die without an indisputable heir. If the choice were between his daughter Mary and his sister Margaret, wife of the King of Scotland, there would most probably be a civil war, plunging the kingdom back into that anarchy from which it had only recently emerged. No, Henry must have a son for the Tudor line to be safe.

Thus, when the alluring but elusive Anne Boleyn refused to become the King's mistress and held out for legal marriage, Henry had little incentive

Catherine of Aragon in middle age

to remain married to Catherine. With a divorce from her, he could marry Anne and beget male children.

But the only way to obtain a divorce in the 16th century was by proving to the Pope that the original marriage was invalid. Since a pope had granted a dispensation to validate the marriage in the first place, this seemed a difficult task. The only way to undo the dispensation was to prove that Catherine and Arthur had had physical relations after all, which would make the dispensation invalid. There were plenty of courtiers willing to oblige the King with 'evidence': one quoted (or fabricated) Arthur's remark of his wedding morning that he had 'been in Spain'; others 'remembered' that Arthur had said that 'it was good pastime . . . to have a wife'. No one would listen to Catherine's ever-repeated assertions that she had come to Henry a virgin, and no one of any power cared to champion so obviously lost a cause as the Queen's integrity.

The only factor in Catherine's favour was the fact that her nephew, that son of Philip and Juana who was now the Emperor Charles V, held the Pope in the palm of his hand. Charles would not allow so shameful a proceeding, Catherine was sure. Nor, one might suppose, would the King of England risk offending the mighty Emperor by so humiliating his aunt. But Henry was daring – and desperate. When he found that he could not gain his divorce by orthodox methods, he broadened the entire issue and renounced all allegiance to Rome: henceforth he would himself be head of the Church in England – with the power, of course, to pronounce on such matters as divorce. Catherine might weep, men who had been his friends might go to the block for their loyalty to the Church, but Henry was adamant in his will. 'The King's Great Matter', as the divorce was called, moved inexorably to completion. Though Rome decided in Catherine's favour, that her marriage was valid, on 24 March 1534, it was too late; on 28 May 1533, Henry's obedient Archbishop of Canterbury had pronounced the marriage null and void. Four days later Anne Boleyn, who had secretly married Henry some months earlier and who was already carrying his child, was crowned Queen of England.

Since Catherine had never, according to Henry, been legally his wife, she could no longer be styled 'Queen'. Henceforward she should be known as the Princess of Wales, or 'Princess Dowager', as the widow of Arthur. Catherine had come full circle back to the days of the reign of Henry VII: a neglected, disdained Princess of Wales.

Fearful for her daughter, who was kept from her; fearful of the peril in which her husband had placed his immortal soul; fearful for her own life – for there were numerous rumours that 'Queen' Anne would have her poisoned – Catherine, 'Princess of Wales', lived on for nearly three years after the divorce, a prisoner. With an impressive dignity she had gone through the humiliation of the divorce proceedings; now, with no less remarkable a steadfastness, she refused to recognise the verdict. Each letter addressed to the 'Princess Dowager' remained unread; each servant who was put into her household who had sworn allegiance to the King as Supreme Head of the Church was ignored. Every so often Catherine would have to suffer searches of her papers and goods for signs that she was plotting treason against the King – no such evidence could ever be found.

One dark night in January 1536 a lady rode up to Kimbolton Castle in Huntingdonshire, in which Catherine lay dying. It was the erstwhile lady-in-waiting Maria de Salinas, now Baroness Willoughby, who for years had been refused permission to attend her mistress. Hammering at the castle door and begging permission to shelter from the cold, Maria gained entrance. She claimed, falsely, that she had a royal permit to see Catherine and was admitted to her chamber. The door closed: she locked it behind her. When the Queen's custodian called to the Baroness that her time was up, there was silence. No threats or cajoling would make Maria unlock the door. She did not come out again until 7 January, after Catherine had died.

When the news reached King Henry, tradition has it, he threw up his hat and cried, 'God be praised. The old harridan is dead.' But later Catherine's last letter was delivered to him, and Henry VIII wept as he read:

> My most dear lord, king and husband,
>
> I commend me unto you. The hour of my death draweth fast on, and my case being such, the tender love I owe you forceth me, with a few words, to put you in remembrance of the health and safeguard of your soul, which you ought to prefer before all worldly matters and before the care and tendering of your own body, for the which you have cast me into many miseries and yourself into many cares. For my part, I do pardon you all; yea, I do wish and devoutly pray God that He will also pardon you. . . .
>
> Lastly, I make this vow, that mine eyes desire you above all things.[7]

Catherine signed the letter not as 'Princess of Wales' or 'Princess Dowager' but as 'Catherine, Queen of England'.

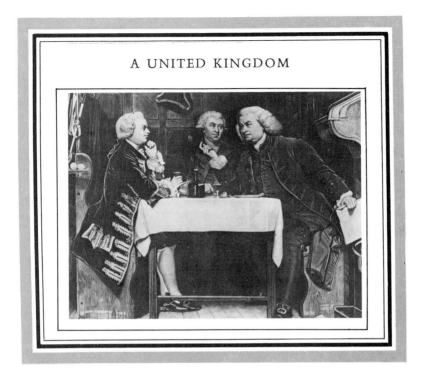

A UNITED KINGDOM

The year is 1714. Catherine of Aragon and Henry VIII are long since dead. The Reformation of the English Church which Henry planted has long taken root and is so firmly implanted that the vast majority of Englishmen now hold fast to Protestant doctrine. So firm is the national prejudice against Catholicism, so great are fears of a return to 'servitude' to Rome, that the succession to the throne has been changed by law to prevent a Catholic's becoming king.

By then, other seeds sown by the Tudors had also come to fruition. The Commons of Parliament had maintained, in the early 17th century, a consistent demand for increased participation in legislation, infuriating Elizabeth I's successor James I by their quite polite requests to share his powers in foreign policy-making, and enraging James's son Charles I with their more forceful expressions against his 'tyranny' of rule without Parliaments. The inevitable head-on collision came in the 1640s, when Parliament took arms against the King. There ensued another civil war, which did not end with Parliament's trial of Charles I for his political crimes and his execution.

In the 1650s the kingdom of England was turned into a republic, in what might have been a noble experiment in democracy but which became yet another form of tyranny. Tired of experiment and failure, in 1660 Englishmen invited home from exile Charles II, son of the royal 'martyr'.

The second Charles was a realist and, for all his political mistakes and despite his frequent betrayal of his Parliaments' policies, had his successors been of the same type, the Stuart dynasty might yet rule in Britain. But Charles was succeeded on the throne by his brother James, a very different man: an idealist who would never compromise his personal conscience, an avowed Catholic (where Charles had hidden his own conversion rather than hazard his throne by offending his Pope-fearing people). James II came to the throne in 1685 amid widespread goodwill in the nation: by 1688 he had alienated almost every section of society, so that his subjects turned to his son-in-law William of Orange to free them from a future in which the King's follies might wreck the nation and in which a line of Catholic Stuarts might drag them unwillingly back to Roman obedience. James was turned from his throne and sent into exile, while his Protestant daughter Mary and her husband William of Orange took his place, on terms dictated by Parliament.

William and Mary were childless, and from the numerous pregnancies of their successor, Mary's sister Anne, not one royal child survived to maturity. Thus, to preserve the Protestant Succession, it was found necessary to enact, in 1701, legislation barring any Catholic from the throne. Anne's Catholic half-brother and later his son made attempts to retrieve the crown, but to no avail. Englishmen might not be fond of Anne's cousin George of Hanover, who succeeded her in 1714, but even he was preferable to a Catholic Stuart.

George came to a land of which any contemporary monarch might have been proud. The nation had recovered remarkably well from the material and psychological effects of revolution, boasted an effective system of government, central and local, and was emerging (after years of Continental warfaring) into a golden age of economic prosperity.

The countryside was more open now – only one-quarter, it has been estimated, was by then left uncultivated. Agricultural techniques were still primitive, with the wasteful 'open-field' system, but, when harvests were good, prices were stable, and even the labouring poor enjoyed a healthy diet of meat, bread, vegetables and beer. But the wealth of the nation did not depend on its self-sufficiency in agriculture: trade, especially the cloth trade, had expanded rapidly in the 17th century, bringing home millions of pounds from foreign and colonial markets. There had also occurred a minor 'industrial revolution' based on an increasing use of coal to fuel large workshops, promoting the establishment of such as iron, steel, salt and glass works and gradually building up many industries whose products increased English exports. At the same time, impetus was given to industrialisation by the streamlining of the nation's financial and commercial institutions, by the creation of new ones, such as the Bank of England (1694). At the beginning of the 18th century, England was the most advanced capitalist nation in Europe, and, as the possessor of vast colonies in America and India (another factor in trade success), a world-power in economics.

London, as the banking, commercial and trading as well as the political capital of England, now assumed unprecedented importance in national life. Its population may have numbered as much as half a million by 1714, while of a total population (England and Wales) of some five million, a million people lived in the counties surrounding London. Indeed, throughout the 17th century, there was a marked shift of population not only towards the south-east but into the many towns of the north, west and midlands.

When James VI of Scotland had succeeded to the English crown of Elizabeth I in 1603, kingdoms which were age-old enemies had been linked, though continuing to operate their individual systems of government and justice. In 1707 the Act of Union was passed, creating a real political unity in the 'kingdom of Great Britain'. Scotland's population numbered only about one million at this time, far more scattered over far less fertile land than in England, with few towns of any size.

Urban life and prosperity in England necessarily promoted intellectual expansion. In the town coffee-houses, men met to exchange ideas and argue over issues of the day, their debates given substance by the factual information which they could cull from the newspapers. The first 'daily' was published early in the reign of Queen Anne: by the time of her death there were seven, while several others were published weekly, including many provincial newspapers. Indeed, there was a new 'golden age' of literature, 'the Augustan Age', at the beginning of the 18th century, graced by Defoe, Addison and Steele, and by the younger Swift and Pope. Controversy was their staple diet, satire their sauce. Not as immediately appealing as the more flamboyant Elizabethan writers, the Augustans were a product of their age in their reasonable and rational philosophy, their economical and exact prose style – worthy forerunners, in this, of the 'great lexicographer' Samuel Johnson.

Religious controversy played a part in the exchanges of literati and coffee-house pundits but, since the 'Glorious Revolution' of 1688, the heat had been taken out of doctrinal debate. Catholics were still much mistrusted, but Anglicans and Protestant Nonconformists had learned to live peaceably. Indeed, religion was in the doldrums in the early 18th century, without persecution and controversy to inspire fervour. The 'squarson' – a cross between a squire and a parson, a typical product of upper-class apathy in religion, lax in his pastoral duties – was occasionally a subject for satire, but in general he was well suited to the taste of his parishioners. However, where sacramentalism declined, moral virtues were emphasised, especially in the middle classes. While books on ethics and manners proliferated, societies were also set up for reforming public morality and spreading the word of 'enlightened behaviour'.

There was more than a little hypocrisy in such a climate. While the middle classes deplored the vices of the poor (though the very rich had their own, no less heinous excesses), they did little to alleviate the conditions which fostered them. London, with its splendid Mall and parks, its great mansions, its wide esplanades where the rich could promenade in the sun, was also the home of thousands of beggars and footpads, thieves and prostitutes, who huddled in the dark alleys by night. Violence and drunkenness were the only outlets for their misery. There was as great a gulf between such unfortunates and the comfortable middle class as between the latter and the aristocrats of title and wealth.

This, then, was the kingdom to which George of Hanover came in 1714. He did not spurn such an inheritance, nor did he embrace it with much joy, seeing Britain as a means of enhancing the prestige of his own petty dukedom in Germany rather than as a prize on its own merits. George brought no consort with him (though he did import an assortment of mistresses), for he had long since divorced his wife, but he did bring his son, George Augustus (the future George II), who was created Prince of Wales. And, since the Prince was married, the nation welcomed the first Princess of Wales in nearly two centuries: Caroline of Anspach.

THE FOURTH PRINCESS
Caroline of Anspach

Caroline of Anspach was born on 1 March 1683, the daughter of John Frederick, Margrave of Anspach, a German state smaller than some English counties. Nearly two hundred years would elapse before Germany was united under its Kaiser: until then it was a conglomeration of states such as Anspach, some large, some infinitesimally small, under rulers whose titles were more imposing than their power and wealth. Owing formal allegiance to the Catholic Holy Roman Emperors, many of the Protestant German princes yet sought to follow policies independent of their overlords and often at variance with them.

By the time of Caroline's birth, Brandenburg-Prussia was emerging as the leader of the German states, extending its territory in the east and everywhere imposing a unifying structure of government. Thus its Hohenzollern dynasty set out on that path which would bring its members to imperial glory in the 19th century and destruction in the 20th.

The family at Anspach was an offshoot of the Hohenzollern line, but by the late 17th century it had acquired none of the prestige of its Prussian cousins. The Margrave John Frederick cared nothing for the arena of politics and was content to be known as 'the delight of his people' by a complaisant peasantry.

Caroline was born of John Frederick's second marriage, to Eleanor Erdmutha Louisa of Saxe-Eisenach. When her father died in 1686 and was succeeded by her half-brother George Frederick, Caroline and her brother William Frederick left Anspach for her mother's old home at Eisenach. The new Margrave, a minor, was under the protection of Frederick, Elector of Brandenburg-Prussia, head of the House of Hohenzollern, who supervised the upbringing of the younger Anspach children also. On the eve of George Frederick's majority, the widowed Margravine and her children visited the Prussian Court at Berlin, and there Eleanor became betrothed to John George, Elector of Saxony. It was certainly no love match: as a protégée of Prussia, Margravine Eleanor was compliant in sealing Prussia's alliance with Saxony by this marriage – at the same time gaining a friend for Anspach.

After the wedding at Leipzig, the new Electress Eleanor took her place at John George's Court at Dresden, settling her children in their new home. At nine years old, Caroline must have found these changes exciting but, a sharp child, she could not have failed to notice her mother's increasing unhappiness. Having married for policy, the Elector saw no reason to give his love with his title to Eleanor and continued to live openly with a young Saxon beauty, Magdalena Sybilla von Röohlitz. Soon Eleanor came to fear for her life, with her husband's mistress casting jealous eyes at her rank: Magdalena would not be the first mistress to poison a rival. Eleanor withdrew with her children to her dower house at Pretsch, a town on the River Elbe near Wittenberg.

She did not live long in such fear, however. In 1694 Magdalena Sybilla von Röohlitz succumbed to an epidemic of smallpox and died. Eleven days later, her lover, who had risked his life to nurse her, followed her to the grave. Thus widowed for the second time, Eleanor lived on at Pretsch for only two years, herself dying in 1696.

Caroline was now thirteen years old and, with no right to remain at Pretsch, would have returned as 'a poor relation' to Anspach, but for the fact that her guardian, Elector Frederick of Brandenburg-Prussia, took his responsibilities seriously. 'I will never fail as your guardian', he wrote to her, 'to espouse your interests and to care for you as a loving father, and pray your Highness to have me in the same confidence your mother always had, which I shall perpetually endeavour to deserve.'[1]

It was a heady experience for a young girl, used to a quiet country life, to be thrown into the brilliant Court of the Prussians. Elector Frederick was a universally admired military commander and statesman – and by judicious aid to a needy Emperor won himself the title of 'King of

George I's mother, Sophia of Hanover, by Andreas Scheits (1706). Sophia was Queen Anne's heir for many years and looked forward eagerly to becoming Queen, but she died just a few weeks before Anne, leaving her claim to the British throne to her son, the future King George I

Prussia' in 1701; his wife, Sophia Charlotte of Hanover, was a renowned patron of the arts. Her palace of Lützenburg was full of treasures, and its gardens were designed by the famous Le Notre on the model of Versailles. Indeed, French culture was paramount, from décor to discourse, and Sophia Charlotte was a real *femme savante*, delighting in the select *réunions* at which she reigned over men of learning and wit. So advanced were her views, in religion and politics, that she was known as 'the Republican Queen'.

The Prussians had only one child, a son, Frederick William, and Sophia Charlotte readily adopted Caroline as a daughter. In return, the Princess so admired the Queen that she turned herself into a youthful facsimile of her, striving to emulate her sophistication and learning. In the informal atmosphere of Lützenburg, Caroline found her greatest friends not among the titled courtiers but among such men as the philosopher Leibniz, the Queen's confidant. And frequently the Queen's mother, the Electress Sophia of Hanover, would pay a visit to her daughter, and Caroline would have the benefit of the old lady's wisdom and erudition.

At seventeen Caroline was one of the most cultured and sophisticated princesses in Europe – and a beauty too, with a Germanic fairness and statuesque figure. For all the comparative insignificance of her birth and the paucity of her dowry, she was a prime candidate to share some great man's throne.

King Frederick found her an incomparable match: Archduke Charles of Austria, second son of the Holy Roman Emperor and himself titular King of Spain (though armies were even then in battle to win him the kingdom against the rival claim of a French prince). No more splendid prospect for Caroline could be imagined. She was at Freiberg, in Saxony, in the autumn of 1703 when she was hurriedly summoned to meet her prospective husband at Weissenfels, through which he was travelling on his way to Spain. They spent five hours in each other's company, and Charles went on his way full of hopes of wedding Caroline.

The only drawback was that the House of Habsburg insisted that the Princess must become a Catholic before entering its ranks. Other princesses had been ready and eager to forsake the faith of their childhood to gain a throne; indeed, princely parents educated their daughters with that possibility in mind. When the mother of Sophia Charlotte, the future Queen of Prussia, was questioned as to her daughter's faith, the insouciant Sophia of Hanover replied: 'She has none as yet; we are waiting to see whom she will marry.'[2]

One Father Urban, a Jesuit, was employed to introduce Caroline to the tenets of the Catholic Church – only to be dismayed at her hesitation to submit. 'When Urban comes to see the Princess,' wrote Sophia of Hanover to a niece in November 1704, 'the Bible lies between them on the table and they argue at length. Of course, the Jesuit, who has studied more, argues her down, and then the Princess weeps.'[3] Caroline may have been frustrated at losing an argument; more likely, she was doing battle with

Caroline of Anspach: a portrait from the studio of Jervas

her conscience, angry at her own inability to acquiesce and thus gain a husband. Infuriatingly, she would change her mind from day to day, now professing conversion, now rebuffing it. King Frederick was pressing her urgently to smooth her path to marriage; Sophia Charlotte, a free-thinker and Cartesian in religion, left her protégée at liberty to make up her own mind. After months of indecision, the Princess cast her vote against the Catholic Church – and lost the Archduke.

Fortunately for Caroline, she had not thrown away all chance of a good marriage. Even by the spring of 1705 another was in the offing.

By then, Caroline was no longer attached to the Court in Berlin. In January of that year Queen Sophia Charlotte had died, aged thirty-six, and, with Frederick still fuming at his ward's refusal of the Archduke, Caroline found Anspach a happier place to pass the summer months. She was unaware of plans being formulated in the north for her marriage when she received a small party of Hanoverian gentlemen that June and enjoyed animated conversation with one of their number, a young man of about her own age. She did not know that he was George Augustus, son of the Elector George of Hanover (brother of the late Sophia Charlotte and son of the sprightly Electress Sophia), sent to assess her beauty and virtues as a prospective bride.

Only a month later, after the Hanoverians had left Anspach, a formal proposal arrived, addressed to William Frederick, Caroline's full brother who was now Margrave of Anspach, asking for his sister's hand. It was accepted with alacrity, Caroline admitting that she would rather marry into the Hanoverian family, from which she had already received much kindness, than into any other. On 26 July the announcement of the forth-coming wedding was made: Electress Sophia was delighted, though piqued at having been left out of the secret (she was a notorious gossip with a Continent-wide network of royal confidants); King Frederick of Prussia was furious – he had still cherished hopes of the Austrian match's eventually transpiring.

On 2 September 1705 Caroline married Prince George Augustus of Hanover.

The Hanoverian dynasty was formally known as the House of Brunswick-Lüneburg, after a division of territory among scions of the ancient House of Brunswick earlier in the 17th century. In fact, Hanover was the centre of their territory, the mainspring of their careers. In the ranks of the German states, it followed only Prussia and Saxony in terms of wealth, territory and prestige. However, it had one unique advantage: already, by the time of Caroline's marriage, the Hanoverian dynasty had been promised the crown of Great Britain, in succession to the ageing Queen Anne.

It was the Electress Sophia, the matriarch, who brought such good fortune to Hanover. She was Anne's immediate heiress, as a granddaughter of the first Stuart monarch of England, James I, also King of Scotland. Since the British people had rejected the senior, Catholic line of Stuarts as their kings, the succession was passed to the line descended from James I's daughter Elizabeth; since some of Elizabeth's children were Catholics, and those who were not were devoid of legitimate heirs, it came about that the youngest of them, Sophia, Electress of Hanover, was prescribed the future Queen of Great Britain.

Sophia was delighted at her prospects. In her youth, it had seemed at one time that she might marry her cousin King Charles II, but it had not transpired. Now she lived for the day when she should be called to the throne in her own right. Her son George, the Elector, however, valued his maternal inheritance more for the increased prestige it would give to Hanover than for its own sake. He was prepared to take up the crown one day and to give as good value to England as lay in him, but mainly for the sake of Hanover and its place among German states. To Caroline, however, the future crown (though three lives stood between it and her husband) must have been a triumphant consolation for the loss of Spain.

In the meantime, there were delights enough in Hanover. George Augustus had professed himself in love with Caroline from their first meeting, writing ardent love letters to her in the months before their wedding and after it according her a warm devotion. Though the Elector himself had initiated the match, he was a cold, unwelcoming father-in-law, having little love for any member of his family (he had had his own wife imprisoned many years earlier, on a charge of adultery, though his own open *affaires* went unrebuked in Hanover), but the Electress Sophia more than made up for her son, giving Caroline the place in her heart which had been left empty by the death of Sophia Charlotte.

Caroline was fortunate to have the Electress's sympathy for her intellectual pursuits, for neither George Augustus nor his father had any interest in the arts or philosophy. Professing to hate all painters and poets, they preferred the vigorous pleasures of hunting and Court festivities to *salon* subtleties. Caroline's apartments at the Leine Palais were filled with sages and wits, and her old friend Leibniz was a permanent fixture.

The Princess was twenty-two years old when she married, several years older than most brides of her rank. She brought to her marriage sufficient maturity to cope with the many problems which she was to encounter over the next few years. First, she found that her husband's affection was not exclusive to herself. Though George Augustus never ceased to love his wife and to admire her ripe beauty, monogamy was just not in the Hanoverian blood. Realising that neither protest nor reprisal would reform him but would rather weaken her own hold on him, Caroline bore gracefully with her husband's infidelities, though making sure that George Augustus fell under no influence than her own. With his stubborn nature and irrational temperament, he was a man who would not be ruled by a woman but who would quite peaceably succumb to persuasion. If he could believe that he had chosen a certain line independently, he would happily follow it, unaware that he had been manoeuvred there by a clever woman. With consummate skill, Caroline early established her ascendancy over George Augustus, and though he might philander and stray, she always retained sufficient attraction for him never to be averse to sharing her bed, while her management of his career was so tactful that he never fully realised the extent of her power.

One of Caroline's first manipulations of her husband was in the matter of the English inheritance. Elector George paid little heed to the English emissaries who frequented his Court: there were suitable celebrations when an English ambassador brought news of the important Regency and Naturalisation Acts in 1706, but when Queen Anne created George Augustus Duke of Cambridge, the young man's father vetoed plans for a ceremonial investiture. The Elector was wholly unperturbed at Queen Anne's refusal to summon her heir to England in her lifetime, but, through Caroline's prompting, George Augustus came to resent it. If his father should not go, there was no reason why he could not. If the Hanoverians seemed now to show no interest in their inheritance, they would receive no warm welcome when they took the crown, it was reasoned.

The fact was that Queen Anne feared the growth of an Opposition party round a future king. Her detested Whig party, out of power in the last years of her reign, were always clamouring for George Augustus to be brought over and seated in the House of Lords. It was obvious that they intended to woo the Hanoverians with an eye to taking over the government from Anne's Tories at her death.

The Electress Sophia reputedly declared that she would die happy if the words 'Sophia, Queen of Great Britain' could be incised on her tomb. In 1714, she was in her mid-eighties, some thirty-five years older than Anne, but the Electress was hale where the Queen was always sickly. Sophia was fully as resentful as her grandson that she received no summons

Caroline's husband, George, Prince of Wales – the future King George II – after Kneller (1716)

to appear in London and would occasionally assume the title of 'Princess of Wales', to which, of course, she had no right. On 6 June 1714 Sophia, George and George Augustus received letters from Anne, strongly affirming her resolution not to have any Hanoverian in England in her lifetime. So distressed was Sophia that she felt ill that day and the next, but on the third day she was able to resume her active round, taking a brisk walk with Caroline that afternoon. When it began to rain while she was promenading, she even refused to return to the Palace in a sedan chair. Then, suddenly, the Electress felt faint. She was laid down on the garden path, her head in the lap of a lady-in-waiting. Within minutes Sophia was dead.

Six weeks later, Queen Anne died, and it was George, not Sophia, who became ruler of Great Britain.

Nearly nine years had passed since Caroline's wedding to George Augustus of Hanover. Seventeen months after the wedding she had given birth to a son, who was named Frederick Lewis, and three daughters, Anne, Amelia and Caroline, were born to the couple in the years before their removal to England. In the feverishly busy weeks before the new King George I left Hanover, it was arranged that though his son would travel with him, Caroline and her three daughters should follow in October (in the event, the youngest Princess was ill, and remained at home when her mother left Hanover). The seven-year-old Prince Frederick would stay behind to represent the family in the Electorate: though Caroline and George had taken care to learn to speak English and would now set about winning acceptance by their new countrymen, George I remained solidly German, speaking not one word of English, and he was adamant to have his grandson brought up as a German.

On 20 October 1714, a few days after her arrival in England, Caroline witnessed her father-in-law's coronation. Since his wife, Sophia Dorothea, remained confined in the fortress of Ahlden, as she had since the discovery of her adultery in 1693, there was no consort queen to be crowned, no procession of peeresses at the ceremony, and Caroline was a mere spectator. Five months later she saw her husband ceremonially seated in the House of Lords, as Prince of Wales.

Though the Hanoverians had not set foot in England before Elector George became King, there were many familiar faces at their new Court of St James's. First, there were the Germans who had accompanied them: Robethon, Bothmar and Bernstorff, George's confidential advisers – always a source of suspicion to the English; the King's mistresses, the grossly fat Madame Kielmansegge and the gaunt Madame Schulenburg –

Caroline's chief rival for the love of George II: his mistress Henrietta Howard, Countess of Suffolk: a portrait by C. Jervas

'the elephant and the maypole' sneered the irreverent English courtiers. But among the ladies and gentlemen-in-waiting were numbered many English men and women who had had the foresight to present themselves in Hanover in the years before George's accession and who were now reaping the rewards of their ploy. For Caroline the most important among them was one Mrs Henrietta Howard, who had arrived in Hanover with her husband and who, having won the approval of Electress Sophia, promptly became George Augustus's mistress. Caroline made no objection to this state of affairs. Besides her policy of non-intervention in her husband's *amours*, she had sufficient sagacity to realise that the possession of an English mistress would do George Augustus's reputation no harm in the eyes of his future subjects. As Caroline later admitted,

> knowing the vanity of her husband's temper, and that he must have
> some woman for the world to believe he lay with, [she] wisely suffered
> one to remain in that situation whom she despised and had got the

better of for fear of making room for a successor whom he might really love, and that might get the better of her.[4]

Rather surprisingly, the majority of George I's new subjects made no demur at accepting a German king, with all the drawbacks of his interfering Hanoverian advisers and his rapacious mistresses. True, there was a rising in favour of the Stuart Pretender in 1715, but that was put down with ease.

George I and his son had never been on good terms. George Augustus could remember just enough of his gay young mother to resent his father's cruelty to her, and, besides, he had grudges on his own account: he had longed to make his name as a military commander in the War of the Spanish Succession which raged on the Continent in the early years of the century: at first his father had refused to allow him to hazard his life until he should produce a son to safeguard the Electoral succession; after the birth of Prince Frederick, George relented so far as to permit his son to campaign for a brief season, during which he displayed praiseworthy bravery at the battle of Oudenarde; then, perhaps jealous of George Augustus's prowess, the Elector had recalled him to the idle round of attendance at the Hanoverian Court. Now, in England, though the King would not permit the Prince any real share in or training for power, he could not prevent his son's taking a leading role in politics; he was furious to see the Prince's open alliance with the Tory party against his own government of Whigs.

Nor did Caroline, whose lively Court attracted far more adherence than George's sombre apartments, scruple to make her voice heard. She spoke openly against her father-in-law's employment of German advisers and criticised his trust in the rising young politician Robert Walpole to his face. Walpole, she said, was leading the King by the nose. 'That she-devil,' muttered George I.

By the spring of 1716 the King was not on speaking terms with George Augustus, a situation of the greatest embarrassment to the Court since father and son could not avoid meeting many times a day. Hitherto, the King had managed to prevent the Prince's participating fully in any government affairs, but now the King was pining for Hanover and managed to obtain the permission of Parliament for leave of absence: his ministers pressed him to make the Prince of Wales Regent, citing law and precedent. George I utterly refused. He had himself been lax in his supervision of his government, rarely attending meetings of the Cabinet; he could well envisage that an English-speaking Prince of Wales, able to understand all that went on and eager to make his mark, could easily win far more power than his father (who spoke no English and understood but little) had ever cared to obtain. When George returned to England, he would find that his son had usurped his throne, he feared, in fact if not in name. Though nothing would have pleased the King better than to return permanently to his Electorate, he had too much *amour propre* to see his son king in England in his own lifetime. With all this in mind, he named George Augustus not Regent but 'Guardian of the Realm and Lieutenant', without any of the powers which usually accompanied a formal regency.

Nevertheless, George Augustus and Caroline did not waste the months of the King's absence. While the Prince of Wales took his seat in the Cabinet Chamber, making brave attempts to understand the Whig point of view, Caroline played hostess to Society at Hampton Court. Nothing could have been more brilliant than her drawing-rooms, more stimulating than the cultured private parties of her intimates. When George I returned, he found all he had feared come to pass. It had the effect of rousing the King from his former apathy as to English popularity, and from this time onward he began to vie with George Augustus and Caroline for public plaudits.

On 2 November 1717 Caroline gave birth to another son, an event which might surely have been expected to aid a reconciliation between the King and the Prince of Wales, since the baby's father asked the grandfather to stand sponsor. Another godfather was to be George Augustus's uncle Ernest Augustus, Duke of York, but at the last moment the perverse King insisted that the Lord Chamberlain, the Duke of Newcastle, should take his place. The Prince had long despised and hated Newcastle as incompetent and corrupt, and throughout the baptismal ceremony he fumed with anger. As the King departed, George Augustus could restrain himself no longer, walking up to the Duke and declaring, 'Rascal, I find you out!' Unfortunately an extra element of drama was introduced by the Prince's bad pronunciation of English. Newcastle thought the Prince had said 'fight' not 'find'. Appalled, he hastened to the King, under the impression that he had been challenged to a duel by the heir to the throne. Though George Augustus later explained the mistake, he did so without concession of an apology. The King ordered his son's arrest.

When the royal ministers refused to have the Prince of Wales sent to the Tower, George resorted to ordering his son to leave the Palace immediately. He would allow Caroline to remain with her children, he said, if she would break with her husband; if she would not, she too must go, leaving them in his charge. Caroline refused. Her children she said, were not 'a grain of sand' to her compared with her husband. However, when the Waleses left St James's, Caroline was weeping bitterly at parting from her daughters and baby son. When the latter fell fatally ill the following February, the Princess was allowed unlimited access to him, at Kensington Palace, but when he died, her bitterness against the King increased.

George I announced that whoever was received by the Prince of Wales would not be received by him, expecting dutiful obedience from his politicians and courtiers. To his chagrin, he found that the many politicians and courtiers not sharing the plums of royal favour flocked to pay court to his son, on whose future reign and power to reward loyalty they set their hopes. Peers and politicians foregathered at Leicester House, the Waleses' new residence in London, and a cross-party unity of interests, against the Crown, gave substance to the 'Leicester House set'. Caroline attracted all the leading ladies of the capital to her Court, providing a far more informal atmosphere at her house than at St James's and varying the customary receptions and balls with lively masquerades and charades. Leicester House and the Prince's lodge at Richmond were certainly the focal point of social life in the years of their banishment from Court.

Not since the reign of Charles II had a royal household comprised such beauties and lively wits as Caroline employed. Among the belles were the friendly rivals Molly Lepel and Mary Bellenden, lauded by poets, courted by numerous gallants, and Sophia Howe and her cousin Margaret – saucy, pretty Sophia was 'ruined' by the rake 'Nanty' Lowther, and died young, reputedly of a broken heart. The Prince of Wales himself laid siege to the virtue of Mistress Bellenden, but he never succeeded in making her *his* mistress. Mrs Howard still reigned supreme; Caroline still tolerated her presence in her own household, where she was a woman of the Bed-chamber, but the Princess's own favourite, Mrs Charlotte Clayton, had several disputes with the lovely Henrietta. The latter was placid and peaceable, beloved of the maids-of-honour as their champion and con-fidante; Mrs Clayton had a fiery temper, which she would not scruple to turn on anyone she fancied had hurt her Princess. Neither of these two ladies, however, had the influence over the Prince and Princess which was commonly attributed to her. The Prince still relied wholly on his wife, and, if Caroline ruled George Augustus, no one ruled her.

However, it was at this period that the Princess of Wales began a political alliance which (though interrupted for a while) would last until her death. She struck up a friendship with Robert Walpole, whom she had formerly regarded with suspicion and dislike. The bluff Norfolk

Leicester House as it was in the early 18th century, when first George and then his son Frederick Lewis made it the meeting-place of 'Opposition' politicians

Whig who, with his brother-in-law Lord Townshend, had left government office in the spring of 1717, now set about ensuring his future with the prospective King George II by promoting the latter's present interests. It was Walpole who mustered support in the Commons in the spring of 1719 to prevent the passing of the Peerage Bill which, had it gone through, would effectively have robbed George Augustus of many friends, since it prohibited the future creation of new peerages – to the self-seeking, it was only the hope of future honours which kept their loyalty to the Prince in the face of his father's spite. It was Walpole, too, who bid for the reconciliation of father and son, towards the end of the year. He was himself then sure of an imminent return to power, since only he could win the Commons over to granting the King money to pay his debts. With strenuous diplomacy, Walpole persuaded the King that his son would be less troublesome in future, George Augustus that he would not be humiliated again by his father, and Caroline that she would regain custody of her children. In the event, he had been over-optimistic: a formal reconciliation was achieved, but beyond the restoration of royal honours to the Prince, such as a bodyguard and salutes, nothing tangible was gained. Caroline was permitted to visit her children more freely, but they were

Robert Walpole: a portrait by J. B. van Loo. Caroline's influence as much as Walpole's own merits brought him to the forefront of George II's government; his extensive powers have caused him to be named the first 'Prime Minister'

kept under the care of their grandfather. The young Princess Anne was once heard to say, 'We have a good father and a good mother, and yet we are like charity children.' When asked if her grandfather ever visited the nursery, she replied, 'Oh, no. He does not love us enough for that.'[5]

When the King heard of this plaintive remark, he took the trouble to see the children, who in fact became quite fond of him.

Nevertheless, with only this slight concession of visiting, Caroline was furiously angry with Walpole for his failure to win the children back for her. He was riding high now, especially when, that summer of 1720, he proved himself the only man able to save England from the chaotic aftermath of crazy speculation – the South Sea Bubble. George Augustus found, too, that the new First Lord of the Treasury was wooing the most useful of the 'Leicester House set' into government office, or at least into his own orbit, which only added fuel to the fires of the Waleses' wrath.

After the reconciliation of 1720, relations between the King and his son remained cool and distant. They rarely spoke to each other, maintaining a tense politeness in public. In politics, though the Prince still had friends to tease Walpole with their criticism of his ministry, he now lacked the biting power of former years and on the whole remained in the background. Naturally, when George I retired to Hanover for his holidays, he did not make his son Regent.

The King was on his way to his beloved Hanover in the summer of 1727 when, on 11 June, he died of a stroke.

George Augustus, now King George II, at first attempted to vest control of the government in the hands of his friend Sir Spencer Compton, 'a worthy mediocrity', but it soon became apparent that only Robert Walpole could manage the Commons. Walpole had long since tentatively re-opened relations with his former friend Caroline, and it was she who now promoted him in the King's favour. Henceforth, while Caroline lived, she and Walpole were the real rulers of Britain. A contemporary wag gave the nation a new rhyme:

> You may strut, dapper George, but 'twill all be in vain;
> We know 'tis Queen Caroline, not you, that reign . . .
> Then if you would have us fall down and adore you,
> Lock up your fat spouse as your dad did before you.[6]

There was no possibility of George's ever considering locking Caroline up, or resenting her influence. To the end, he remained devoted to her, so admiring her ample physique that he 'never described what he thought a handsome woman but he drew her picture'.[7] She continued always to live equably with her often irascible and always unfaithful husband – even, it was said, providing suitable ladies to supplement the charms of Mrs Howard, who was elevated to the rank of Mistress of the Robes to the Queen when Mr Howard succeeded to the earldom of Suffolk. When George II finally tired of Henrietta Howard, who had grown tediously deaf and vacant, Caroline actually told her that she was sorry that they must part company after so many years. The King's new love was one Amelia Sophia von Walmoden, a lady of Hanover who remained in the Electorate while Caroline lived, and whom George would visit from time to time, leaving his wife as Regent in Britain.

Not long after George Augustus became king, he sent for his eldest son, Frederick, to join the family. After fourteen years' absence from the home circle, the Prince was ready to please his parents – but he could not: soon, the old familiar situation of King versus Prince of Wales in politics was renewed, and Queen Caroline herself became her son's most bitter critic, reviling him in terms such as few mothers have used of their sons. Frederick's younger, only surviving brother, William, Duke of Cumberland, on the other hand, was all that his father most admired, proving a valuable military leader and obedient son. Often George II and Queen Caroline would sigh at the dictates of fate which gave Frederick precedence over his brother in the line of succession.

The eldest of their daughters, too, was aggrieved at the prospect of Frederick's reigning: Anne, Princess Royal, was convinced that she would make a great queen if given the chance. When she was sixteen years old, there came a proposal from France that she should marry King Louis XV, but again the religious prohibitions came between a princess and her king. In 1734 she married William, Prince of Orange – she would have taken any reasonable offer by then, to leave home and rule her own establishment. The fact that her bridegroom was deformed and ugly did not deter her: she would have married a baboon, she told her father. William died in 1751, leaving his wife to enjoy the power of regent during their son's minority. The fact that she drew the Netherlands into an unpopular alliance with France, which did great harm to the prestige of the Orange family among the Dutch, gives rise to the suspicion that it may have been fortunate that she never became Queen of Great Britain. She died in January 1759.

Anne's younger sisters Amelia and Caroline remained unmarried, impatient attendants on their dominating mother. The youngest princesses, however, did marry – though neither found happiness: as the wife of Prince Frederick of Hesse-Cassel, Mary had to bear with brutality and the horror of her husband's conversion to Catholicism, which drove her to leave him; Louisa married King Frederick V of Denmark and, having lived humbly under the regime of his mistresses, died at twenty-seven.

If Queen Caroline ever regretted that she had missed the chance of an imperial diadem (for her old suitor Archduke Charles became Holy Roman Emperor), she could be well satisfied that her talents had been worthily employed in giving Britain stable government, through her ally Walpole. The 18th century saw several great women rulers – the finest of them Empress Maria Theresa of Austria and Catherine the Great of Russia, but Caroline, as the greatest British Queen since Elizabeth, also had an undeniable place in the first rank.

Caroline might have lived into an honoured and influential old age but for her scrupulous care never to offend her husband: George II was so antipathetic to all forms of illness that Caroline would, she felt, lose her power over him if she admitted, and gave in to, the pain of a hernia from which she had suffered since the birth of her last child. Leaving her ailment untreated until the last days of her agony, Caroline died on 20 November 1737.

Reputedly, on her deathbed she begged her husband to marry again. 'No,' he wept, 'I shall have mistresses.' It was a typical, back-handed compliment which she could appreciate.

INTRIGUE AND CHANGE

In studying the life of the fifth Princess of Wales, Augusta of Saxe-Gotha, it is hard to estimate exactly how much the Princess knew of the country to which she came to be married in 1736 and in which she spent the rest of her life. Although the Hanoverians were becoming anglicised in political outlook and interests, Augusta might as well have been in her native Germany or in any other part of the Continent for all the 'national awareness' which she would have imbibed in the self-absorbed royal Court.

The royal family resided, for the most part, at Whitehall Palace and at Hampton Court and Kew south of the Thames, rarely making a foray beyond the nearest home counties. They drove through the thoroughfares of the capital but never penetrated the mean streets in which the majority of citizens lived. The men and women with whom they consorted were gathered from many parts of the kingdom, but the great majority of them were aristocrats, themselves divided by class and wealth from the bulk of the population; the Princess's intimates, her ladies-in-waiting, were of the nobility, her husband's associates noblemen and upper-middle-class politicians. Unlike her mother-in-law, Augusta was no bluestocking, and the talk of her drawing-room would be only of fashion and the arts, occasionally coloured by more robust discussion of the hunt and the stables when her husband and his cronies were by. Augusta would have heard talk of politics: she could not avoid it, as her husband's hostess at Leicester House; but such talk was not of policies and social reforms but of the manœuvring of parties and the infighting of the leaders of government. In all, Augusta's view of England would take little account of the habits and aspirations of the great majority of her father-in-law's subjects.

Royal ladies were not alone in their ivory towers. Few upper-class women of the time came into contact with their 'inferiors' and the harsh realities of their life. All over the land were dotted palatial mansions of luxury and elegance, far removed from the solid comforts of the bourgeoisie and even farther from the squalor of that amorphous mass 'the poor'. Nor was a woman's mind now broadened by formal education: the Georgian lady did not study the classics and distinguish herself in literature and scholarship as the Tudor lady had once done; in France there were the *femmes philosophes* and *salonistes*, but they had no counterparts in England. Georgian noblewomen were real 'ladies of leisure', their only business their own appearance and entertainment, and the pursuit of love.

The old values of housewifery, which a century before not even duchesses had despised, were unknown to the sophisticated belles of 'society'. The domestic arts flourished still in the ranks of the middle classes, where a woman was supported by her husband and free to give undivided attention to family welfare, but increasingly lower-class women were taken from kitchen and garden by pressure to add to the family's cash income. Thousands of women were forced to take in work to do at home and, as the century progressed, thousands more toiled in factories, on farms and even in mines, to swell the family budget to mere subsistence level. The employment of women was regarded by theorists as of considerable benefit to the nation, a blessing to the domestic economy of the poor: in fact, the increased employment of women outside their homes, and the employment of their children from an early age, had a demoralising effect on family life which came to be understood only very much later.

The famous Industrial Revolution was, of course, responsible for this development, even though the trend towards female 'out-work' and factory-work had long been advancing. The textile industry employed the majority of women, who could card and spin wool at home while bringing up a family – though they had to toil long hours, to the detriment of their housework, to earn more than a pittance; the cotton-mills took them out of their homes, toddlers clinging to their mother's skirts as they worked the looms, while even children of nine or ten could be utilised in fetching and carrying, turning wheels and brushing droppings into piles for re-use.

The widespread employment of women and children arose from the demand for increased productivity which, in an only slowly rising population, men could not provide alone. In the first half of the 18th century opportunities for trade at home and abroad were expanding everywhere, as Britain entered a phase of general peace with the Continent and as colonial markets were opening up in America and Asia: thus the need for a greater output of manufactured goods, especially the prized British textiles. The broadening facilities for the raising of capital to fund large-scale industrial enterprises to cope with demand for higher productivity were provided by a diverse and generally efficient network of financial institutions.

But labour and capital were only part of the Industrial Revolution. New machinery, new techniques, were devised in these years to swell output, not only a tribute to man's inventiveness but also the result of the expansion of the iron and steel industries, themselves the result of more extensive use of coal power. The machines were made of iron and steel, eminently durable and capable of moulding and tooling to unprecedented precision; and, in the 1780s, steam-powered engines made of iron were developed to drive the machinery.

One drawback to the viability of higher production was the immense difficulties encountered in transporting goods on the still untreated surfaces of British roads. Road-engineering became a vital aid to industry, providing highways to connect manufacturing centres with trade outlets, and, with rivers fully utilised in trade already, long stretches of canal were also cut to add to waterway usage. By these means delivery was speeded and manufacturers' costs and retail prices were cut, thus opening yet another new market by making the purchase of manufactured goods possible to the lower paid.

The term 'Industrial Revolution' and the customary landmark of 1760 for its beginning have been increasingly challenged in recent years by historians who have pointed to trends in industrialisation long before that date. Nevertheless, the expansion of British industry before 1760 was so gradual, after 1760 so rapid, bringing revolutionary changes in British economy and society, that the old theories still retain much weight.

The Industrial Revolution was to prove a mixed blessing. To the manufacturer, wholesaler and exporter, it came as a boon from heaven, a means to seemingly limitless wealth; to the poor, it meant only a new sort of poverty, infinitely more oppressive than the age-old round of agriculture, as family after family was swallowed up in the miasmas of the new industrial towns. At the end of the 18th century the population was still largely rural, but thirty years later the picture was different, with Manchester, Birmingham, Sheffield, Leeds and Glasgow swollen to twice their proportions of 1800, and the birth-rate rapidly rising in urban communities. Men and women accustomed to open landscapes were enclosed from dawn to dark within the walls of factories, to emerge only into grey streets and crowded hovels, but now there was also a new generation, town-born, slum-bred, completely divorced from the measured round of the countryside.

In the 18th century, in the first phase of the Industrial Revolution, there was little organised rebellion against the new conditions of life. In the brightly lit, hysterically gay 'gin-palaces' oblivion from daily misery could be purchased for a farthing; in the Methodist chapels which scattered town and country by the end of the century, visions of a future heaven went a long way towards compensating for a present hell on earth. Where there was rebellion, it was often curiously irrelevant to the situation: men protested not against the decline in the quality of their life-style but against the new machinery which, they thought, would rob them of their livelihood. Some attempt was made by workmen (in agriculture before industry) to band together to demand higher wages and the improvement of working conditions, but everywhere such embryo unions were repressed. In 1799 the Combination Acts firmly put 'right' on to the side of employers stung by workmen's appeals and protests, making the outcries of organised labour a matter for criminal law.

This was one rare case of government intervention in industrial practice in the 18th century. For the most part, the government found its duty to the economy to lie mainly in the protection of foreign trade. Wars of ideology and of European frontier disputes did not cease in the 18th century, but for Britain wars for profit in trade were the most alluring. By mid-century Britain's wars were trade wars, fought in defence of lucrative colonies, to expand the territories of the British Crown and trading companies, and to defend the rights of British merchantmen on the high seas. When, in the second half of the 18th century, the founding fathers of the United States primed the revolt against Britain, they did so on high-minded principles of political theory – but also to protect themselves from

Britain's greedy commercial ploys: Britain fought back to maintain her dignity and authority – but also to retain her profits from American trade.

In the 18th century property and political power still went hand in hand. In theory, every male freeholder of forty shillings per annum had a free vote in Parliamentary elections: in practice, elections were rarely contested in most areas, and where they were, bribery and intimidation accounted for many votes cast for the candidates put up by rival parties. Nor did the return of M.P.s correspond to the distribution of the population: five counties in southern England returned one-quarter of the members of the Commons; some boroughs with the right to return M.P.s had become greatly depopulated over the years, while the industrial cities growing up in the 18th century had only minimal representation. Any attempt at reform, such as was mooted by radicals towards the end of the century, was fiercely rejected and combatted by those with vested interests in maintaining the *status quo* and came to nothing. While the power of the Commons had increased, little advance had been made towards the Parliamentary democracy which we know today.

The century-long striving of Parliament against the Crown had, by 1714, seemed to be resolved by the terms of the settlement of the Crown which Parliament had laid on William and Mary in 1689. Kings still appointed their governments, but their ministers had a dual responsibility, to the King and to Parliament, an anomaly which was to remain a problem and matter of controversy even in the 19th century. As the 18th century progressed, it became ever more apparent that no king could maintain in power a government which could not command a majority of members' support in Parliament. However, there was little difference between the two parties (the Whigs and the Tories, who had evolved in the years after the restoration of the monarchy in 1660), for both operated only on the broadest of principles, without political doctrine or programme of reform to mark their difference: their only object being to take power as a government and enjoy the prizes of state office, Court appointment, and access to wealth and title which accrued to government ministers and their protégés. 'Party' politics may have dominated the 18th century, but in a form unrecognisable today.

King George III attempted to break the stranglehold on power of the aristocracy and to regain the powers which his two predecessors had lost, but in so doing he immeasurably damaged the prestige and influence of the monarchy: both parties buttressed their powers by bringing into their ranks men of the middle classes, intellectuals and businessmen of talent and strong will, and by utilising the volatile emotions of the mob in violent agitation against royal policies. 'Radicalism', a force towards change in politics, economics and the social structure of the land, burst into British politics in the last years of the century with a violence which many feared would end only in revolution.

By the end of the 18th century, the constitution was outmoded, the power base unstable, the economic structure of the nation too complex for existing institutions, so that Great Britain was ready and waiting for the all-embracing reforms which inevitably followed in the 19th century.

THE FIFTH PRINCESS
Augusta of Saxe-Gotha

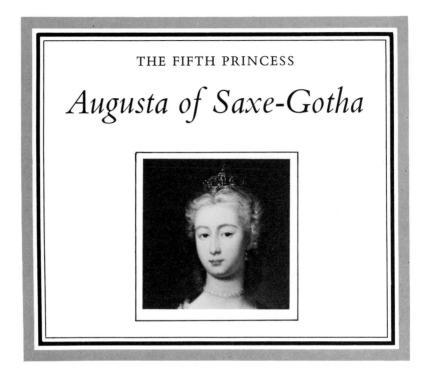

After the harsh treatment meted out to George II and Caroline of Anspach by George I, one might expect that they would treat their own heir and his wife rather better. In fact, relations between George II and Frederick, Prince of Wales, could scarcely have been worse, and after Frederick's death (nearly ten years before his father's), Augusta, Princess of Wales, carried on her late husband's opposition to the King's domestic and political authority.

When Queen Anne died in 1714, and George I and his eldest son left Hanover for their new kingdom, the seven-year-old Frederick was left behind. His elders were determined that the future King should be educated as a German, and it was to be fourteen years before the Prince was allowed to join his family. Throughout that period, the boy never once saw his parents or his sisters and brother, though he did occasionally see his grandfather, who, on his visits to Hanover, actually displayed some affection for him in an entirely uncharacteristic fashion.

In the absence of the Elector-King, Hanover was administered by Frederick's great-uncle, Ernest Augustus, who was also his guardian. On ceremonial occasions the boy was brought out to make his bow to Court and Council; for the rest, he was left in the care of servants. His education was entrusted not to internationally respected scholars but to teachers in the local schools, but somehow the boy managed to imbibe the basic principles of politics and government and to become immeasurably more cultured in the arts than his father and grandfather. In 'polite society', he had a charming social manner, but left to his own devices he had his share of youthful dissipation: early learning the pleasures of 'low company', he could often be found drinking in taverns with pages and stable-boys, wandering the town at night, carousing and breaking the windows of honest burghers. Whatever his earliest sexual adventures may have been, the Prince's first acknowledged mistress was one Madame d'Elitz, a Court lady of ripe age, who had ministered to the lusts of his father and grandfather before him. None of his misdeeds went unnoticed of course, for regretful reports were sent to Frederick's parents by his governor.

The Prince was a mere child when the first plans for his marriage were set in train. His grandfather was anxious to conclude an advantageous treaty with the rising power of Prussia, whose king was his own son-in-law, and he proposed that his Hanoverian grandchildren Frederick and Amelia should marry his Prussian grandchildren Princess Wilhelmina and Crown Prince Frederick respectively.

George I himself later went to Berlin to supervise negotiations and at the same time took a good look at the prospective bride and groom. The then fourteen-year-old Wilhelmina, tall, well-made, intelligent and already fluent in English, was an ideal candidate for a throne. George I was not easily impressed, however. 'As soon as I entered the room,' wrote Wilhelmina in her memoirs, 'he took a wax light and examined me from head to foot; while I all the time remained immovable like a statue and very much disconcerted. All this passed without his saying anything.'[1]

Through all the years of their engagement, Frederick never met Wilhelmina, but that was no bar to his fancying himself in love with her. When, soon after the death of George I, negotiations for their marriage were broken off, Frederick remained determined to wed Wilhelmina and at one point even suggested an elopement; but his aunt the Queen of Prussia, a party to the secret, proved untrustworthy, and the news arrived in London before the romantic adventure had been accomplished. After that, of course, it was impossible. King Frederick William of Prussia, whose violent temper bordered on madness, beat his daughter mercilessly, and his Queen retired to her bed in hysterics.

Soon after this incident, Frederick, now twenty-one-years old, was summoned to England.

George II had long resented his father's kind treatment of Frederick and the praises he lavished on him – so different to the snubs and rebukes he was himself accustomed to receiving. Frederick's obvious independence of his father, accentuated by his plans for the Prussian marriage, was disconcerting to the King, who now called his son to London where he might be more closely supervised.

The summons came suddenly, one winter night in 1728. Frederick was called out of a Court ball to receive his father's envoy, only to receive orders that he must leave for England at once. Through the bitter, snowy weather, he travelled at full speed, but on his arrival in London, on 7 December, he found no ceremonious reception and scarcely a warm welcome from his own family.

Within a month, Frederick had been created Prince of Wales – though his father grudged him the title and withheld its usual pecuniary advantages, bestowing the honour only under great pressure from his chief minister, Robert Walpole. The title proved an empty one, bringing with it neither responsibility nor power, nor even a formal training for his future rule. Even when, a few months later, George II departed for Hanover (where he stayed for two years), he left no share in the regency to his heir.

After years of independence, the Prince of Wales was forced to live *en famille*, with three sisters he scarcely remembered and a brother and two sisters who had been born after their parents' arrival in England. At first, all went well. Queen Caroline proved responsive to the affection of her long-lost son, and 'Fretz' was popular among his older sisters. It was not to be expected, however, that the Prince could live in virtuous idleness for long. Soon he was gambling beyond his means (he had only infrequent small sums of money allowed by his father's provisions), and he began roaming the London streets with hooligan gangs of 'Mohocks' for amusement, finding his mistresses among actresses and 'ladies of the town'. In 1731 his father returned to find his heir one of the most debauched young rakes in the capital.

Over the next few years, relations between Frederick and his parents worsened considerably. The various and disparate parties of the political 'Opposition' looked to Frederick to make their fortunes and give them power when he came to reign. To George II it was a severe blow to his pride to find his son courted and fêted by so many of his own enemies, while to Caroline, the real ruler of Britain, her son's new circle of friends posed a threat to her power. Even Robert Walpole, who had tried at first to temper the King's and Queen's growing antipathy to their son, gave up

A music-party at Kew *by P. Mercier (1733): Frederick Lewis, Prince of Wales, with his sisters* (l.-r.), *Anne, Caroline and Amelia*

when it became apparent that the Prince of Wales had become a focal-point and figurehead for his opponents. The Prince's 'Boy Patriots' – with the future great Earl of Chatham, William Pitt, among their number – were a force to be reckoned with in the 1730s. Even in music, one of the few tastes shared by the King and the Prince, there was a ridiculous but acrimonious rivalry: George II favoured the works of Handel and other Germans; Frederick was the patron of the Italian master Buononcini and his fellows. Partisans of the King and of the Prince flocked to the rival theatres, irrespective of their own preference, simply in order to demonstrate loyalty to their royal leader.

In 1734 Frederick applied to his father for permission to marry. He had no specific lady in mind, he said, and would willingly accept his father's choice. To prove his good faith, he even gave up his long-time mistress Anne Vane (who was, in fact, more trouble than she was worth, 'two-timing' the Prince secretly with Queen Caroline's confidant Lord Hervey).

The future Princess of Wales must be a Protestant, so much was demanded by English prejudice. To please George II, she must be a German. A princess of Denmark was put out of the running when reports came that she was deformed, a dwarf and mentally retarded; Princess Wilhelmina of Prussia had married in 1731, and her younger sisters were rejected because of the reputed madness of their father; a Princess of Württemberg was considered – until it was remarked that her grandmother would not let her own husband lie with her after the birth of their first child, while her great-grandmother would reputedly lie with anyone. Consideration was still being given to the problem of who should become Princess of Wales when Frederick himself received the offer of an English girl with fortune enough to balance her non-royal birth. The proposal came from the Duchess of Marlborough, the former favourite and *éminence grise* of Queen Anne, who had outlived her beauty and political finesse to a meddlesome old age. Duchess Sarah offered Frederick her granddaughter, Lady Diana Spencer, with the remarkably useful sum of £100,000. The Prince was more than willing to take such a dowry, and to win even more popularity in the country by espousing a native, the descendant of the famous warrior John Churchill, Duke of Marlborough. Walpole, however, ended the Duchess's daydream by informing the King and setting him firmly against the match.

Not long after, the name of Princess Augusta of Saxe-Gotha was mooted. There was no fortune or real political advantage for Britain in an alliance with her brother's petty duchy, but it was an unexceptionable match. George II inspected the girl during one of his periodic visits to Germany and saw nothing in her to deter him. Britain's proposal was made; Saxe-Gotha accepted; Frederick concurred.

On 25 April 1736 seventeen-year-old Princess Augusta disembarked at Greenwich. Though she received no official reception, Frederick himself soon arrived from St James's, and over the next two days he was almost continually with his future wife. They talked together, ate together, danced together and went for little trips on the Thames, with musicians following their barge. Frederick knew how to be pleasing.

On the 27th Augusta set off for the Palace. She was late, her couriers having misjudged the height of the river tide. George II was working himself into a rage in the waiting, but when Augusta finally appeared, she melted his cold heart by prostrating herself first at his feet, then at Caroline's.

One of the first courtiers to see Augusta, the Earl of Egmont, noted that she 'is about [the Prince's] height, much pitted with the smallpox and had a great colour from the heat of the day and the hurry and surprise she was in. But she has a peculiar affability of behaviour and a very great sweetness of countenance, mixed with innocence, cheerfulness and sense.'[2]

Frederick Lewis, Prince of Wales: a portrait by P. Mercier, in about 1736–8

Lord Hervey, unwilling to admire the girl who was to marry the Prince he hated, wrote:

> The Princess was rather tall and had health and youth enough in her face, joined to a very modest and good-natured look, to make her countenance not disagreeable; but her person, from being very ill-made, a good deal awry, her arms long, and her motions awkward, had, in spite of all the finery and jewels and brocade, an ordinary air, which no trappings could cover or exalt.[3]

To complete the picture, Queen Caroline informed her eldest daughter, Princess Anne of Orange, that the girl 'far from being beautiful, has a wretched figure', adding that her blonde hair was of 'a sheep's colour', though she admitted that Augusta had 'pretty eyes and a good mouth', adding, 'She is as anxious as a good child to please.'[4]

The wedding was to take place that very evening. First, however, the Princess was sent up to the royal schoolroom, to partake of a meal with her future husband and his brother and sisters. Perhaps Frederick was revelling in being the centre of attention and lost his head; perhaps he was trading on the occasion's excitement to score off his father; perhaps he merely, kindly, wanted to establish his bride's precedence over his brother and sisters: whatever the reason, Frederick made the unwise move of ordering that while he and Augusta were to be seated in arm-chairs at the table, and to be served on bended knee, the Prince and Princesses were to sit on their usual stools and serve themselves. The elder Princesses, Amelia and Caroline, were furious at the insult and refused to concede the honours: the King was consulted, and he coldly counter-manded his son's orders. It was a sore embarrassment to the newcomer, and her first taste of the family squabbles that were to colour the next twenty years and more of her life.

At nine o'clock the royal family took their places in the Chapel Royal. The pews had been moved so that as many people as possible could cram in, craning for a view from tiers of benches. Augusta entered 'wearing a crown of one bar, as Princess of Wales, set all over with diamonds; her robe likewise, as Princess of Wales, being of crimson velvet, turned back with several rows of ermine, and having her train supported by four ladies, all of whom were in virgin habits of silver, like the Princess, and adorned with diamonds not less in value than from twenty to thirty thousand pounds'.[5]

For all her splendour, Augusta was terrified. Unused in Gotha to such

Princess Augusta: a portrait by C. Phillips in 1736, the year of her marriage to the Prince of Wales

magnificence, unable to understand a word of English, she turned appealing eyes to Queen Caroline.

> I told her to look at me and I would make a sign when she ought to kneel [wrote the Queen to her daughter in Holland later]. She clung to my skirt and said, 'For Heaven's sake, please don't leave me,' but [Frederick] bawled in her ear, making her repeat the marriage sentences. She did not want to let go of my skirt. After the service, she and her husband knelt to ask the King's and my blessing, which the King bestowed most benignly, and she, poor creature, just as one has seen in plays – she was sick . . . .[6]

Then Augusta had to go through the ordeal of a supper-party, amid an immense crowd of onlookers. Frederick, completely unperturbed, ate jelly after jelly, winking largely at his friends.

The custom of centuries was for the royal family to 'bed' the newly married couple. Augusta was released from the agony of her stays and put into an ornate nightgown by the Queen herself, then led to her bed. In nightshirt and lace cap ('a grenadier's bonnet',[7] scoffed his mother), Frederick joined her. Side by side they sat while the Court streamed by them, avid to lose no detail of the scene. Then candles were dowsed and Frederick and Augusta, Prince and Princess of Wales, were left alone.

In the first months of her marriage, Augusta walked a tight-rope, and it was much to her credit that she had no serious fall. 'She is the best creature in the world,' said Caroline in those first days, 'one puts up with her insipidity because of her goodness.'[8] Of course, there was the problem of her lack of English to be overcome ('I could scold that old Duchess of Gotha for not having given the poor good child a better education,'[9] wrote Caroline), but Augusta proved willing and quick to learn.

The Princess made mistakes; that was inevitable. She was discovered playing with a doll, 'a great jointed baby, and dressing and undressing it two or three times a day',[10] in full view of sniggering guards and servants. More heinous was her persistence in taking the Sacrament at the German Lutheran chapel rather than among Anglicans. But this error was blamed on the Princess's German governess. Left behind on the Continent on the King's orders when Augusta came to England, the old lady had been summoned by Frederick at Augusta's urgent request. The mistake was soon rectified: Madame Rixleiven was dismissed.

The lively minded Queen Caroline found Augusta's company tedious, but, determined not to quarrel with the Prince of Wales in the King's absence, she was frequently in the young people's company. Though

Augusta was invariably polite to her mother-in-law, Caroline noted that the Princess never took a stand against Frederick's petty insults to his parents or against his Opposition friends. In justice, Caroline had to admit that, 'Poor creature, if she were to spit in my face, I should only pity her for being under such a fool's direction, and wipe it off.'[11]

That summer after the wedding, Frederick and Augusta were due to pass their holiday under the Queen's eye, with the rest of the schoolroom flock. Instead, Frederick bore his wife off to St James's, holding great court there, against the express orders of his absent father. Nor did his conduct receive royal approval when, having put himself at risk to help fight a fire in the City (like Charles II in 1666), the London mob greeted him with shouts of 'Crown him! Crown him!' That same month, January 1737, there was every chance that Frederick would soon be crowned, for reports came to London that the King, on his way home, had been drowned at sea. When George II finally arrived home, alive and well, he was less pleased at the prudent conduct of his son during the crisis than angry to find that so many of his subjects had greeted news of the supposed disaster with glee.

By then Augusta was pregnant, though Frederick did not inform his parents of the fact until the beginning of July. The King and Queen, who expressed doubts as to their son's ability to beget children, were determined that Augusta's baby should be born in their sight, so that there should be no possibility of a changeling's being foisted on the royal dynasty. Frederick, however, had other ideas, and when his wife went into labour, on the evening of Sunday, 31 July, he conveyed her out of Hampton Court Palace, where his parents and all the Court were making merry, and into a coach. With total disregard for Augusta's comfort and safety – though urging her continuously to have courage, Frederick sped her to St James's. Inevitably, nothing was prepared, and the neighbourhood was scoured for napkins and implements; without sheets to hand, the Princess lay between two table-cloths.

At a quarter to eleven, a princess was born: 'a little rat of a girl, about the bigness of a good large toothpick case,'[12] wrote Lord Hervey.

The King and Queen were asleep when the Prince's messenger reached Hampton Court, and they were still unaware of the Waleses' 'moonlight flit'. A lady-in-waiting broke the news that Augusta was in labour.

'My God, my nightgown!' exclaimed Caroline. 'I'll go to her this moment.'

'Your nightgown, madam,' said the lady, 'and your coaches too; the Princess is at St James's!'[13]

By four o'clock the angry King and Queen reached London, to be met with the news that they had a granddaughter. Caroline congratulated the mother more kindly than she might have under the circumstances and kissed the baby. Later she was heard to remark that she was sure that the child was her son's true-born, though she admitted that 'if, instead of this poor, little, ugly she-mouse, there had been a brave, large, fat, jolly boy, I should not have been cured of my suspicions . . .'.[14] Nevertheless, the Prince's trick had been unforgivable.

Earlier in the year, Frederick had driven the King to fury by having his Parliamentary friends put pressure on the Government to give him control of his allowance, the bulk of which the King was still appropriating. The motion was defeated by a small majority, but it had left the bitterest aftermath in the royal family. Now, after the birth of Frederick's child, the King was in a desperate rage, threatening to disinherit the Prince. While appearances were kept up in public, George and Caroline sought a means to discredit their son and to drop him into such base ignominy that his partisans could not but desert him. On 10 September Frederick and Augusta received a notice of eviction: they were to leave St James's within three days. An announcement was made to the effect that whoever showed friendship or rendered service to the Prince would never be received by the King and Queen. Not many months afterwards, the Waleses found a home at Leicester House: thus closely did the pattern of events follow that of the previous reign.

When Caroline lay dying, that November, Frederick was refused permission to see her. She died unforgiving.

George II's intentions to humiliate his son and isolate him were thwarted. Not only did 'the people' – that nebulous mass who formed their own opinion of events, despite propaganda – cheer Frederick and Augusta as they drove away, but all the Prince's friends rallied to him now. After all, George II was an old man, and many thought – mistakenly as it proved – that it could not be long before Frederick succeeded to the throne. A new King, indebted to his friends, would prove, they thought, a rich fount of bounty.

From this point, Frederick became a major political figure. Before, he had always been careful to demand only his rights, to attack his father and the royal government only obliquely. Now, he and his supporters mounted a full-scale attack on Robert Walpole. First, he forced the King's chief minister into war with Spain, which he had tried desperately to avoid, and then he allowed Walpole to take the blame for Britain's failure in the war. Complex alliances of politicians and subtle shifts of policy, combined with a little judicious bribery and corruption, produced Walpole's downfall, and he resigned on 2 February 1742. But all the vaunted plans of the Opposition, under the Prince, to reform the British constitution, came to nothing, for Walpole's successors, the Pelham brothers, wooed the majority of them into the government, whereupon the sweets of office made them forget their supposed ideals. Frederick, of course, could not be won over, for there was nothing in Parliament's gift which he could desire. He was left in the political wilderness, too dispirited to gather up his remnants and form a new Opposition to the coalition government.

However, by then a reconciliation between father and son had been engineered. In his last days in power, Walpole himself had opened up the possibility. Now George II and Frederick were outwardly at least on terms of mutual respect. In fact, Frederick was still given no power, nor was he permitted any part in Britain's military ventures. While his brother, the Duke of Cumberland, was making his name in England as a military hero in putting down the Jacobite rebellion of 1745 and in the wars on the Continent, Frederick fumed impotently at home.

He had his consolations. On 4 June 1738 Augusta had given birth to a son, the future King George III, and in the following years the royal nursery was filled with five more boys and three girls (a fourth daughter was born posthumously in 1751). The marriage was undoubtedly happy, and Augusta was Frederick's constant companion, sharing his interest in music, painting and literature, and in planning the landscaping of his gardens. They took more interest in the education and amusements of their children than many contemporary parents, and, with his love of amateur theatricals, the Prince would patiently rehearse his growing family in home-made entertainments.

This is not to say, however, that the Prince of Wales was the ideal husband. Augusta had to bear with his infidelities from the earliest years of their marriage. When she arrived in England, Frederick told her that she must not be perturbed by rumours that a certain Lady Archibald Hamilton was his mistress. Perhaps he deceived his wife, for everyone else thought Lady Archibald shared his bed, for all that the lady was middle-aged and plain, the mother of several children. Frederick persuaded Augusta to beg the Queen to allow the lady to serve her in her household, and whether the two were rivals for Frederick's affections or not, they always maintained good relations. Grace, Countess of Middlesex, was certainly the mistress of the Prince of Wales. Described by the memoirist Horace Walpole as 'very short, very plain and very yellow; a vain girl, full of Greek and Latin and music and painting, but neither mischievous nor political',[15] Lady Middlesex never interfered with her lover's home life. Since scarcely one princess in Europe could claim perfect fidelity from her husband, perhaps Augusta was fortunate: she never had to submit to humiliations which royal mistresses imposed on many other royal wives.

By 1747 the Prince had re-entered the political arena, gathering a new faction which drew up a manifesto for reform. But though his partisans hovered around the Pelham Government, like gnats at dusk, they scored no real hits and drew no blood. Frederick was staking everything now on a speedy accession to the throne, and made elaborate plans for his assumption of power. But they were never to be put to the test.

On 5 March 1751 the Prince of Wales put in some hours in his garden at Kew. It was a bitterly cold day, with rain, and he came into the house wet through. Then he went off to sit in the musty, oppressive heat of the House of Lords, in heavy robes. He returned to Kew in an open chair but was soon off again, this time to Carlton House, where he sat three hours by an open window. Not surprisingly, the next day he was suffering from a chill and had to submit to being bled and blistered by his surgeons.

By the 15th the Prince seemed to have made a good recovery, but on the night of the 20th he relapsed into a prolonged fit of coughing, followed by a sharp pain (from an abscess which had burst in his chest, it was later found).

'*Je sens la mort*,' gasped the Prince.

'Good God! The Prince is going!' exclaimed his German valet.

Augusta had been standing at the foot of the bed, but even before she could reach her husband's side, he was dead.

The Princess refused to believe it. Four hours she stayed by the corpse, watching for signs of life. Then, after two hours' sleep, she feverishly sorted the Prince's papers, burning many – probably those in which he reviled his parents.

On 13 April Frederick, Prince of Wales, was buried. His epitaph on his tomb was of the conventional sort, listing his titles; a less formal tribute was distributed anonymously:

> Here lies poor Fred
> Who was alive and is dead;
> Had it been his father,
> I had much rather;
> Had it been his brother,
> Still better than another;

The Prince of Wales and his family at Henley-on-Thames, c. 1743, by J. Wootton

Had it been his sister,
No one would have missed her;
Had it been the whole generation,
Still better for the nation;
But since 'tis only Fred,
Who was alive and is dead,
There's no more to be said.[16]

It is hard to assess the character of 'Poor Fred': so much was written against him by the royal toady Lord Hervey and by the credulous gossip Horace Walpole, so little on the other side, so little by neutral sources. He was certainly a man of some intelligence and ability, no worse in his morals than any monarch of his dynasty; a loyal Briton, he was hurt at being denied a part in the nation's defence and government; what talents he had in politics, historians will never agree on, some saying that he was the mainspring and inspiration of his party, others that he was the dupe of ambitious men using him for their own future power. A man of culture and good taste in the arts, he was a keen gardener and cricketer; he had good humour and good manners. He was an affectionate and considerate husband and father, and he might have been a good son in different circumstances. He has often been compared with his Prussian first-cousin Frederick, who embarked on a campaign against his own father similar to the Prince of Wales's against George II: but Frederick William of Prussia was of a different stamp from his brother-in-law of England – he had his son imprisoned for his rebellion. The two Fredericks were much alike in taste and ambition, but where the one died, the other lived to become 'Frederick the Great', one of the most notable kings of Prussia.

Hervey wrote that Frederick 'used always to say a prince should never talk to any woman of politics, or make any use of a wife but to breed; and that he would never make the ridiculous figure his father had done in letting his wife govern him or meddle in business'.[17] It certainly seems as if for once Lord Hervey was telling the truth, for though Princess Augusta was a fine hostess to the 'Leicester House set' and though she always maintained polite relations with her in-laws, she never once, in her husband's lifetime, figured in his intrigues or openly influenced his judgement. In the usual controversy over historical motive, some writers have deemed her prudent and patient, and have imputed to her the power of foresight that she would have a chance to rule through her son; others have read into various incidents 'proof' that she was behind such incidents as the

Augusta and her children in mourning for the Prince of Wales, whose portrait hangs in the background: a painting by G. Knapton

removal from Hampton Court for the birth of her first child; others congratulate the Princess of Wales on the wisdom of her acquiescence to her husband and simultaneous show of submission to the King and Queen.

It seems most likely that Augusta had been primed, before her arrival in England, to be as complaisant as possible to the will of those who elevated her to her rank, and that this advice, and her obedience to it, stood her in good stead over the first years of her marriage, but that she also, having a sharp intelligence, learned from those around her how to manage affairs once she had an independence. Certainly, she took the best possible line towards her father-in-law on Frederick's death.

George II was undoubtedly shocked at the loss of his heir. He wrote kindly to his daughter-in-law. With consummate tact, she replied:

The sorrow which overwhelms me does not make me the less sensible of the great goodness of Your Majesty. The only things, Sire, which can console me are the gracious assurances which Your Majesty has given me. I throw myself, together with my children, at your feet. We commend ourselves, Sire, to your paternal love and protection.[18]

When the King arrived to see her, he found the Princess, flanked by her sons George and William, kneeling before him in a room hung around with black curtains. With apparent sincerity, he wept with her.

The future King George III was only twelve years old when his father died and when he was himself created Prince of Wales, and an immediate consideration was the arrangement of a regency, in case George II should die before the boy gained his majority, at eighteen.

The King himself was in favour of his son the Duke of Cumberland's becoming regent: he had always favoured Cumberland against Frederick, letting it be known that he thought that his second son would make a better king than his first. But 'Butcher' Cumberland was grossly unpopular in the country and in Parliament, and the leading politicians, Newcastle and his brother Pelham, combined to prevent the King's getting his own way. Augusta was the most viable alternative, as the future King's mother, and in the end it was she who was nominated and accepted for this power. Nevertheless, she was not to rule with real monarchical authority: she would not be allowed to dismiss ministers

Scotch broomstick and female besom: *a cartoon by George Townshend (1762) against the supposed liaison between Princess Augusta and Lord Bute and their influence over the young George III*

formerly appointed by George II without the consent of a majority in her Council or the assent of both Houses of Parliament.

Less than three months after the death of her husband, Augusta gave birth to her ninth child, a daughter, who was named Caroline Matilda. Though this last of her children became a favourite, always daring to contradict or tease her mother where the others quailed, in the main the Princess concentrated her affections and attentions on her eldest son to the detriment of the emotional development of the others. But she continued Frederick's regime for the nursery and schoolroom, with regular hours and simple food. She also kept the family circle tight, not allowing her sons to associate with young scions of the nobility, deeming them 'ill-educated and so very vicious' and justly fearing that they would corrupt her innocents.

'Princess Prudence' was the name Horace Walpole gave Augusta in these years, and she certainly lived up to it with her diplomatic dealings with her father-in-law. But at the same time, she also kept open those relations with Opposition politicians which her late husband had cherished. Perhaps, however, her personal political skill should not be exaggerated, for in her widowhood Augusta increasingly bowed to the judgement of one very shrewd and far-seeing man: John Stuart, Earl of Bute.

Frederick had known Bute for several years before his death and had made quite a favourite of him, though he had no high opinion of his political weight (Bute would make a very good ambassador at a foreign Court of little consequence, Frederick once said). To Augusta, the Earl was the chief director of her life in her widowhood; to her son George, he was mentor. Bute was a Scotsman, none too rich at the time, though he later inherited a large fortune. He had great ambition and just enough intelligence to warrant his hopes for future power.

It was, of course, rumoured that although a married man with several children he was Augusta's lover: it cannot be definitely proved or disproved. However, it is certain that Augusta was a good friend of Bute's undoubted mistress, her own maid-of-honour Miss Vansittart, which she surely would not have been had they been rivals for his favours. At the same time, the future George III was quite a prude about sexual relations, and yet he was a fervent admirer of Lord Bute, which would surely not have been the case had he had any suspicion of an intimacy between his mother and his friend. When, in the summer of 1756, it was represented to George that Bute was his mother's lover, he would not believe it:

They [the scandal-mongers employed by his grandfather] have . . . treated my mother in a cruel manner (which I will neither forget nor forgive to the day of my death) because she is so good as to come forward and preserve her son from the many snares that surround him. My friend also is attack'd in the most cruel and horrid manner, not for anything he had done against them but because he is my friend and wants to see me come to the throne with honour and not with disgrace and because he is a friend to the bless'd liberties of his country and not to arbitrary notions. I look upon myself as engag'd in honour and justice to defend these my two friends as long as I draw breath.[19]

Though George II had left his heir in Augusta's care, he demanded a share of control in the boy's education (it was actually the Duke of Newcastle who nominated members of the boy's staff and his tutors, but George liked the semblance of power). Then, in 1755, when his grandson was seventeen years old, the King proposed his marriage with Princess Sophia Caroline of Brunswick-Wolfenbuttel, and that of his sister Augusta with Sophia Caroline's brother Charles. The Princess of Wales had no desire to see her son marry as intelligent and masterful a princess as the Brunswick girl was reputed to be, nor was she pleased to allow George to obey his grandfather: if the boy must marry, there was her own niece Frederica Louisa in Gotha ready and willing to be Queen of Great Britain and to be grateful to the kind aunt who gave her that chance. So heartily did Augusta throw herself into denigrating the Princess of Brunswick, declaring that she was deformed and ugly, that George declared himself terrified of being 'bewolfenbuttled'. The younger Augusta eventually married Charles of Brunswick, but George's match never transpired.

Within the year, the Prince of Wales attained his majority, and the King offered him an independent household, but the dutiful son refused, claiming that his happiness depended on his remaining with his mother. Nevertheless, though the Princess of Wales kept a firm grip on her son's personal affections, his political confidence rested with Lord Bute. To his credit, the Earl did manage to prime his charge with sound political principles – though they tended somewhat to exaggerate the potential of his royal power, but it cannot be denied that Bute had an eye to his future, when he should become his pupil's chief minister.

Suddenly, at breakfast time on 25 October 1760, George II had a heart-attack and died.

As George II had feared, 'that puppy Bute' directed all the policies of the

George III as Prince of Wales, by Reynolds (1759)

new King. In the midst of the Seven Years' War, which ranged from Europe to the New World and India, Britain remained at first in the control of the 'hawks' Pitt and Newcastle; naturally, they were appalled to hear George III, under Bute's tutelage, denounce their efforts in proclaiming his intention of concluding 'honourable peace'. Soon, with Newcastle and Pitt at each other's throat, Bute became leader of the Government. His position was confirmed in the spring of 1762.

When George III drove out to see his mother in those days, the crowd would shout after him: 'Are you going to suck?', under the mistaken impression that Augusta had the real power in the kingdom. In fact, the Princess had little political influence. She could nominate candidates for titles, household posts and honours, but all her political connections looked to Bute as their leader and the 'great provider' of office. And Augusta was content that this should be so.

However, she realised that her son was of an age to leave her and fall under the spell of any pretty woman clever enough to charm him. Shrewdly, she managed to retain his affections all the rest of her life by selecting for him a wife no less docile than she had herself once been and who would pose no threat to her own influence.

She was prompted to hasten George's marriage when she saw him ready to embark on one of his own choice, not at all to her taste, with a potentially masterful Englishwoman. This was the beautiful young Lady Sarah Lennox, who came of one of the greatest families of England and who might well have graced a throne. George certainly paid court to the adolescent beauty and certainly intended marriage with her. But it came to nothing. Augusta saw to that.

Princess Charlotte Sophia of Mecklenburg-Strelitz, young, plain and without a political idea in her head, was the ideal match. So overjoyed was her family to hand her over to her grand destiny that within a week of their informing her of her good luck, Charlotte was on her way to England. Forgetting her own tears at the loss of her old governess, Augusta would not allow the Princess to bring any large retinue of familiar ladies with her, and the few she did bring were regarded with suspicion. The Princess of Wales advised her son to keep his wife well protected from Society and from politicians who would encourage her to influence her husband on their behalf, so much so that the poor girl was isolated and lonely in her first years in England. So jealous of her son's affections was Augusta that when the King fell ill in 1765, she kept it from her daughter-in-law as long as possible.

George III, with Bute to manage his kingdom and Queen Charlotte to fill his nursery, was in safe harbour. But by now, Augusta had other preoccupations to fill her mind and hours. Several of her children were frail: already, in 1759 Princess Elizabeth had died, aged eighteen, and Princess Louisa was a permanent invalid. Prince Frederick William died aged fifteen in 1765, and his elder brother Edward, Duke of York, two years later; Princess Louisa gave up the struggle for life in 1768.

York was little loss: a debauched weakling, he had been a continual annoyance to his mother and had shocked his pious eldest brother. William, Duke of Gloucester, was more like George, but even he had his faults: in 1766 he secretly married Maria, Lady Waldegrave, the illegitimate daughter of a milliner; so shameful was his secret that not even his family knew of it until 1772. His fond mother, unsuspecting, cherished William (who had once feared her and bemoaned that he should not know a mother's love), and he was certainly her favourite son once George had grown away from her. Henry, Duke of Cumberland, also married 'beneath him': having made a name for himself in all the brothels of London and having scandalised the nation by figuring in a court case of adultery, he married a widow, Anne Horton, who was an artful coquette with eyelashes reputedly 'a yard long'.

Augusta married her surviving daughters more suitably. In 1764 Princess Augusta the younger was dispatched to Germany to be the wife of the Duke of Brunswick-Wolfenbuttel, and two years later the youngest princess, Caroline Matilda, aged fifteen, married King Christian VII of Denmark. Neither, however, found happiness. Augusta was miserably unhappy with her husband, and of her six children, two were mad and one was blind. Caroline Matilda found her husband a pervert and a brute, but she managed to console herself by taking over his political role and finding a lover, a Dr Johann Struensee, whom her authority made Prime Minister.

The world of the Princess of Wales seemed rather bleak in the late 1760s. Though George was all that could be expected of a son, he had his own family to occupy his first affections. At the same time, Bute had lost power. Having concluded the Peace of Paris, which ended the Seven Years' War, in 1763, he resigned in the face of his rivals' growing power in the Commons. His influence over George III continued undiminished for some time, but it was increasingly unpopular in the country. Augusta, with whom the mob identified 'the Scotch favourite', was booed as she rode through London, and more than once she fled from a theatre amid cat-calls and obscenities. When George was taken seriously ill in 1765 and a Regency plan was urgently required, it was made perfectly clear to

Princess Augusta in old age, by J. E. Liotard

the King that the country would not tolerate his mother in power, with Bute at her elbow. To spare Augusta the humiliation of rejection by Parliament, George had to change his nomination. In the political chaos of May 1765, with the King forced to grovel to George Grenville for the sake of stable government, the prospective Prime Minister agreed to deliver the King from his problems only if he would ban Bute from ever

Augusta's daughter, Queen Caroline Matilda of Denmark, who, with her lover, for some time ruled the Danish King but was later sent into exile

again participating in government. George was forced to submit. (Later, Bute was able to wreak revenge by refusing Grenville his help when he needed it.) Government spies would occasionally report that Bute had met the Princess of Wales at Miss Vansittart's house, which was continually watched, but Bute and the King had little or no known contact.

In June 1770 the Princess of Wales set out on a pleasure-trip to Germany, to visit her daughter Augusta at Brunswick. But the unhappy Duchess, who blamed her mother for arranging such a life for her, let her mother know whom she held responsible for her misery. Then, at Lüneburg, the Princess had a meeting with the King and Queen of Denmark, finding to her horror that Christian was undoubtedly mad and Caroline Matilda enslaved to Struensee's charms. The Queen of Denmark would hear no word of criticism and advice from her mother, and when the Princess spoke scornfully of her liaison with Struensee, the merciless daughter threw back Bute's name in her teeth.

The year 1772 threw Augusta into despair. Not only did she hear at last of William's secret marriage but news came from Denmark that Caroline Matilda and her lover had been arrested. For the few years of life which remained to her, the luckless Queen was kept in comfortable captivity in Germany.

Already stricken with cancer of the throat, Augusta refused for months to acknowledge that she was ill, not permitting any doctor to prescribe for her pain and relying on the dubious skill of one of her German servants. But to the end she forced herself to activity, and on the very day of her death she took a carriage ride. That evening she conversed for some four hours with George III and Queen Charlotte, but she died during the night.

It was Horace Walpole's contention that Augusta ruined the lives of her younger children by neglecting them in their childhood through her over-care of the future George III. Walpole estimated the Princess's ruling passion to have been that of seeking absolute power for the monarchy: it was her fulminations, he said, against Parliamentary restrictions on British monarchs which drove George III to make so many and so wilful political mistakes and Caroline Matilda to seek absolute power for herself in Denmark, to her doom. This is strong criticism. Contemporaries were too ready to blame a foreigner for the failings of the British political system, and women for the failings of men.

Augusta had faults undoubtedly, but they were the faults of weakness not of a strong will. To her credit, she retained the love of her husband, whom it would have been impossible for her to move from his long-established antipathy to his parents, and she worked tirelessly for her son George III, despite constant criticism from all sides, believing that she was serving his true interests. She had been unexceptionable in her conduct and respected in the country until she formed too close an alliance with the unpopular Bute and became so closely identified with his hold on George III. But George himself sought out Bute's friendship and advice, long after he might have taken an independent line, and Augusta allowed the Earl to control her son's policy at the expense of her own influence. As to Caroline Matilda, she ignored her mother's repeated warnings against meddling in Denmark's affairs and against her infatuation with Struensee.

To blame Augusta for the mistakes of her son and daughter would be to reverse the adage and visit the sins of the children on the mother.

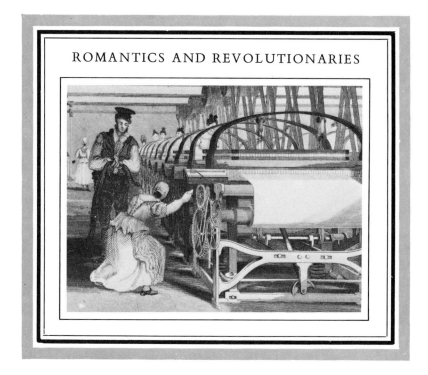

ROMANTICS AND REVOLUTIONARIES

When Caroline of Brunswick-Wolfenbuttel travelled through Germany and the Low Countries to England to become the bride of George, Prince of Wales (the future King George IV), in 1794–5, she crossed lands torn by war. Everywhere Frenchmen were on the move, in defence of the new Republic which they had set up after their Revolution in 1789.

There were many men in Britain who had hailed the French Revolution with wonder and joy, turning a blind eye to its savagery and destruction and seeing in it a nobility of ideal and a miracle of national reorganisation which they longed to emulate at home. 'Bliss was it in that dawn to be alive,' wrote the poet William Wordsworth, voicing the emotion of those who cherished the illusion that Britain too might be purged and revitalised by revolution. But Wordsworth and his fellows were to be disappointed. Conditions for a revolution were present in their society, but government had too many means at its command to suppress an uprising for it ever to be feasible: Habeas Corpus was suspended, radical leaders were rounded up and imprisoned, new treason acts were passed, 'corresponding societies' on the lines of the influential French political clubs were outlawed. And, while statesmen and aristocrats thus protected themselves, the middle class, too, experienced a revulsion against the extremes of political change, an equally adamant force against national upheaval.

The war with the French Republic, and subsequently with the Napoleonic Empire, confirmed national identity and concerted national effort and went a long way, in itself, towards staving off reforms which revolution might have brought about.

Nevertheless, the mood of revolution prevailed, leaving its mark on the nation's social life and attitudes. In the arts, for example, the 1790s and earliest years of the 19th century witnessed a new era of energy and vitality, marked by individual genius. The 18th century had been an age of disciplined form and style in architecture, painting, poetry and music; at the end of the century, Romanticism replaced Georgian Classicism in exuberant and unrestrained displays of excess in the arts and the 'artistic' life. The human passions were laid out for inspection in the verses of Byron and Shelley, in the pictures of William Blake; and the lives of such artists themselves read like epic romances, full of amoral and immoral licence, of absorption with the vagaries of emotion and ego. Even the solid middle classes, virtuous and placid, self-righteous in their own stalwart morality, were caught up in the excitement of the new arts, snatching new volumes as they poured from the presses and adorning their estates with the Gothick whimsicalities of the new architecture.

Inevitably, there was a section of society merely amused by romantic excesses and wholly dismayed by 'artistic licence' in literature and life. William Wordsworth was weaned from revolutionary idealism and philosophical anarchy to become a leader of the milder Romantics, the poets of the Lakes. John Constable was totally uninfluenced by the bright visions of his contemporaries, Turner and Blake, and presented the nation with a calm view of idyllic countryside. Jane Austen, the country gentlewoman turned novelist, wrote the main canon of her works during the Napoleonic Wars, but the contemporary ferment of conflict and political controversy no more intrudes into the 'polite society' which she created than do the harsh realities of urban life and industrialism, while the ideology and expression of Romanticism drew from her only gentle mockery.

While the extreme Romantics examined every facet of the human emotions, many of their contemporaries were studying life in a more tangible form. Novels and verses formed only a part – though a satisfyingly lucrative part – of the publisher's output: for the rest, there were the great encyclopedias and compendia of knowledge, the tomes on foreign travel and history, which were offered in ever-increasing numbers to assuage the middle-class appetite for educative pabulum. While some men turned their innovative talents to the service of the new technology, others began investigation into the natural sciences: zoology and biology, botany and horticulture, chemistry and physics, both extending and codifying knowledge of the natural world.

There was a vast gulf in late 18th-century society, not only between the rich and the poor but between the romantic idealists and those who transformed their ideals into reality. The latter were products of mid-century developments in religion and ethical thought: the revival in the Church of England brought with it demands for a reform of morals throughout society, the founding of new schools and hospitals for the worthy poor, an effective campaign against the sin of slavery within the British colonies. Later the ideals of such philanthropists would become enacted in the reform of social conditions: they were the forerunners of the Victorians.

By the end of the 18th century, such gentlemanly reformers were beginning to find a place in the House of Commons, occasionally incongruously aligned with the more stringent Radicals. In deference to common humanity, such idealists and philosophers sought to bring in true democracy: to have a Parliament to govern the land which represented not property but individuals, to extend the franchise from property-owners to every mature man, however poor. They found little sympathy. The Tories still clung to hierarchical notions, adamant in their protection of their own power, fearful of 'Jacobins under the bed' throughout the abrasive last years of the century; the Whigs were timidly in favour of change, but they sought to extend the franchise only on the property basis, to provide more effective representation in Parliament for the commercial interest which had too long, they felt, been kept from its right by the landowners: the Whigs sought to transfer power from the aristocracy of title and land to the aristocracy of industry and commerce. It was the Whigs who brought in the Reform Bill of 1831-2, and they who (as the Liberal Party) agitated successfully for further parliamentary reform later in the 19th century. Only in the 20th century did the franchising demands of the long-dead Radicals find satisfaction.

In 1815 Britain emerged from the long war against France as one of the leaders of the victorious allies, her system of government intact despite fears for its safety, her industries agog for new opportunities for expansion and growth. In 1815 the population of Britain stood at some thirteen millions; by 1851 it had doubled. By then, the nation was approaching the zenith of its power, owing her world eminence to a combination of many favourable factors: the fund of a large and increasing labour-force; possession of vast resources of the major fuel of the century, coal; her head-start on the other nations of Europe in industrialisation and the development of capitalising institutions; the control of colonies all over the world; a stable, elastic system of government, efficient and incorrupt; and, less tangibly, honest citizens, eager for self- and national improvement, confident of the benefits of 'progress' and 'enlightenment'.

The period 1760 to 1830 was a great melting-pot, capable – on the vagaries of men and mood – of destructive revolution or constructive reform. It was Britain's good fortune, and not a little to her credit, that fate determined the latter course.

THE SIXTH PRINCESS

Caroline of
Brunswick-Wolfenbuttel

When the future King George IV decided to marry, in 1794, there were numerous princesses of suitable religion, status and virtue who might have satisfied the British nation, the royal family and the then Prince of Wales himself. Two were short-listed: a niece of King George III, Caroline of Brunswick-Wolfenbuttel, and a niece of Queen Charlotte, Louise of Mecklenburg-Strelitz. The latter, beautiful, well-educated, discreet and courageous, was unfortunately discarded: she married the future King of Prussia and, later, during the Napoleonic Wars, became her country's heroine for her diplomatic dealings with the French conqueror. Caroline, on the other hand, had little to recommend her besides her rank, but the King's choice of his son's bride prevailed. The English envoy sent to collect the Princess found her attractive enough, in a florid, blowsy fashion, but lacking in good manners, courtly reticence and feminine sensibilities – and she had no idea of personal cleanliness. And this was the woman who was to marry the most fastidious prince in Europe, a connoisseur of beauty and charm!

George, Prince of Wales, had been born in August 1762, the first child of George III and his consort Charlotte. Blessed with simple tastes and high principles, the royal couple presented the nation with an edifying picture of domestic bliss, bringing up their children (fifteen in all) in rural seclusion at Kew and the then Buckingham House, a large but unpretentious mansion on the outskirts of the expanding metropolis. They neither spared the rod nor spoiled their children, and the boys, at least, were given a good grounding in education. However, it was not in the Hanoverian blood for an heir to the throne to live harmoniously with his family, and from his teens George proved a sore disappointment to his parents.

At seventeen, the Prince followed a flirtation with a Court lady, six years his senior, with a passionate *affaire* with an actress, Mrs Mary Robinson, twenty-one years old. Having seen her first in the role of Perdita in Shakespeare's *Winter's Tale*, he proclaimed himself her Prince Florizel, writing fervent letters to her which had to be redeemed at great expense when the passion cooled. At the same time, the Prince trod the familiar road of his ancestors by espousing the cause of the Opposition party in Parliament. The King was a Tory; the Prince must be a Whig. Though the well-meaning George III tried to win his son back to the family fold, it was impossible.

In 1783 the Prince of Wales came of age, and there began the age-old wrangle over his allowance. Already he had debts totalling some £30,000, to his father's horror, and though he was now allowed £50,000 (like his father and grandfather before him), George could never live within his means, spending lavishly on his new residence, Carlton House, and regaling his raffish friends with far more brilliant entertainments than were ever seen at his parents' staid Court.

His most heinous crime, however, was committed in 1785, when the Prince secretly married Mrs Maria Fitzherbert, not only a commoner but also a Catholic. The Act of Settlement of 1701 had ordained that any member of the royal family marrying a Catholic would automatically forfeit his right to the throne; the Royal Marriage Act of 1772 invalidated the marriage of any member of the family who wedded without the King's permission before the age of twenty-five. Both Acts applied to the Prince of Wales, aged twenty-three.

In fact, George married Maria with Anglican ritual (the ceremony being performed by a clergyman who had been brought out of the debtors' prison for the occasion), though that would make little difference under the 1701 Act as Mrs Fitzherbert continued to practise as a member of the Catholic Church. Whether Maria herself regarded the marriage as binding (which she might not, since the Catholic Church did not recognise non-

George's secret wedding to Mrs Fitzherbert in 1785. The artist has portrayed Charles James Fox (at Mrs Fitzherbert's right) and Lord North (sleeping) though neither attended or knew of the ceremony

Catholic sacraments), it later transpired that George certainly did not, in law at least. He had no qualms of conscience to make him proclaim it and opt out of the royal succession. Nevertheless, honour satisfied by both parties, George and his Maria lived together happily for some twelve years. Officially they had no children – nor has evidence of any come to light, but, to the end, Mrs Fitzherbert would never quite admit that her union with the Prince had been without issue.

In London and at the Prince's Pavilion in Brighton, Maria acted as her 'husband's' hostess, held in universal esteem and attempting to check the worst excesses of the Prince's dining, drinking and gambling. Even his closest friends could never be sure if she was mistress or wife, and when the question was raised in Parliament, even the Prince's political confidant, Charles James Fox, denied that George was married.

Of course, perfect fidelity could not be expected of this typical Hanoverian product. By the end of 1793 the Prince was deeply infatuated with Frances Villiers, Countess of Jersey, who, though nine years his senior and already a grandmother, had a sophisticated charm and coquettish manner which the religious, decorous Maria so signally lacked. It was she, Lady Jersey, who reputedly advised George to marry (to re-marry?), intending, no doubt, to maintain her own rule by overshadowing the prospective Princess of Wales.

George was not averse from the idea. Though in 1787 he had solemnly promised his father that he would never go into debt again, by now he owed some £700,000 which he had no hopes of paying off. Only by marrying and giving the nation an heir to the throne in the younger generation could he win the national approval which would bring him financial relief and an increased annual income. Accordingly, the Prince put the matter to his parents and settled down while they wrangled over the rival merits of their respective nieces as his bride.

Though George III had formerly gone on record as being wary of the mating of blood-relations, he forgot his principles in championing the candidature of Caroline of Brunswick–Wolfenbuttel, daughter of his sister Augusta. This bitter Princess, with her unloving husband and unsatisfactory children, was a great favourite of her brother the King – as small children, they had shared a cot for years. And it was this Augusta's daughter Caroline whom the King deemed best suited for his son. George

George IV as Prince of Wales, by Matthew Brown (c. 1790), a detail

III made some devastating mistakes during his long reign, but this was among the worst.

In the distant past the House of Brunswick had split into two dynasties, in terms of family possession of its territory. The House of Brunswick-Lüneburg was the eventual inheritor of Great Britain, by its connection with the House of Stuart, while that of Brunswick-Wolfenbuttel remained in comparative obscurity.

Though undistinguished territorially, in the 18th century the duchy had already provided several princesses as consorts to the most illustrious rulers of Europe. Two Brunswick princesses had shared the throne of Prussia, one wore the crown matrimonial of Denmark, another became the mother of Tsar Peter II of Russia; a duke of Brunswick-Wolfenbuttel married a Romanov princess and begat Tsar Ivan VI. Of course, happiness was not an inevitable consequence of such great matches: Elizabeth Christina of Brunswick-Wolfenbuttel separated from her husband Frederick the Great of Prussia; King Frederick William of Prussia repudiated his Elizabeth; Ivan VI's parents, trying to flee from the usurping Tsarina Elizabeth, were caught and sent to Siberia, while the boy himself spent all but the first three years of his life in prison.

The latest matrimonial disaster in the family was the Princess Augusta (elder sister of Caroline, prospective bride of the Prince of Wales). She had married a future King of Württemberg, then an officer in the Russian army, and had travelled to St Petersburg with him. Soon after, she disappeared, to live out the rest of her life in prison, for unnamed misdemeanours. With such an unsavoury story lingering about the family name, and in full knowledge that two of the Princess's brothers were subnormal, if not imbecile, in mentality, the Duke and Duchess of Brunswick readily agreed to dispatch their daughter Caroline to mingle her tainted blood with that of England. At twenty-six, in 1794, she had failed to accept in marriage a Prince of Orange and scions of the Houses of Darmstadt and Mecklenburg. Now, the English proposal was a godsend, the match the envy of all the princesses of Protestant Europe.

Many of the faults of Caroline's character may well be ascribed to her parents – in the environment and education with which they provided her, as well as in their heredity. Her father, whom she much admired, especially for his brave part in the defence of Germany against the invading French in 1792–4, was a strong character but lacked, as many biographers have noted, 'moral courage'. And in his dealings with his daughter he scarcely exercised his usual impeccable judgement: though he allowed her the same education as her normal, intelligent brothers and wisely kept her on a short rein, he spoiled the girl hopelessly. Her mother, the English Augusta, was a cipher at her own Court, and Caroline was not restrained in her open contempt for her. In fact, she far more admired her father's mistress of thirty years' standing, Fräulein von Herzfeldt – though she failed to emulate that lady's smooth manners or acquire her common sense.

In the months which the English envoy, James Harris, Earl of Malmesbury, passed at Brunswick and *en route* to England with Caroline, he came to have a good grasp of her failings. Refusing to be fettered by the petty restrictions of protocol and etiquette which ruled the lives of so many of her contemporaries, she had become hoydenish and coarse – her speech was often extremely indelicate; some might say that she was honest and open in her dealings with others, her detractors would say that she was 'blunt'; vulgar, noisy and not in the least amenable to correction, she seemed to Malmesbury the last person in the world to hold Prince George's affections. What Caroline needed, he thought, was a strong hand and a gentle but firm guide: then her good qualities could emerge.

Fräulein von Herzfeldt herself warned Malmesbury of the evils which might follow if Caroline were not properly handled:

I conjure you [she said] to induce the Prince, from the very commencement, to make the Princess lead a retired life. She has always been kept in much constraint and narrowly watched, and not without cause. If she suddenly finds herself in the world, unchecked by any restraint, she will not walk steadily. She has not a depraved heart – has never done anything wrong, but her words are ever preceeding her thoughts. She gives herself up unreservedly to whomsoever she happens to be speaking with; and thence it follows, even in this little Court, that a meaning and intention are given to her words which never belonged to them. How then will it be in England, where she will be surrounded, so it is said, by cunning and intriguing women, to whom she will deliver herself body and soul, if the Prince allows her to lead a dissipated life in London, and who will make her say just what they please and that the more easily as she will speak of her own accord without being conscious of what she has uttered.

Besides, she has much vanity, and though not void of wit, she has but little principle. Her very head will be turned if she be too much flattered or caressed, or if the Prince spoil her; and it is quite essential that she should fear as that she should love him. It is of the utmost importance that he should keep her closely curbed; that he should compel her respect for him. Without this she will assuredly go astray.[1]

Malmesbury listened closely and attentively to Fräulein von Herzfeldt, her assessment of the Princess agreeing well with his own fears.

On the long journey to the coast, begun at the end of December 1794, the Earl attempted to warn Caroline of the pitfalls of her new life and tactfully tried to suggest certain reformations:

> I had two conversations with the Princess Caroline [Malmesbury recorded], one on the toilette, on cleanliness and on delicacy of speaking. On these points I endeavoured, as far as it is possible for a *man*, to inculcate the necessity of great and nice attention to every part of dress, as well as to what was hid as what was seen. I knew she wore coarse petticoats, coarse shifts and thread stockings, and these never well-washed or changed often enough. I observed that a long toilette was necessary and gave her no credit for boasting that hers was a *short* one.[2]

Embarrassed, Malmesbury persuaded one of Caroline's ladies to enlighten her as to details of more personal hygiene, and he was pleased to note that the Princess emerged from her dressing-room next day 'well washed *all over*'.

Fears of the swarms of French still in Germany delayed the journey to England, and it was not until April 1795 that Caroline's party landed at Greenwich.

Malmesbury had been expecting to be met by a large band of courtiers, headed by the Princess's future ladies-in-waiting. Inexplicably, they seemed to have been delayed. In fact, it was Lady Jersey who offered this first slight to the future Princess of Wales. She, reputedly the mistress of the Prince and certainly so high in his favour as to have ousted Mrs Fitzherbert, had been made chief lady to the Princess and had deliberately delayed the cavalcade to establish the upper hand from the first. Nor, when she arrived, did she mend matters by throwing up her hands in pretended horror at the Princess's clothes. For once, Caroline looked her best, in a morning gown of muslin, with a fine hat and jacket, but Lady Jersey hurried her into a Court robe of satin, applying jewels and *maquillage* with a free hand – thus spoiling the Princess's advantage over her, her freshness and comparative youth. Now she seemed a clownish copy of the suave elder woman.

When, having arrived in London, Malmesbury led Caroline into George's presence, the bridegroom took one look at her and gasped,

The wedding of George and Caroline in the Chapel Royal, St James's Palace, 8 April 1795: a painting by Singleton

'Harris, I am not well, pray get me a glass of brandy.'[3] Thereafter, he was never wholly sober until the day after the wedding.

Caroline was at her worst that day at dinner, talking volubly in her guttural English and shocking even the hardened Prince with her snide references to Lady Jersey, whom she had immediately recognised as his favourite. And far from evincing any fear or respect for George, she had already openly voiced her disappointment at finding him grossly fat, scarcely resembling the flattering portrait with which she had earlier been presented.

Nevertheless, there was no room for romance in this royal marriage, and both parties were determined to fulfil their contract. On Wednesday, 8 April 1795, George and Caroline were married in the Chapel Royal, St James's.

'Judge what it is to have a drunken husband on one's wedding day and one who spent the greater part of his bridal night under the grate where he fell and where I left him,' said Caroline to a friend in later years. She added: 'If anybody were to say to me at this moment, will you live your life all over again or be killed. I would choose death, for you know sooner or later we must all die, but to live a life of wretchedness twice over – oh, *mein Gott*, no!'[4]

In fact, the first months of marriage, overshadowed as they were by the hovering Lady Jersey (who was always ready to show the Princess in a bad light), had some quite happy moments for both George and Caroline. They spent the summer and autumn of 1795 at the Brighton Pavilion, and a few of the letters of the royal family at this time reveal that George had hopes that his wife might improve on acquaintance. However, he was still surrounded by his bottle-cronies and their women, and Caroline was definitely made to feel unwelcome at their carousals.

The Brighton Pavilion, George's exotic palace by the sea. Caroline was not a welcome guest there

Princess Caroline in 1804, by Sir Thomas Lawrence. Caroline is wearing a red velvet dress and hat, which heighten her already florid complexion

Nor was her husband pleased with the financial settlement for which he had been so eager. True, Parliament did increase his allowance to £125,000 a year but, with the nation already in financial difficulties through the long war with France, no one would consider paying off his debts outright. The Prince was appalled to find that he must contribute £65,000 a year, and the total revenues of the Duchy of Cornwall, towards liquidating his debts. This did not improve his temper.

It should not be thought that George was an utter villain. Though it was certainly neither reasonable nor kind of him to have taken a dislike to his future wife on sight, merely because her looks did not please him (shades of Henry VIII and his 'Flanders Mare', Anne of Cleves!), he soon had cause to deepen his dislike, to persuade him that Caroline would never suit him – for she did nothing to temper her vulgarity or amend her disorderly dress. To his sisters, indeed, George was a tender, loving brother, who would take the utmost care to please them; to the wives of his friends he was ever courteous and gallant; to Mrs Fitzherbert, he had been a doting husband and, as we shall see later, when he subsequently returned to her, he evinced sincere repentance for his infidelity. But where he could not respect, he could not love: he took mistresses who attracted him, but they were all 'of easy virtue', and he could discard them with no compunction, no regard for their feelings. In the same way, he could find nothing respect-worthy in his wife and treated her as if she could feel no pain at his sneers.

Nevertheless, within a few days of her wedding, Caroline had conceived the child for which the marriage was largely made – fortunately for George, for he did not relish sharing her bed and was only too glad to leave it. And on 7 January 1796 the Princess gave birth to a daughter, who was named Charlotte Augusta, for her two grandmothers.

The Prince had been under great strain in the days before the birth, fearing, perhaps, that should the child be born dead, he would have to go through the misery of cohabitation with his wife again to produce the necessary heir to the throne. Still wrought up and somewhat hysterical, a few days after Charlotte's birth George wrote his will, cutting Caroline off with the proverbial shilling and swearing eternal love for Mrs Fitzherbert, his 'wife in the eyes of God, and who is and ever shall be in mine'.

Despite King George III's attempts to repair the marriage before it was too late, and despite Caroline's avowed willingness to live in her husband's house if he would promise never to renew marital relations, George was adamant in his desire for a separation. He wrote to Caroline on 30 April 1796:

Madam,

. . . Our inclinations are not in our power, nor should either of us be held answerable to the other, because nature had not made us suitable to each other. Tranquil and comfortable society is, however, in our power; let our intercourse, therefore, be restricted to that, and I will distinctly subscribe to the condition which you required . . . that even in the event of any accident happening to my daughter, which I trust Providence in its mercy will avert, I shall not infringe the terms of the restriction by proposing, at any period, a connection of a more parti-cular nature. I shall now finally close this disagreeable correspondence, trusting that as we have completely explained ourselves to each other, the rest of our lives will be passed in uninterrupted tranquillity.

I am, Madam,
With great truth,
Very sincerely yours,
George P.[5]

On 6 May Caroline sent her reply, affirming every point of her hus-band's letter but making it clear that the separation should be laid to his aversion from her rather than to her own desire.

Thus this strange marriage came to an end.

Caroline had been assured that she would have custody of her daughter until she was at least eight years old. In the event, however, the Princess Charlotte was kept at Carlton House even when her mother moved to the country, south of the river, that spring.

At Charlton and later at Montague House, Blackheath, Caroline filled her days with some small-scale farming and large-scale charity. Her main occupation was the care of certain orphans and children of the poor, who compensated her for the loss of Charlotte. One of their number, William Austin, the son of a dockyard labourer, was brought to Caroline soon after his birth and became her especial favourite. She spoiled him thoroughly, and her guests were amused and repelled by the 'little, nasty vulgar brat' whom the Princess named her 'Willikin'. Nevertheless, this pastime would have been harmless enough but for the interference of a one-time friend of Caroline's who became her most dangerous enemy.

This was Lady (Charlotte) Douglas, the wife of one of Caroline's Blackheath neighbours and, for an appreciable period apparently, her confidante. But, having gossiped indiscreetly about the Montague House *ménage*, and hinting that the Princess did not scruple against multiple adultery, she lost Caroline's favour. Certainly there is valid evidence that decorous 'gentlemen callers' were horrified by the Princess's flirtatious behaviour with them, and there were always plenty of men ready to say that they had been intimate with the Princess of Wales, but Caroline's guilt has never been definitely proved.

However, Lady Douglas went further. She claimed that Caroline had told her that William Austin was her own son, and George's too. If true, this would mean that William, not Princess Charlotte, would eventually inherit the throne. Though the whole business was plainly preposterous, it would not do to leave doubts as to the legality of a future Queen Charlotte. King George III, who had been kind to his niece/daughter-in-law all along, now insisted on a commission of inquiry, under royal warrant, to look into the allegations, and thus there began, on 1 June 1806, that 'delicate investigation' in which many charges were laid against Caroline, none proved. In fact, it was easily demonstrable that Austin was not her son, that Lady Douglas must have fabricated the whole story of the Princess's claim that he was – laying her other allegations wide open to question. However, though Caroline's name was cleared in January 1807, the matter was not permanently closed.

George had attempted a reconciliation with Mrs Fitzherbert as early as May 1796 while he was even then in negotiation for the separation from Caroline. But Maria's conscience troubled her, and it took four years – of wooing, gifts and ardent protestations of repentance – before she would return to her 'husband'. And then it was only after Pope Pius VII had assured her that she would not jeopardise her immortal soul by doing so. Then, for some ten years, she reigned supreme once more. Re-established at Carlton House and the Brighton Pavilion, Mrs Fitzherbert set about regulating George's habits and extirpating his vices, restoring him to a measure of health by weaning him from his brandy again. But ten years was a long time for a man of George's propensities, and no one, not even 'Princess Maria' herself, could have been surprised when his roving eye lighted on yet another buxom grandmother, Lady Hertford. Maria bore no grudge and tried to turn a blind eye, but the new royal mistress was too forceful a character to tolerate a rival for long.

Early in 1811 the Prince of Wales was appointed Regent for his supposedly mad father, George III, and though even he, gleeful at being in power at last, could not openly celebrate such a nationally mourned event, he used the current visit of some French princes as an excuse to put

Carlton House into gala rig and arrange festivities.* When Mrs Fitzherbert found that she had been demoted to a lowly place at table for one of the grand banquets, she knew that her day was over. On 7 June she wrote a last letter to the Prince Regent and withdrew from his life.

The Princess Charlotte was now a teenager, remarkably like Caroline – in character more than in looks, being open and frank, rather boisterous and noisy. Treated coldly by her father and openly disliked by her grand-mother, she had an engaging affection for all who showed her kindness. Above all, she was thoroughly loyal to her mother, refusing to believe the royal family's tales of Caroline's misdemeanours.

When it was decided that the Princess should be formally presented at Court to mark her 'coming out' in January 1813, she insisted that she should be sponsored by her mother. In fact, Caroline arrived at St James's Palace for the ceremony only to meet her sister-in-law the Duchess of York, who had been delegated by the Prince for the same task. Charlotte refused to be presented by anyone but her mother; the royal family refused to receive the Princess of Wales: therefore Charlotte was not presented.

The Prince of Wales had means to hand for spiteful retaliation. He requested that a committee of the Privy Council should advise on the desirability of his wife's having access to her daughter – the decision being easily inferrable. By then, however, the Princess herself had quite a following in the House of Commons and was able to force a debate on her situation. Though she could not gain any redress for the calumnies against her, she was so fulsomely praised and pitied by the speakers that George's plan failed.

Undeterred, the Prince had Caroline evicted from her rooms in Kensington Palace and refused Charlotte permission to see her mother at all. So, on the advice of her close friend and counsellor, the politician Henry Brougham, the Princess of Wales made one public appearance after another, graciously acknowledging the cheers of a populace which saw her as the persecuted, pitiful victim of a tyrant. (In fact, through all her troubles, Caroline remained remarkably cheerful and well able to hold her own in every phase of battle.)

* Recent research has produced the argument that George III was not mad but suffering from a blood disease, porphyria. However, his symptoms suggested madness to the physicians of the day, and he was treated as a madman, subjected to gross brutality and put under restraint.

In the summer of 1814 the Prince pressed his daughter into an engagement with Prince William of Orange, an unattractive young man ('Little Frog', Charlotte called him) who was sufficiently ambitious to take on the difficult girl for the sake of her future inheritance. Though Charlotte at first acquiesced, expecting more freedom to result from her marriage, she soon came to realise that she would have to leave England. Unable to gain reassurance that she would be allowed to return at will, she set the whole family in defiance and, after a quarrel with Orange, broke off the engagement.

George was furious. In the evening of 16 July he burst into his daughter's rooms at Warwick House and presented to her a set of new ladies-in-waiting to replace Charlotte's friends who, the Prince believed, were encouraging her in rebellion. He told his daughter that she must prepare to leave London immediately, to take up residence in the seclusion of Windsor Forest, at Cranbourne Lodge. Outwardly quiet, respectful and humble, inwardly Charlotte seethed. No sooner had her father departed than she swept out of the house and ran as far as Charing Cross, where she found a hackney coach. Thus incognita, the potential heiress to the throne arrived at her mother's house in Connaught Place – only to find that Caroline was at Blackheath.

In the hours that followed, several persons converged on Connaught Place, among them Brougham and Caroline, summoned by Charlotte, then emissaries of the Prince Regent (who had discovered his daughter's flight), then even the Archbishop of Canterbury and the girl's uncles the Dukes of York and Sussex, come to plead with her to see reason. Messages flew between Charlotte and her father, with threats and attempted compromises.

By dawn the Princess was worn out and at the end of her tether. The mother to whom she had come for protection seemed to be casting her off: Caroline protested that she was powerless against her husband and advised Charlotte to submit to him.

A royal coach drew up in Connaught Place, and Charlotte entered, to be carried away to 'captivity'.

When Caroline left the country, shortly afterwards, she had a chance to bid farewell to her daughter. However, it cannot have been a harmonious meeting. Charlotte was amazed and angry that her mother should think of leaving her when she most desperately needed her help. 'She decidedly deserts me,'[6] Charlotte wrote to a friend.

Brougham (who needed the Princess of Wales as a focal point for Radical propaganda against the Regent) and Caroline's *preux chevalier*

Samuel Whitbread (a credulous, idealistic man who would believe no ill of her and who called up the ancient liberties of England to vindicate her, without success) both begged the Princess not to leave England. They reminded her that her prime weapon against her husband was her identification with the popular Princess Charlotte: a mother and daughter fighting for their rights, two innocents against the black tyrant and rake who persecuted them. They warned her that abroad she would be surrounded by spies, unable to refute their scurrilous stories of her conduct. But Caroline was adamant: she had spent years being hounded by her husband, and now she needed to escape from the small world of London society and its malice. With the European wars at last over and Napoleon penned up on Elba, this was the time for flight.

It is hard to know what would have followed had Caroline gone her way quietly and lived respectably in some out-of-the-way corner of the Continent. Probably her husband's spies would have been able to concoct some stories of hole-in-the-corner crimes. But, true to form, Caroline provided them with plenty of spicy copy.

In Switzerland she met Napoleon's faithless wife the Austrian Archduchess Marie Louise; in Italy she consorted with the downcast scions of the Bonaparte family now in exile; at Naples she was so intimate with the fallen conqueror's brother-in-law Joachim Murat that their adultery was soon the talk of London. In her fifties now and no less portly than the Prince Regent himself, Caroline everywhere disported herself in the dress of a young *fille de joie*, at Genoa shocking all who saw her as she drove out in a coach shaped like a shell, garbed in a pink feathered hat, a pink bodice not pretending to cover her breasts and a white skirt well above her knees. At a ball in the city she appeared in a black wig and wreath of pink roses with a *décolletage* which disgusted all spectators.

These displays alone would have given the spies a chance to justify their wages, but they could also add that everywhere the Princess went, she was now escorted by a tall, majestic man with curling black hair, flashing eyes and amazing mustachios: he was Bartolomeo Bergami (or Pergami, as he preferred to be called), a self-proclaimed aristocrat fallen on hard times, who was her secretary and courier. When this colourful couple trailed across Europe and took ship for the East, they did so in the grand manner, calling at Sicily, Tunis, Malta, Athens and Constantinople before disembarking in the Holy Land. There Caroline rode at the head of a noisy cavalcade into Jerusalem itself, surely one of the most incongruous pilgrims ever to tread the Holy Way.

Settled at Como, and later at Pesaro, from the autumn of 1816, Caroline still had Pergami with her. Even Brougham's brother James had to confess that they were 'to all appearances man and wife'.

While Caroline was at Pesaro, in the last months of 1817, she received the news of her daughter's death.

Charlotte had survived the rigorous regime imposed on her by her father in 1814 and had actually found happiness with the husband of her choice, Prince Leopold of Saxe-Coburg-Saalfeld. This young man, ambitious and shrewd, had taken the girl in hand and had made her so anxious to please him that she had tempered all her hoydenish manners and noisy tantrums. But she had died, in childbirth, on 18 November 1817.

Thus Britain was left without an heir in the younger generation. George III still lived out his unhappy days in his padded cell at Windsor, one day to be succeeded on the throne by the Prince of Wales, but after George the line of succession comprised only a dozen or so elderly princes and princesses, his brothers and sisters, none of whom could muster a legitimate child between them. While the younger royal dukes scrambled hastily to marry and beget a potential king or queen, the Regent himself thought of divorcing his erring wife and taking another whom he might still be able to impregnate.

Accordingly, the Prince appointed a commission to look into Caroline's conduct, to find grounds for divorce. In August 1818, armed with the reports of the Prince's spies, they foregathered in Milan to assemble their evidence. At last, Caroline was stirred to action. Through Brougham she made representations in London for a formal separation, with her guarantee that she would never claim the title of Queen, if only her husband would settle a suitably generous pension on her. Inevitably, George refused.

Then, on 10 February 1820 Caroline received the news that her father-in-law had died: her husband was king and, whatever he might say or she might wish, she was queen.

After some twenty-five years as Princess of Wales, Caroline lived only eighteen months more to enjoy her new title.

She landed in England in June 1820, everywhere hailed as a heroine and favourite. Pergami, who had tyrannised over Caroline – and her money – for too long, had been left behind on the Continent, angry but powerless to retrieve his position. Henceforth the Queen must seem the spotless angel of popular legend, and an Italian adventurer of dubious origins and outrageous behaviour had no part in the plans which she hatched with Brougham.

The 'trial' of Queen Caroline – more properly the hearing of the royal divorce case in the House of Lords, 1820, by Sir George Hayter

While Caroline received loyal addresses and heart-bursting cheers, George IV had troops brought up to London in case of riots. Demands for political reform were rife; the whole nation had been thrown into panic in August 1819 when a peaceful demonstration in Birmingham had been broken up by armed yeomanry – the 'Peterloo Massacre'; within weeks of George's accession, a plot to murder his whole Cabinet had been discovered – the 'Cato Street Conspiracy'; revolution seemed imminent. In fact, it may well be that the coming of Caroline averted revolution: by concentrating on her cause, politicians and agitators were diverted from the grievances and complaints which might have triggered off national revolt.

Soon after the Queen's arrival, the Tory Government put through Parliament a 'Bill of Pains and Penalties', to dissolve the royal marriage and deny Caroline her title as queen. In August the House of Lords was packed, as the 'trial' (as it was called, though in fact it was merely an investigation of Caroline's relationship with Pergami) began.

Caroline was not permitted to give evidence, but she was allowed to hear all the proceedings, and every day the Queen was ushered to her place in the Chamber – George remained hidden in his cottage in Windsor Park. Yet, for all the formidable array of witnesses against the Queen, from servants' gossip and spies' reports, only circumstantial evidence could be found. Despite the fact that few of her 'judges' believed her innocent, nothing could be proved. So small was the Government vote on the Bill's third reading that the Prime Minister, Lord Liverpool, dared not introduce it in the Commons, where most of Caroline's supporters sat. The Bill was withdrawn.

London went wild with joy, and throughout the country the Queen was cheered and the King reviled. For a time there was even the danger that the Government might fall, with the King's anger against the ineptitude of Liverpool and his Tories.

Queen Caroline in the last year of her life: a portrait by Samuel Lane

THE GRAND CORONATION of HER MOST GRACELESS MAJESTY C-R-L-E COLUMBINA the first QUEEN of all the RADICALS &c &c JULY 9th 1821.

The Grand Coronation of Her Most Graceless Majesty: *one of many cartoons issued during the royal scandal of 1821*

The next pitfall was the coronation, which had been postponed too long already in the hope that the King might be free of embarrassment before he was seated on the throne of his ancestors. Now, with that hope dashed, the coronation was scheduled for 19 July 1821. It was not to be expected, of course, that Caroline would stay away. In fact, in May she wrote to the Prime Minister asking for details of the arrangements made for her at the Abbey. After George made clear his refusal to have his wife there at all, there was an ominous silence from her quarters.

Caroline might well have expected, after the recent demonstrations in her favour, that when she was refused admittance at each door of the Abbey on coronation day, the mob would rise and break down the doors for her. They did not. The fickle populace, tired of drama and anti-climax, turned on their former darling, and she was booed and hissed as she drove disconsolately away.

Three weeks later, on 7 August, the Queen died. It was not a broken heart which caused her death, whatever her few surviving friends might claim, but an obstruction of the bowels. She was taken ill at Drury Lane Theatre on the night of 30 August and lived through the first week of August in full knowledge that it was her last. There was no death-bed reconciliation with her husband, no last-minute appeal for forgiveness: none of the elements of drama so dearly loved by moralists.

It would be pleasing, perhaps, to present Caroline as a victim of persecution, of calumny and malice, totally innocent and pitiful. But it would not be the truth. She was vulgar and dirty; she not only rarely spoke the truth but seemed to enjoy fabricating lies (perhaps even the assertions of Lady Douglas in 1806 were based on Caroline's tall stories, invented to horrify a gullible listener); whether she was faithful to her husband before 1814 or not, she was certainly adulterous with Pergami; the love which she evinced for her daughter would not stand up to the test in 1814. Even the most earnest seeker for 'redeeming features' would be hard put to it to find any in Caroline.

King George IV outlived his wife by nearly ten years, dying in June 1830. He did not marry again, and his elderly mistresses succeeded each other with tedious regularity to the very year of his death. Had Charlotte lived, she would have been in her mid-thirties when she succeeded to the throne and might well have made a good queen with the help of her excellent husband Leopold.

As it was, nothing remained of the 'disastrous marriage'. George IV was succeeded by his brother William IV, a reformed wastrel and the father of some dozen illegitimate children who had been taken in hand by 'the love of a good woman'. William's legitimate daughters died in infancy, and in 1837 he was succeeded on the throne by his niece Victoria, one of the babies born in 1819 as a result of the royal Dukes' undignified marriage-rush after the death of Charlotte.

Queen Victoria, encouraged by her impeccable consort Albert, lived in such unimpeachable respectability that the very word 'Victorian' now connotes a high standard of morality. But when she was a young, unmarried girl, she was known to look admiringly, if with some trepidation, on a flamboyantly handsome young man, too shocking a character for her to be allowed to meet, who was her distant cousin Charles, a nephew of George IV's Queen Caroline.

EMPIRE AND PROGRESS

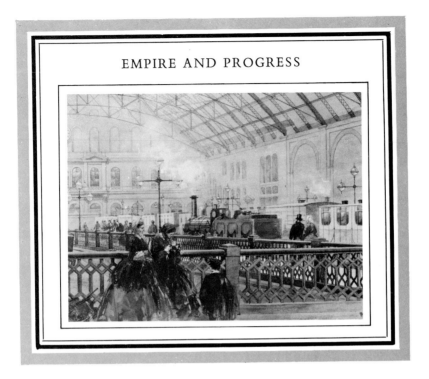

In 1837 died the last Hanoverian king of Great Britain, William IV, a better-conducted, better-intentioned man than he was generally accredited, but still little regretted by the majority of his subjects, associated as William was with the political self-interest and guile, the dubious sexual morals and the careless extravagance of his family. William's successor on the throne was an eighteen-year-old girl of untarnished reputation and reputed dedication to duty, his niece Victoria, from whom much good was to be hoped and expected.

Few could then have foreseen, however, that, by the time the slim girl had become a portly matriarch, the nation would have arrived at such unprecedented size, prosperity, good order, peace and international prestige as it did, that the Victorian Age would be so long and, in the eyes of contemporaries, glorious. Of course, the triumphs of the age were not the achievement of Queen Victoria herself: the days were long gone when a monarch initiated or even greatly influenced national developments. Victoria was merely the symbol of Britain's eminence and virtue, a mother-figure to the generations who lived through her long reign (1837–1901) in Britain and the mighty Empire beyond the seas. There was no single benefactor to 19th-century Britain, neither the monarchy nor the Empire, nor Parliament, nor religion, nor industry, nor trade, nor even the era's numerous men of genius and vision, though all were factors in the nation's rapid development and improvement.

A comparison between the conditions of the nation in 1837 and 1901 reveals at a glance the advances of which late Victorians were so proud. Between those dates the population of the British Isles had more than doubled to some thirty-two million, as had the area of the British Empire, while overseas trade almost quadrupled in value to a total of nearly £870 million a year; the electorate was some ten times the size of that of 1837, at almost seven million approaching a quarter of the nation.

These were the most easily quantifiable advances of the century. As well as increasing in number, the population was living longer, more healthily; infant mortality was falling; medical discoveries provided not only cures to once fatal diseases but gave relief from pain in anaesthesia, while improved sanitation and hygiene eradicated the source of many ills. Labour was still often sweated, hours long, but legislation and social conscience had improved the lot of the 'labouring poor'. Slum housing remained at the end of the century, a blot on the land, but few in work need be homeless.

While industry was mechanised with steam-power and, later, gas and electricity, agriculture too underwent rapid change, with the improvement of crop-raising and stock-breeding, though the use of machines in ploughing, reaping and threshing was viewed with concern by those who saw their livelihood threatened by depopulation of the land. Transport, the servant of productivity, was transformed by the age of steam: there had been few railways in Britain in 1837, but by the end of the century there was a nationwide network for freight and passenger travel; at the same time, British steamships, of iron then of steel, plied every ocean.

Cheap food and manufactured goods contributed to public welfare, feeding, clothing and supplying the population as never before (and thereby contributing to health and well-being), but the quality of life was also improved in public order, education, social intercourse and standards of social morality. Die-hards had forecasted anarchy when liberals insisted on removing centuries-old penal laws from the statute book – laws which had awarded the death-penalty for sheep-stealing, transportation for life to proven pickpockets; in fact, though the crime rate continued high to the end of the century, public order was generally improved, not least by the respect earned by the nation's 'peelers', the police force. Reactionaries had expected revolution from mass-literacy but lived to exploit it, propagandising the populace in the new Press and in the 'moral tales' which flooded the nation at the end of the 19th century. In fact, Britain became a thoroughly 'moral' nation, at the worst self-righteous in its own morality. Hypocrisy there was, but there was much genuine religion too, with church-going a national pastime, interest in missionary endeavour fervent, while the practical results of personal religion were everywhere expressed in philanthropy and neighbourliness. Even where daring spirits doubted the existence of God and the validity of the Bible, few challenged contemporary ethical standards, and that Victorian demigod, the family, with its stance for personal and corporate morality, was worshipped by all but the most 'outrageous' free-thinkers.

If the Victorian era was an age of self-confidence, it was also an age of self-consciousness. The immigrant revolutionary Karl Marx was not the only sociologist to take a long, detailed look at his world; everywhere there were scholars, statisticians, reformers and publicists researching and counting and taking statements and making reports, adding to contemporary knowledge of society and its shortcomings. The fragmentary, often inadequate, social legislation of the 19th century went far towards alleviating real hardship and injustice, but the work of Victorian social-inquirers provided a firm base for those who followed, legislating in this century for the Welfare State.

So rapid had progress – social, political and educational – advanced by the end of the 19th century that late Victorians could afford to sneer at the values and aspirations of their grandfathers: a 'new woman' of the 1890s, with her bicycle, typewriter and latch-key could cheaply deride the mincing, crinolined miss of 1860 in subjection to mamma and papa, absorbed in her embroidery and novelettes. Nevertheless, in general the Victorians were the greatest admirers of their era's achievements, and it was only in the early years of the 20th century that reaction set in. Those who came through the First World War could see more clearly than their parents the pre-war trends towards national decline, and by the end of the 1920s the inadequacy of pre-war reform was everywhere apparent. It became fashionable to sneer at Victorian architecture, art and literature, Victorian bourgeois society and, above all, Victorian 'cant'. The Victorians had, it was argued, cleansed only the veneer of their society, never daring to look into the dark recesses of their own minds. New psychological theories attributed to Victorians all sorts of emotional, sexual and intellectual repressions which the new world would not tolerate, bravely freeing mankind from the timid respectability of its forebears and bestowing genuine freedom.

Since the Second World War, historians have not been so arrogant. They have seen the snail's pace with which men have advanced towards Utopia even amid the rapidly accelerating forces for material improvement in this century. They have seen also that the vaunted liberation of mankind has released new ills, when self-interest and self-absorption go unchecked by idealism and altruism. It is therefore not surprising that many now hark back to the Victorian Age as a time when, despite obvious evils, there was more contentment and optimism than there is today.

Facing: *Princess Alexandra and her younger sister Dagmar (later, by marriage, the Tsarina Marie Feodorovna of Russia), painted by E. Jerichau-Baumann, 1856*

THE SEVENTH PRINCESS
Alexandra of Denmark

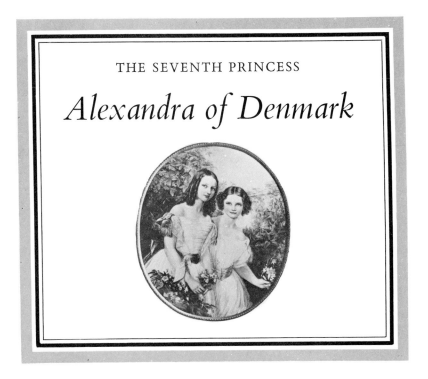

Alexandra of Denmark was Princess of Wales for almost thirty-eight years (1863–1901) as the wife of Queen Victoria's eldest son, Albert Edward, the future King Edward VII, endowing her title with more dignity and grace than any of her predecessors. Her problems were remarkably similar to those of the 18th-century princesses of Wales: her husband was embittered by denial of a real share in, and training for, power, and he was consistently unfaithful to her. However, fortunately for Alexandra (and for Britain), the Prince had a sufficiently responsible attitude to his position never to seek leadership of a party in opposition to the Crown, and the Princess had neither the intellectual stature nor the forceful will of a Caroline of Anspach to incite her husband's disobedience to his mother. Though Alexandra was undeniably aware of the many mistresses whom her husband took, many of whom she was required to receive in her own house, she was no Caroline of Brunswick to make public gestures of defiance against the man who so frequently humiliated her.

Prince 'Bertie' did his best to be a good husband, never consciously cruel to his 'Alix', but he had the hereditary moral weakness of his

Hanoverian forebears, and he never found his wife an adequate intellectual companion – though it is hard to see who, among contemporary princesses, would have suited him better. Alexandra recognised her own shortcomings, and so far did she manage to curb all jealousy and resentment that she continued to keep her husband's respect and affection.

The situation could easily have been worse: had Alexandra been jealous and demanding, she might have made a public scandal even worse than those occasioned by her husband's indiscretions; had she sought to rule him and to interfere in his political aspirations, she might have alienated him completely. Princess Alexandra was not a clever woman in the accepted sense, but she had good judgement.

Queen Victoria and her husband, Albert of Saxe-Coburg-Gotha, early recognised the deficiencies in their son's character; unfortunately, they became so obsessed by them, and by righting them, that their remedies were over-harsh and failed. Both were keenly aware of the qualities of character demanded of a king in government, and of the educational attainment needed for such a career: over-anxious, they sought to bring their son to a standard which he, though eager to please them, could not reach. From nursery days onwards, the Prince suffered from having an unusually brilliant elder sister, 'Vicky', with whom he was forever being unfavourably compared. No wonder then that he was often sullen and resentful, though he had moments of sincere repentance and dedication to duty.

The Queen revered and doted upon her husband, who combined not only remarkable male beauty but high principles, a sure grasp of the ways of government and perfect fidelity to herself and her interests. Though, in the early years of their marriage, Victoria had frequently rebelled against her husband's masterful temperament, she soon came to depend on him completely, in government and in the home. It was inexpressibly painful to her to compare her son with her husband, and it is not too fanciful to suspect that she saw many of her own shortcomings in Bertie, reinforcing her determination to mould him on his father's model, as she herself had striven to live up to her husband's ideal.

Albert and Victoria agreed that an early marriage would keep Bertie from moral pitfalls and give him that sense of responsibility which he so lacked. Their son was only some seventeen years of age when they began their search for a suitable wife for him. That she must be a Protestant went without saying; for the rest, 'Good looks, health, education, character, intellect and a good disposition, we want; great rank and riches we do not,'[1] averred the Queen. Whatever their own ideas of the future Princess of Wales, however, both Victoria and Albert knew that she must be beautiful if she were to attract their son: the young Albert Edward had already made his tastes quite apparent.

An invaluable aid to the royal search was Vicky, Princess Royal, who had in 1858 herself been married suitably and happily to the eventual heir to the throne of Prussia. Vicky was charged to review all the eligible princesses in Germany (the main source of Protestant candidates) and to report back on their comparative suitability.

On the surface, there seemed a broad choice, but it proved surprising how many young ladies seemed to be deficient in one attribute or another. Princess Anna of Hesse, with her 'flat, narrow and upright forehead', 'gruff, abrupt way of speaking'[2] and twitching eyelids, was soon put out of the running; Marie Hohenzollern was lovely – but a Roman Catholic; a Princess of Saxe-Meiningen was 'not strong'; Marie of the Netherlands was 'clever and lady-like, but too plain and not strong';[3] 'Addy' of Prussia was 'not clever or pretty';[4] a princess of Dessau was too old – and her family had a bad reputation; 'the Weimars' were pronounced 'very nice girls but delicate and not pretty',[5] and the Princess of Sweden 'a dear little girl, pretty and nice but of course much too young for Bertie'.[6]

Princess Elizabeth of Wied was the favourite for a time, even though Vicky wrote that the girl

is not tall and has an underset figure not graceful, very fresh complexion and nice white teeth, a great many freckles and a mark of a leaf on one cheek but which does not show much. She has not a pretty nose and rather a long chin. She is what you would call a strong, health-looking girl – nothing more – she does not look very ladylike and head not well dressed – whether she is clever or not I cannot say. . . .[7]

Later Vicky saw that Elizabeth was noisy and 'odd', displaying forward manners and coarse speech which shocked the prim English Princess. By then, however, another, far more suitable candidate had been presented, and Elizabeth of Wied lost her chance – she later married the future King of Romania, published her charming fantasies under the name 'Carmen Sylva' and proved one of the most eccentric queens of the eccentric 19th century.

Elizabeth's rival was Princess Alexandra of Schleswig-Holstein-Sonderburg-Glucksburg. It was very good-natured of Vicky to speak kindly of 'Alix' to the Queen, for the girl's connection with the Danish throne (her father was the King's heir) was not a recommendation in

Prussian eyes, since a long and bitter territorial dispute was then raging between the two kingdoms. But so glowing were the reports of her beauty, goodness and sweet temper that she could not be overlooked. Vicky was delighted with her when they finally met.

Queen Victoria had some reservations at first. Alexandra's mother was a sister of the Queen's aunt-by-marriage, the Duchess of Cambridge, an ambitious, showy woman who had once tried to marry her own son to the then youthful Queen; the Duchess's daughter Mary Adelaide had the reputation of being 'fast'. Victoria feared that so close a relation of the Duchess as Alexandra was would fall under her influence, once in England, and would be 'spoiled' by the mischief-maker. Vicky put her mother's mind at rest. Princess Christian of Schleswig-Holstein, she said, was as careful of her children's morals and manners as anyone could wish and had herself remarked to the Princess Royal that she would not allow Alexandra to have anything to do with her aunt and cousins, beyond mere politeness, if she went to England. The interview between Vicky and Princess Christian took place in September 1861, a few days after Bertie and Alix had been introduced at a carefully contrived 'accidental' meeting at Speyer. Bertie was sufficiently interested in the Princess to warrant his sister's frankness with the mother of the potential bride.

By then, Queen Victoria was in possession of the full details of Alexandra's family, upbringing and character, and she was convinced that here was the future Princess of Wales.

Princess Alexandra Caroline Marie Charlotte Louise Julie was born on 1 December 1844, the daughter of Christian of Schleswig-Holstein-Sonderburg-Glucksburg and his wife Louise of Hesse-Cassel. She was seven years old when her father, a cousin of the then King of Denmark, was proclaimed heir to the throne. Until then, Christian had lived the strenuous life of an active army officer, supporting his family on his pay, only some £800 a year. Alexandra and her brothers and sisters had a fine Copenhagen address, the Yellow Palace, but it was in fact nothing more than a large house in an ordinary street. They were brought up simply, with plain food and plain clothing, which the little princesses themselves helped to sew. In later years, Queen Victoria would write that 'they are wonderfully united – and never breathe one word against each other, and the daughters remain as unspoilt and completely children of the home as when they were unmarried. I do admire this.'[8] This early security and stability gave Alexandra an enormous advantage over Prince Bertie, who had never been at ease with his parents, who resented the superiority of his elder sister and who was deprived of the company of his nearest brother, Prince Alfred, of whom he was particularly fond, at an early age, when their training diverged. Where Bertie, now a young man in his early twenties, sought his pleasures in the beau monde, Alexandra found hers at home.

Unknown to his parents at the time, the Prince of Wales had already embarked on the sexual adventures for which he would one day become renowned. A pretty actress, Nellie Clifden, had been smuggled into the Curragh, his army training-camp, one night, and when she left, the Prince was no longer a virgin. It was November before Albert learned of his son's 'fall', as he termed it, and when Victoria was informed, she was furious. Bertie, confronted by his father, evinced repentance and begged forgiveness. But Albert had been overwhelmed by the shock. Coming hard on the heels of a trying summer, in which the Queen noisily and uncontrolledly bemoaned the recent death of her mother, demanding her husband's constant attention, it was all too much for him. The Prince Consort was already ill when he travelled to Cambridge to see his son, and a soaking in torrential rain worsened a cold from which he was suffering. He continued his work, struggling to avert war between Britain and the northern states of America after an embarrassing confrontation at sea, but early in December he took to his bed. Typhoid was diagnosed. On the 14th Prince Albert died.

Queen Victoria was overcome with grief. She exhausted herself with tears. When calmness, in some measure, came at last, it was to her second daughter, Alice, that the Queen turned, not to Bertie. Victoria could not stand the sight of him, she said, remembering how much sorrow he had caused his father. In February 1862 he was dispatched on a tour of the Near East.

Still, in the months that followed, the Queen was determined to marry her son to Alexandra. When she set off for Albert's old home at Coburg in the autumn of 1862, Victoria paused a few days in Belgium, to meet the Danish family at Laeken. She thoroughly approved of Alexandra, whom she now saw for the first time, making sure both that the girl was truly fond of her son and that she had been warned of his failings. Bertie dutifully proposed; Alexandra accepted.

After such brief encounters, it could not be expected that either of them was in love. But princesses had to marry someone, and Bertie was certainly a fine, elegant, if not handsome young man, with the dazzling prospect of a crown; the Prince found Alexandra one of the most beautiful women he had ever seen – and, besides, marriage would give him the freedom from rigid parental control which he had long craved.

Whatever the Queen might say about the need to play down the role of the Danish royal family in future plans, Britain rejoiced in the match, as a counterbalance to the overwhelming German connection.

The poet Tennyson offered characteristic verses to welcome the bride:

> Sea-kings' daughter from over the sea,
> > Alexandra!
> Saxon and Norman and Dane are we,
> But all of us Danes in our welcome of thee,
> > Alexandra!
> Welcome her, thunderers of fort and fleet!
> Welcome her, thundering cheer of the street!
> Welcome her, all things youthful and sweet,
> Scatter the blossom under her feet!
> Break, happy land, into earlier flowers!
> Make music, oh bird, in the new-budded bowers!
> Welcome her, welcome her, all that is ours!
> Warble, oh bugle, and trumpet, blare!
> Flags, flutter out upon turrets and towers!
> Flames, on the windy headland flare!
> Utter your jubilee, steeple and spire!
> Clash, ye bells, in the merry March air!
> Flash, ye cities, in rivers of fire!
> Welcome her, welcome her, the land's desire,
> > Alexandra!
>
> Sea-kings' daughter, as happy as fair,
> Blissful bride of a blissful heir,
> Bride of the heir of the kings of the sea,
> Oh joy to the people and joy to the throne,
> Come to us, love us and make us your own;
> For Saxon or Dane or Norman are we,
> Teuton or Celt, or whatever we be,
> We are each all Dane in our welcome of thee,
> > Alexandra!

Obedient to these injunctions, the people of Britain fêted the Princess on her arrival in Britain in March 1863. But the royal wedding itself was a comparatively quiet affair, celebrated at St George's Chapel, Windsor, where the Queen might retain her privacy – she had rarely been seen in public since her widowhood. Victoria stood, clad in her mourning black, on the grilled balcony overlooking the nave known as 'Catherine of

The wedding of Albert Edward, Prince of Wales, and Princess Alexandra of Denmark, in March 1863 in St George's Chapel, Windsor. Queen Victoria looks down from 'Catherine of Aragon's closet'

Aragon's closet'; below, an ocean of white silk and satin mingled with the bright colours and glittering gold of men in uniform. Alexandra, in a floating white crinoline festooned with flowers and foliage, took the hand of Albert Edward, Prince of Wales.

Thus, at nineteen years old, the shy, simple Princess from Denmark, who had never had fine jewels, *grandes toilettes* and Paris gowns in her life, became the second lady in the realm, mistress of Marlborough House and the mansion of Sandringham in Norfolk, commander of a seemingly limitless fortune of pin-money. She, who had only recently romped in Danish fields with her younger sisters and brothers, now led processions and opened balls, in the arms of a fairy-tale Prince. For so, at first at least, did her new life and her husband seem to Alexandra. With the Queen in retirement at Windsor and on the Isle of Wight, the young Waleses were the leaders of fashion and frivolity in the capital. Of faultless instinct where lavish display and elegant entertainment were concerned, Bertie led Alix into fairyland.

The idyll ended the following winter. Alexandra's father succeeded to the throne of Denmark that November and in the following month faced the advancing troops of the Prussian army, challenging for possession of the disputed duchies of Schleswig and Holstein. The Prussians were, they maintained, acting on behalf of the rightful Duke, Frederick of Schleswig-Holstein-Sonderburg-Augustenburg, a cousin of the new King Christian IX; in fact, they were seizing the opportunity to extend Prussian influence over long-desired territory. So far, Queen Victoria had been more than satisfied with her daughter-in-law; now, seeing Alexandra wander, with tear-stained face, through her apartments, fearful for the very lives of her family in Denmark, Victoria was irritated. The Queen herself was firmly pro-Prussia, whose Crown Prince was her own son-in-law; Vicky's letters to her mother were now full of passionate feeling for the war. The British Government, on the other hand, insisted that the nation must remain neutral in a conflict which in no way concerned it.

The royal household itself was turned into a battlefield. Alexandra and her husband spoke out firmly for the Danes; the Queen's visiting half-sister, Feodora, who was the mother-in-law of the claimant Prince Frederick, was equally vehement for her Ada's Fritz. Victoria, at her wits' end to keep the peace, declared that she sorely regretted having made the Danish match if it brought so much trouble.

In the midst of this furore Alexandra gave birth to her first child on 7 January 1864. The strain of the past weeks had taken its toll, and the child was a puny seven months' baby, weighing only three and three-

Marlborough House, the Waleses' London home

Sandringham House, Norfolk, where the Prince and Princess of Wales entertained their friends with lavish house-parties: out of doors the Prince slaughtered hundreds of game birds; indoors his prey was beautiful ladies

189

quarter pounds, born suddenly and inconveniently before adequate preparations could be made. Bertie and Alix were at Frogmore House on the Windsor estate when her labour began – or rather, in the grounds, watching the skating on Virginia Water. Rushed back to the house, Alexandra was put to bed and, since the royal doctors would not reach her in time, a local physician was called in. Lacking any proper layette, the baby Prince was delivered into the flannel petticoat of his mother's lady-in-waiting.

As the war continued, with the Prussians overrunning Schleswig, Alexandra's recovery was held back. The fact that her father's name was allowed in the list of her son's, 'Albert Victor Christian Edward', was the only comfort the Princess could derive from those dark days, though the Queen managed to conceal her continuing annoyance with her daughter-in-law for the sake of her tranquillity.

In July Denmark admitted its defeat, losing Schleswig and Holstein, some half of its former territory. Only the fulfilment of Bertie's promise that they should visit her home together, that autumn, could console Alexandra for her country's humiliation. Henceforth she never relaxed her hatred of Prussia which, joined to her husband's wariness of that kingdom's increasing power and influence in Germany, presaged a formidable turn-about of royal policy in future years.

Queen Victoria was no longer so enchanted by the Princess. Where, before the Schleswig-Holstein affair, she had sung Alix's praises and admired her tactful management of her difficult husband, now nothing the Princess of Wales did was right in the Queen's eyes: Bertie and Alix, complained Victoria, were marring the reputation of the monarchy with their informal but costly and vulgar entertaining at Marlborough House – courting popularity, in fact, while she, the poor 'Widow of Windsor', sat neglected and alone. Her son's devotion to the social round, and his dedication to winning the flattering adulation of the nobility and their parasites, was a sore point with the Queen for the rest of her life. Alexandra, she said, did nothing to curb her husband's excesses, aiding and abetting his folly. Victoria was easily beguiled by her daughter-in-law's charm when they were together – the 'Alexandra fascination' was hard to withstand, but she could never really forgive her for not measuring up to her ideal – or perhaps, again, Victoria blamed herself for not providing her son with a better wife.

Over the next few years, Princess Alexandra's time was divided between her formal Court duties, her social life and the care of her growing family of children.

The rare, the rather awful visits of Albert Edward, Prince of Wales, to Windsor Castle: *a satire by Max Beerbohm in his book* Old and New (*1923*) *on Queen Victoria's disapproval of her heir*

The birth of her second child, Prince George, in June 1865, was again premature, and in the weeks that followed, the Princess was gravely ill with rheumatic fever. Fortunately, her heart was left unscathed, but the rheumatism settled in a knee, leaving her permanently lame. Between 1867 and 1869, three daughters were born – Louise, Victoria and Maud, and then, in 1871, a last son. He, named Alexander, lived only a few hours.

Nothing could have been less regal than the upbringing of Alix's children. The boys – especially the elder, 'Eddy' – were, of course, subjected to rigorous regimes of education from early childhood, but for the most part the Wales children ran wild. They became a curious mixture of shyness and boisterousness, a constant irritant to their Grandmamma, who infinitely preferred the docile German grandchildren who so often visited her. In childhood and adolescence, all Alexandra's children adored their 'Motherdear', whom they treated with a jocular familiarity amazing to the Prince of Wales, with his memories of his own early relationship with his parents. In later years, however, even the most devoted of the brood, the Princess's own 'Georgie', could admit his mother's selfishness and possessiveness, though all came to realise that her cloying love was a result of their father's failure to respond fully to her affection.

Despite all his parents' care, the Prince of Wales was treading the beaten paths of his Hanoverian forebears through the low-life brothels and high society boudoirs of London and Paris and the German spas. Though his good looks faded fast, with increasing *embonpoint*, Prince Bertie had a charm which few women could resist. Appreciative of pretty women, admiring wit and grace, generous – though not to excess, the Prince inspired real affection from his mistresses. Besides the many *filles de joie* who fleeted through his nocturnal adventures, the Prince numbered among his mistresses such 'society beauties' as Lady Warwick and the occasional actress – Lillie Langtry lasted the longest.

While the Prince was scrupulously discreet, never embarrassing his wife intentionally (though she was expected to receive ladies of sufficient rank in her drawing-room, knowing full well, or suspecting, that they had met her husband in a bedroom), his way of life left him always open to discovery. While the Prince was generally shielded from publicity by a coterie of men friends, he could not avoid being implicated in some of the most colourful scandals of the century. First, in 1869–70, there was the case of Lady Mordaunt: she admitted to her husband having committed adultery with several men, the Prince included. Only narrowly did Bertie avoid being named as a co-respondent in the subsequent divorce case, but he was called as a witness for the lady and was given a chance to deny any

'Bertie' and 'Alix' at Cowes in 1870

The Prince and Princess of Wales with their children aboard a yacht in 1880

improper relationship. Wisely, Alexandra refused to be cowed by the general feeling against her husband, and she appeared everywhere in his company – though her private feelings may be surmised. When, in the following year, the couple lost their son Alexander, they were drawn more closely together than ever before, and when, that autumn, Bertie nearly died of typhoid, the reconciliation was completed.

Nevertheless, there were more troubles to come. In 1890 the Prince was staying in a house, Tranby Croft, in which a fellow guest was accused of cheating at cards, and though the heir to the throne himself was not under any personal suspicion, his involvement with the principals of the affair brought national censure. Then, before that scandal had abated, he was entangled in an unsavoury marital dispute, with the classic 'revealing' letters, jealous husband, frail-virtued lady and all: the Beresford case.

Alexandra never retaliated. Not one whisper of suspicion ever marred her reputation. True, she had a devoted cavalier in Oliver Montague, one of the more circumspect members of the 'Wales set', but though he avowedly loved the Princess, it was with an idealistic romanticism which never went beyond the bounds of confidences, courtly attentions and sympathy. Other men admired Alexandra – but from further off, repelled by her dignity and air of aloofness, which was, in fact, a result of her increasing deafness.

No, Alexandra found solace for her husband's failings rather in her children and in the almost unceasing round of visits which she exchanged every year with her parents and brothers and sisters.

Since the days when they had played together in Copenhagen, counting the few pennies of their pocket-money and trying to 'make do and mend' their few possessions, Alexandra's brothers and sisters had gone far. Her brother Frederick did not succeed their father on the throne of Denmark until 1906, but in 1863 William had become King of the newly independent Greek state, as King George I. Of their sisters, Dagmar was now the consort of Tsar Alexander III of Russia. Occasionally the Prince of Wales would accompany his wife on visits to her relations – though the atmosphere of quiet Denmark bored him infinitely; more often the Princess went alone or took only her daughters.

These family connections abroad of the Princess's were a continuing source of annoyance to Queen Victoria. Though the Queen herself knew the sorrow of conflicting family loyalties (the German husbands of her two elder daughters found themselves on opposing sides in the war of 1866), she so revered her late husband's concept of a united Germany under Prussian leadership that she could find no sympathy for her daughter-in-law's anti-Prussian relations and her involvement in issues which conflicted with Britain's interests. While the British people – and the Queen and her eldest son – were disposed to favour Turkey in international diplomacy, both the Russian and the Greek interests made them firm enemies of the Sublime Porte, and Alexandra championed her brother of Greece and her sister of Russia. With a mixture of passion and reason she begged the Queen not to allow Britain to enter a war against Russia on Turkey's side – a war which, if won by Turkey, could only result in a debilitation of Turkey's former province of Greece also. 'Excuse me, dearest Mamma,' wrote Alix in November 1879, 'for worrying you with all this, but the fact is that I am really distressed about my poor brother's position, that I feel I must make *one* more appeal to you on his behalf and on that of his country, before it is *too late!*'9

In fact, the tragedy which the Princess feared was averted – though not by Victoria's influence: it was the anti-Turkish policy of Gladstone when Prime Minister which kept Britain out of the 'Eastern affair'.

In 1887 Queen Victoria celebrated her Golden Jubilee, having reigned for fifty years – though even now, in her late sixties, she relegated none of her constitutional powers to her son. The following year, Bertie and Alix had their own festivities, for their Silver Wedding.

Twenty-five years of marriage had given each clear insights into the other's character. Alix knew exactly what she could and could not expect of her husband; Bertie knew full well the strengths and weaknesses of his wife's character, admiring the greater virtues – such as her forbearance of his own vices, but continually deprecating her minor faults of vagueness, unpunctuality and obtuseness, though he never ceased to admire her unfading beauty.

In July 1889 the Princess Royal (Louise) married the Earl of Fife, to Alexandra's joy – she had feared a German match. She was similarly contented when her daughter Maud married Prince Charles of Denmark – though she would have preferred her to remain single, a constant companion. In the event that duty fell to Princess Victoria, who was fated to live out her days as 'a glorified maid' to her mother, constantly at her beck and call.

Scarcely had the Prince and Princess of Wales rejoiced in the engagement of their elder son 'Eddy', second in line to the throne, to Princess Mary of Teck, however, than the young Prince died. He had been a trial to his parents, displaying his father's vices and propensity for expensive trouble without his father's charm, but he was still a sad loss to his mother. Nevertheless, both parents and the nation could not but be relieved that

Lillie Langtry, the 'Jersey Lily'

'Skittles' Walters, the girl from the Liverpool slums who made a successful career as a courtesan in high society

Daisy Brooke, Lady Warwick, who lost her place in the Prince's harem when she turned Socialist and demanded his help in her schemes for reform

such an unreliable, wayward young man would never be called upon to reign: his replacement, Prince George, was a far more promising heir.

On 22 January 1901 Queen Victoria died. After more than sixty years on the throne, she had relinquished power to her son by the only means acceptable to her. Albert Edward, Prince of Wales, became King Edward VII, and Alexandra was Queen.

For some nine years Britain had a king entirely devoted to its interests – surprising to the many who had doubted his talents and dedication. Though with as little experience of government in his sixties as his mother had had when she came, in her teens, to the throne, Edward VII had made good use of past years in formulating an understanding of international relations. For both personal and political reasons he feared the German Empire (created after the Franco-Prussian war of 1870–1) and its Kaiser, his nephew Wilhelm; consequently, Edward built up his ministers' own suspicions of German ambition and was himself instrumental in forging links with Russia and France, the basis of the Alliance so vital in combating Germany in the coming World War.

Alexandra had always loathed Kaiser Wilhelm II, whose pressure on Turkey in the late 1890s had pushed that nation into war with Greece at last – to the eventual humiliation of the Danish King of the Hellenes. Wilhelm was also pro-Boer during British hostilities in South Africa, while Alexandra had thrown herself whole-heartedly into organising nursing staff – the sisterhood later named Queen Alexandra's Imperial Nursing Service – to tend the army shipped to Africa. But in fact, the Queen had no political influence: she had not in the past managed to enlist her mother-in-law's support for any of her Danish relations and their subjects; now, her husband's policies were so close to her own, more personal, sympathies that the Queen had no cause to seek influence over them – fortunately, for it is very doubtful that Edward VII would have been swayed by personal considerations if those had conflicted with his diplomatic designs.

In other matters, too, Alexandra's life continued in the course set when she was Princess of Wales: Edward VII had replaced Lady Warwick with one Mrs Alice Keppel, a plump but lively woman who kept him from ennui for the whole of his reign. The Queen tolerated and respected her, though she could never like this rival as much as she once had the long-since-discarded Lillie Langtry. And there were no more scandals to blacken Bertie's name. Relations between the King and the Queen were cordial and peaceful, though they still needed to take frequent holidays apart.

Alexandra as queen

A family card-party: Alexandra with her brother King Christian IX of Denmark and her sisters, the Tsarina and the Duchess of Brunswick

In fact, the Queen was returning from a short stay on the Greek island of Corfu in 1910 when, at Calais, she was met with news of her husband's illness – the last attack of his old bronchial trouble which resulted in his death. With characteristic generosity, Alexandra sent for Mrs Keppel to come to the deathbed. On 7 May King Edward VII died.

Alexandra lived on until 1925, still graceful and charming though little trace of that famous beauty remained, bearing the title of Queen Mother with admirable self-effacement. She had the pleasure of seeing her son, now King George V, build up the reputation of the monarchy in Britain and the Empire, and of seeing her daughter Maud become Queen Consort in the newly created independent kingdom of Norway. Alexandra could take comfort too in the vindication of her husband's policies and her own prejudices with the defeat of Germany in the First World War. But, on the other hand, she lived to see the death of her brother, the King of Denmark, to whom she was devoted, the assassination of her brother George of Greece in 1912 and the murder of many of her Russian relations (though not of her sister the Dowager Tsarina) in 1918. For years the Queen pestered her son to help his cousin 'Tino', King Constantine of

Alice Keppel,
Edward VII's last love

Greece, to regain the throne which he had been forced to abdicate in 1916, but without success (in fact, Constantine later returned briefly to Greece as King, through internal politics not British pressure).

To the end Alexandra retained her interest in international affairs and in international family gossip. Increasingly cloistered at Sandringham – that once brilliant setting for gay house-parties now desolate and shadowy, Alexandra, partly blind and almost completely deaf, was attended by her daughter Victoria and her long-time companion Charlotte Knollys. Then, on 19 November 1925 the Queen suffered a heart-attack; she died the next day.

Queen Alexandra had requested that, on her death, Charlotte Knollys should sort her papers and burn all those of a private nature. Her friend faithfully carried out this wish – to the impoverishment of those who would know more about Alexandra's private thoughts and motives. But perhaps it is, after all, a fitting loss, since, as Princess of Wales and as Queen, Alexandra so rigorously forced herself to show a bland public face, never offering her own opinions or allowing her own fears and sorrows to be known outside the family circle.

MONARCHY IN QUESTION

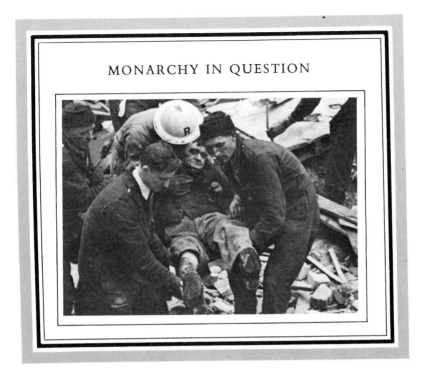

The lifetime of the eighth, and latest, Princess of Wales, Mary of Teck, spanned more than eighty years, over a period when change was more rapid than it had ever been before. She was born in 1867, when Britain basked in an era of peace, at the peak of prosperity, when her royal birth placed her in the highest élite in the world; she died in 1953, having experienced two World Wars, having seen Britain wracked by economic and social upheavals, and having witnessed the downfall of many European monarchies.

It was a bewildering time to live, moving from the age of horse-drawn carriages to that of the jet-plane, from the swirl of bustled skirts to the sight of women in trousers, from the penny-post to the transcontinental telephone call, from the sword and cannon to the atom-bomb, but above all from an age of certainties to an age of political, intellectual and moral doubt.

One of the fundamental certainties of the Victorian Age was that of monarchical government. Switzerland was the only republic in Europe, a freak whose nonconformity with its neighbours was by then hallowed by long time and custom. True, France threw off her Emperor in 1871, but then France was derisorily unstable in political emotion. For the rest of Europe, there remained monarchies like that of Britain, with origins far back in history, while all the time new kingdoms were being created from artificially formed states: Belgium, the Netherlands, Italy, Greece, Bulgaria, Romania – each chose a king from the great dynasties of the Continent. The power of the various monarchies varied enormously, from the constitutionally demarked authority of Britain's sovereigns to the absolutism of the Tsar, 'Autocrat of all the Russias', and national policy could always outweigh the communal interests of the royal caste, but still, the international élite maintained a transpolitical affinity.

Every 'Majesty' and 'Highness' in Europe seemed to be related to each other, since marriage within the caste was, if not wholly compulsory, at least still the norm. But where, in centuries past – even until the 18th century, a marriage between members of two royal Houses could be used to cement an international treaty, now such weddings were largely irrelevant to Continental politics: they no longer marked a formal unity of interests between two nations, nor did mutual support in war automatically follow.

Queen Victoria's husband, the German Prince Albert, hoped that the marriage of their eldest daughter, another Victoria, to the heir to the kingdom of Prussia would ensure a future of Anglo-German peace and mutual support, but, had he lived to see the late decades of the 19th century, he would have been disappointed. By the end of the century, Britain and the new German Empire were the fiercest of rivals, in international trade, in the accumulation of territories beyond Europe and in the struggle for leadership of the Continent itself. Some historians have argued that Kaiser Wilhelm II of Germany would have made war on Britain years earlier than he did were it not for the awe which he felt for his English grandmother, Queen Victoria, and the respect which he accorded to her rule. However, there were many other factors, political and military, which staved off the inevitable Anglo-German conflict until 1914, and though royal personalities did play a part in the drama, there were overwhelming national considerations which forced the cataclysm of the First World War.

Before the first two decades of the 20th century ended, many of the monarchies of Europe had fallen. The Kaiser and the Austrian Emperor had been overthrown in defeat, trailing the hordes of their minor territorial princes and dukes with them. Revolution in Russia in 1917 accounted for the downfall of the imperial Romanov dynasty. By the time of Mary of Teck's death in 1953, another World War and more European revolutions had brought down other thrones, leaving only Britain, Scandinavia and the Low Countries with monarchies unscathed.

Britain's victories in war were not the only cause of her monarchy's survival. A succession of monarchs with respect for representational government had become so divorced from the fount of power, from party politics, from the transitory unpopularity of statesmen and ministries, as to be irrelevant to the real issues of the 20th century. The monarchy, bereft of all but artificial power, took on a new role – one to which members of the House of Windsor were admirably suited: that of national leadership above the wrangles of opposing ideologies within the kingdom.

At the same time, the British parliamentary system of government was itself sufficiently effective and respected to be accepted as the power-base of the nation, an advantage not shared by outworn systems in Europe which only revolution could move. The British system was sufficiently flexible and adaptable already to have coped with the transfer of power from the aristocracy to the middle classes, and, with the growth of working-class political consciousness, was seen to be able to integrate this new force also. The change from Tory-Liberal to Conservative-Socialist confrontation in Parliament was not painless, but it was achieved without any recourse to violence against the constitution.

Outside Parliament however, the 20th century has witnessed a shift in the apportioning of power still bitterly contested. 'Power to the people' at the turn of the century meant mainly the extension of the franchise to all adults (achieved by 1928), yet even then there were signs of the coming struggle for economic power which is still with us today.

Early in the century, organised labour militated for higher wages (that is, a 'fair' share of profit) and improved working conditions, with only a few extremist theorists to challenge the system of privately controlled industry and the gulf between the rewards of capital and of labour. Then the inter-war years, the 1920s and 1930s, revealed the real issue: manpower there was in plenty, urgent in its demands for work, but the capital to fund industry and the commercial outlets for goods had been thrown off balance by seemingly uncontrollable world-wide conditions: capital could no longer supply work where goods could not be sold, and the work-force had to wait, furiously but impotently, until conditions improved. Thereafter organised labour would demand a share in controlling industry and its financing and in creating the political conditions which control demand, as well as a share of the profits of industry. Political and economic power are so interwoven in the modern world that neither can now be considered without the other, and the British debate on the fusion of the two is still a long way from resolution.

The material standard of living enjoyed by British subjects in the mid-20th century would have amazed those who lived in the middle of the 19th. Not only was purchasing power higher than ever before, with a wider range of goods, home-produced and coming from every part of the world, but the Welfare State provided free medical treatment, free education, security in old age and numerous other benefits from the nation's common purse. It would have been as absurd to have expected such facilities from a government of the 19th century as from that of one of the medieval kings, but within the space of a few years, after the Second World War, national resources were mobilised and new aims attained.

Thus the period of the life of Mary of Teck saw immense, speedy changes within national life, in a period of the most rapidly accelerating change ever experienced in human existence. There can be no doubt that material improvement was great, but whether there was an advance in that indefinable commodity 'the spirit of the nation', in the fulfilment of humanity, must be left to the decision of future generations.

THE EIGHTH PRINCESS

Mary of Teck

The last Princess of Wales was Mary of Teck, wife of the future King George V. She and her husband bore their titles from January 1902 until George's succession to the throne in May 1910.

Mary, or Victoria Mary as she was known at that period, was the first Princess of Wales for some four and a half centuries to have had a predominantly English upbringing. Her father was a German duke, of the royal House of Württemberg, but her mother was Princess Mary Adelaide of Cambridge, a granddaughter of King George III. When the First World War drove a wedge between the British royal family and their German kin, the then Queen Mary's British loyalties were never called in question.

When Princess Charlotte of Wales had died in 1817, leaving such a singular dearth of heirs to the throne in the younger generation of the British royal family, George III's seventh son, Adolphus, Duke of Cambridge, had hastened to marry in the hope of providing the eventual heir to the throne. His bride, Augusta of Hesse-Cassel, dutifully gave him a son, George, in 1819, who was the only legitimate grandchild of George III (and thus the presumptive heir to the throne after his father and childless uncles) until the birth of the future Queen Victoria some two months later. Since Victoria's father, the Duke of Kent, was senior to Cambridge in the succession, both Adolphus and young George lost forever their chances of the crown when Victoria was born.

In the years that followed, the Cambridges had two more children, both daughters, Augusta and Mary Adelaide. The latter, born in 1834, was the future mother of Queen Mary.

Mary Adelaide was the family's 'problem child'. She was good natured, well mannered and not unintelligent, but she was seriously overweight: in 1857, when she was twenty-four years old, she weighed some 250 pounds. In 1853 the Emperor Napoleon made tentative offers for her hand (Mary Adelaide being the only British Princess of suitable age to wed) as a token of Anglo-French amity, but on political and religious grounds Queen Victoria felt obliged to refuse on her cousin's behalf. However, since Mary was popular and the possessor of a not inconsiderable dowry, there were other suitors. In 1856 Prince Oscar of Sweden visited England with a view to proposing marriage to the Princess – but, having seen her, he departed without making an offer. Several other prospective husbands were mooted for Mary Adelaide over the next few years, mainly from among the ranks of her German cousins, but, as the contemporary Lord Clarendon wrote, 'Alas! No German prince will venture on *so vast an undertaking.*'[1]

It was not until 1866 that the Princess, already in her thirties, met her future husband. The man who professed himself willing to face a lifetime with such a large lady was himself tall and thin, 'very nice and amiable, thoroughly unassuming and very gentlemanlike and certainly very good looking',[2] as Queen Victoria – not without surprise, one feels – noted when she met him. He was Prince Franz of Teck, four years younger than his bride and vastly her inferior in terms of rank.

He was the son of Duke Alexander of Württemberg, who had been heir to the throne of his country until he had made a morganatic marriage (that is, a marriage with a commoner which necessitated his giving up his rights in the royal line of succession) with a Hungarian countess, Claudine Rhedey. Their son Franz was created Prince, and later Duke, of Teck, by the King of Württemberg, and he had a successful career in the Austrian army behind him (which helped eke out his inherited pittance) when he met Mary Adelaide in 1866.

Their meeting was no accident. Mary Adelaide's cousin Albert Edward, Prince of Wales, was, like the rest of the royal family, frequently given to making plans for marrying off the Princess, and when he met Franz in

Austria, in 1865, he thought he had found an ideal candidate. The Prince invited Franz over to England, introduced him to his cousin (who had been called home, from her sister's Court in Germany, on purpose) and subjected the young man to hints of the most blatant kind as to his matrimonial chances. Fortunately, Franz was acquiescent, and Mary Adelaide was delighted.

On 12 June 1866 they were married. A fortnight later, the couple hastened off to Germany, where Franz was anxious to take part in the war against Prussia which his royal relations and his Austrian patrons were waging (in fact, he arrived too late; the war lasted only six weeks). Then, for the first few years of their marriage, the Tecks' base was in England, first at Kensington Palace, and later at White Lodge, Richmond, but their persistent lack of money (both were spendthrifts) frequently drove them abroad in search of a more economical way of life.

Their first child, the future Princess of Wales and Queen of Great Britain, was born in Kensington Palace on 26 May 1867. Nearly forty years before, in May 1819, Queen Victoria herself had been born in Kensington Palace and was dubbed by her maternal grandmother 'a May-flower': so too was Mary Adelaide's child – for all her formal baptismal names, Victoria Mary Augusta Louise Olga Pauline Claudine Agnes, she was known for years as 'May'. ('Victoria Mary' was her choice in 1902 when she became Princess of Wales; it was shortened to 'Mary' when she became Queen; but she was always known as 'May' to her family.)

Over the next few years May was joined in the Teck nursery by three brothers, Adolphus, a year her junior, Francis, born in 1870, and Alexander, born in 1874. With only some seven years between them, the children grew up together, very close and united.

By 1870 the family was ensconsed in White Lodge, Richmond. The Duke of Teck had almost no occupation, having given up his military service soon after his marriage, and apart from occasional attendance at Queen Victoria's Court (where he was always chagrined by protocol's demand that his rank, inferior to his wife's, placed him at the end of formal processions and at the lower seats at table), he was free to be with his children. In an age when relationships between parents and children of royal families still tended to be of the most formal, the Teck children were unusually free with their parents.

However, the Tecks were only a small part of the international network of royal families, and May was still a very young child when she was introduced into the 'polite world' far from the romps of the White Lodge

Mary Adelaide, Duchess of Teck, with her two elder sons, 'Dolly' and 'Frank', and her daughter 'May', in 1872

nursery. Living in England, the Tecks were on the periphery of Queen Victoria's family circle, now, in the 1870s, spreading ever wider as her children married. Of the Queen's nine children, eight married into foreign dynasties, so May and her brothers had 'cousins', of whatever distant degree, in most of the Protestant Courts of Europe. Then too, there were her mother's relations, the Hesse-Cassel family, with their meeting every year at the family home at Rumpenheim; the Danish royal family, first cousins of Mary Adelaide through her mother; and the grand ducal family of Mecklenburg-Strelitz, connected through the marriage of

May's aunt Augusta. Duke Franz's relations, the royal family of Würt-temberg, were ever ready to welcome visits from the Tecks too. Not a year of May's childhood passed without a visit to or from her German relations, and at home there was always a steady stream of young visitors from among Queen Victoria's grandchildren, May's near contemporaries. Through these myriads of uncles and aunts and cousins, May drifted, a shy child despite her wide social contacts, but definitely a person in her own right rather than 'one of the crowd': already a firm character.

'May', 'Frank', 'Dolly' and 'Alge' were well-sheltered children, learning fast and with a surely unique knowledge of Europe through their network of relations, but guarded against the problems of living with which 'lesser mortals' were familiar. Thus it came as a shock when, in 1883, the Tecks realised that they were too deeply in debt ever to maintain their station as 'royalties' in England. Amid public scandal, their affairs were investigated, their debts and few assets weighed and their solvency barely salvaged.

For nearly two years, 1883–5, the Tecks lived abroad, largely at Florence in Italy, in what the future Queen Mary herself once described as *'short street'*. It was there that she, in her mid-teens, laid the foundation of her passion for antiques and fine art which she later used to transform Britain's royal palaces, so long the repository of negligible Victorian bric-à-brac. Though May's education was by no means broad or deep, she acquired, especially in the Florentine years, a sure insight into the many facets of European culture. At the same time, she was drawn, by her rank, into the brilliant circles of visiting royalty and eminence and, by the age of eight-een, when her family returned to England, had acquired a stately, some-what withdrawn and aloof 'presence'.

In London the Princess 'came out' into Society, first appearing among the royal ladies at Queen Victoria's Court in March 1886. Thereafter she had a regular place in royal processions, ceremonies and festivities. Queen Victoria thoroughly approved of the quiet, well-behaved May (though she had always deplored Princess Mary Adelaide's 'fast', frivolous behaviour before her marriage), and pronounced her 'a very nice girl, *distinguee*-looking, with a pretty figure'.[3] With her social round and charities and studies at home, and her long summer visits abroad, Princess May had a full life and one certainly to her taste: in later years, she always declared that she loved nothing so well as a Court ball, with its elegance and eti-quette – though by the end of her life there remained few vestiges of the ceremonial of her youth.

However, despite May's sharing in the royal entertainment in Britain, on the Continent she was considered very much a 'second-rank' *partie*. Because of her paternal grandparents' morganatic marriage, she was a 'Serene' not a 'Royal Highness', and princes of the various royal Houses in search of brides would not contemplate a match with a princess not *ebenbürtig*. Queen Victoria, on the other hand, cared little for the petty restrictions of German rank, and by 1891, when May was twenty-four years old, the Queen already had her plans for the Princess's matrimonial prospects. Victoria intended that May should marry her grandson Prince Albert Victor, Duke of Clarence and Avondale, second in line to the throne. The Princess, unacceptable as a bride to almost every petty princeling in German royal Houses, should one day become Queen of Great Britain and Ireland, Empress of India and the Dominions beyond the Seas.

Albert Victor – 'Eddy', as he was known in the family – was no Prince Charming. Like his father, Albert Edward, Prince of Wales, before him, he was in his youth an unpromising candidate for a throne. As a child he had shared the lessons and recreation of his younger brother, Prince George, and had made no good showing beside that brighter, more diligent boy. When the two Princes were sent off for naval training, again it was George who showed more aptitude and discipline than Eddy. In the end, it was found necessary to separate the brothers, to send Eddy into the army and to university, to give him a chance to develop without competition.

In his twenties, Eddy had some elegance of manner, though few but his doting mother would call him good looking. Tall and very thin, he had an unusually long neck and wrists: 'Collar and Cuffs' was his father's nickname for him.

Nor could this prospective King be called 'good', in the term which Queen Victoria would use. He had his father's propensity for seeking amusement outside the home and Court circle, with consequences disastrous for his reputation. In the years since his death, many – often contradictory – stories have been told of Prince Eddy's sins: he knew every brothel in London, avers one source; he was a practising homosexual, says another; he was 'Jack the Ripper', murderer of several prostitutes in the East End of London, claims another biographer. Whatever the truth, it is certain that his family was wary of letting the Prince loose in the Courts of Europe and preferred to send him on a tour of the Far East where he could do less harm to the royal reputation.

His marital intentions prove his character's uncertainties. First, in 1889–90, he seemed set on marrying his cousin Princess Alix of Hesse-

Darmstadt and was heart-broken when she refused him (later marrying Tsar Nicholas II of Russia and ending her life in the massacre of the Romanovs at Ekaterinburg in 1918). But scarcely had the Prince ceased sighing for Alix than he was deep in love with Princess Hélène of Orleans, a member of the exiled royal family of France. Hélène herself returned his love, but her father refused to allow her to leave the Catholic Church, a vital step for a prospective Queen of Great Britain. Though Eddy declared that he would give up his inheritance for Hélène, and though the Princess herself made an impassioned plea to the Pope to allow her to change her religion, in the end the lovers had to agree to part.

Two or three months later, Eddy was writing fervently to one Lady Sybil St Clair-Erskine, a young English beauty. It was at this point that Queen Victoria stepped in, proffering the more suitable hand of the Princess May.

May had known Eddy all her life, though merely as one of the many royal cousins with whom she had played in her childhood. There can be no doubt that she knew well all his faults and failings, for her mother was an inveterate collector of royal gossip. On the other hand, the Princess had been brought up to view the career of queenship as the greatest to which one of her rank could aspire, an opportunity for unique service and responsibility as well as of grandeur. She would know, too, how slight were her chances of making any suitable match with a prince and so far she had shown no inclination to find a husband among the English or Scottish nobility.

In November 1891 May paid a visit to Queen Victoria at Balmoral, passing all the rigorous tests of manners, charm and intelligence which the Queen knew so well how to give to a potential royal bride. The Tecks, not a little ambitious and mercenary, were overjoyed by the prospect. The fickle Eddy – though he was known not to care for May at all deeply – was ready to marry (and, for once, to please his family), and on 3 December 1891 he dutifully proposed. May accepted him.

When she returned to London from the house-party at Luton Hoo where she had become engaged, the Princess was greeted with the cheers of the populace. It was her first, heady taste of future majesty.

For two months May was caught up in the joy of the Queen and the Prince and Princess of Wales in having provided so suitable a wife for the future King. She was made much of by the maternal, affectionate Alexandra of Denmark, Eddy's mother, and viewed with pride by the Prince of Wales, a connoisseur of feminine charms. Eddy, on his best behaviour, was attentive and, for once, quite respectable.

*Albert Victor,
Duke of
Clarence,
Mary of
Teck's first
fiancé, who
died in 1892*

The idyll ended the following January. After a bout of influenza, the Prince could not recover his health: pneumonia developed (complicated, say some sources, by the fact that he had contracted syphilis). In the early hours of 14 January the Prince and Princess of Wales, Eddy's brother and sisters and Princess May gathered to watch him die.

The country was shocked at the death of the heir-presumptive. A popular ballad sang:

> A nation wrapped in mourning
> Shed bitter tears today,
> For the noble Duke of Clarence
> And fair young Princess May.

The Princess herself, shocked and grief-stricken, the object of national pity, was immersed in the mourning rituals established by Queen Victoria in the years after the death of her own beloved Albert. 'The dear girl looks like a crushed flower, but is resigned and quiet and gentle,' wrote the Queen, '– it *does* make one *so sad* for her.'[4]

Disappointed as the Tecks were with this cruel blow to their child's happiness, they were not despondent about her future prospects. Duke Francis was heard, to his daughter's embarrassment, to mutter over and over again, 'It must be a Tsarevich, it must be a Tsarevich.' May knew, as did the rest of the family, that he was referring to the death of the Russian Tsarevich Nicholas in 1865, and his fiancée's subsequent marriage to his brother, the new Tsarevich Alexander. Eddy was dead, but now the crown had a new heir-presumptive in the Prince's brother George. It was obviously in the Duke of Teck's mind that May should marry George and retrieve her position.

It was in the mind of the Queen too. Sincere as her grief for Eddy was, she could not be blind to his faults, and she was fully aware that George was a far more suitable heir than his brother. A highly praised naval officer, with both aptitude for and interest in his career, the Prince yet managed delicately to show that he was ready for the new work now inevitable for his future. True, he had not long recovered from the disappointment of discouragement by his cousin Marie of Edinburgh, but he genuinely admired May – for her character as well as her looks and graces, and in the months following his brother's death, kept up an affectionate correspondence with her.

On 3 May 1893 George proposed marriage to May and was accepted. Perhaps it was not a love-match, on either side, but the circumstances fully explained that. Nevertheless, some months after their wedding, George wrote to May,

> You know by this time that I never do anything by halves, when I asked you to marry me, I was very fond of you, but not very much in love with you, but I saw in *you* the person I was capable of loving most deeply, if you only returned that love. . . . I have tried to understand you and to know you, and with the happy result that I know now that I do *love* you, darling girl, with all my *heart*, and am simply *devoted* to you. *I adore you, sweet May*, I can't say more than this.[5]

That Princess May came to reciprocate her husband's love is surely proved by the years of her devotion to him and her help in his work.

They were married on 6 July 1893, in the Chapel Royal, St James's,

George, Duke of York, May's bridegroom of 1893

amid an astounding array of royal relations, weighed down by furs and diamonds in the summer heat.

Then, a brief honeymoon at York Cottage, Sandringham (furnished by the Princess of Wales and her son, to May's disappointment: even then she was an ardent interior-decorator), before appearing at Cowes for the yacht-racing, in the mêlée of the royal family, which always turned out in force for the event, gathering from the four corners of Europe. And for the main it was to be this sort of festival at which the Princess, now

Princess May, photographed in the months before her wedding

Duchess of York, most generally figured over the next years. Since the Queen still refused to delegate any power to her own son, it could not be expected of her that she would treat her grandson any better: like his father, George chafed at inactivity, but no alternative was open to him. Those years at sea, which he had so much enjoyed, were over for good. The most he, and his wife, could expect was to be allowed to represent the family at cousins' weddings abroad or to attend provincial ceremonies, neither onerous nor demanding any initiative.

These were the first years of May's child-bearing – a duty she found tedious and unpleasant. The first child, third in line to the throne, was born in June 1894, within a year of the wedding. This future King Edward VIII was given seven names, and was always known by the last, 'David', in the family. In December 1895 Prince Albert (the future King George VI) was born, and then Princess Mary, the only daughter, in April 1897; three more sons, Henry, George and John, followed in the first years of the 20th century (John, the youngest, suffered from epilepsy and was brought up in country retirement, dying in 1919). In contrast to Princess Alexandra, May was an 'unmaternal' woman, always putting her husband's needs for her company, at home and abroad, before those of her children – but then, so did many women of her time and class, and she had a, surely *avant-garde*, notion of allowing them far more freedom than any earlier royal generation had enjoyed.

The year 1897 gave George and May more scope for their talents and for making a contribution to royal prestige. Two months after Queen Victoria celebrated her Diamond Jubilee, they set off for Ireland, to 'whip up' a little enthusiasm for the Crown. Despite the ever-present spectre of 'Irish troubles', they were well received, especially May in her green dress of Irish poplin, trimmed with Irish lace. Nevertheless, though the Queen approved their efforts, she was not ready to respond to her ministers' suggestion that the Yorks should take up residence in Dublin as permanent representatives of the monarchy.

Then, on 22 January 1901, Queen Victoria died, to be succeeded at last by her son, as Edward VII.

After so many years as Prince of Wales, the new King was loth to grant the title to his own heir (now Duke of Cornwall, a title which came naturally rather than by appointment), justifiably feeling that there would be confusion in the period of transition. It should not be imagined that Edward was miserly in this matter: in fact, he had so learned from his own experience under his mother's rule that he was anxious and eager to share power and ceremony with his son. Coming to the throne at the age of fifty-nine, he was well aware that he could not reign for long (in fact, he nearly died in 1902, from appendicitis), and he was fearful lest his son should come to reign with as little experience as he had. More than any king since the Middle Ages, Edward VII allotted duties and authority to his heir – which George himself was the first to appreciate.

At the same time, the King had a fair estimate of the growing importance of his overseas dominions. His own taste for European diplomacy did not blind him to the fact that much of the nation's international

'Four generations': Victoria with Alexandra of Denmark, Mary of Teck and the infant Prince Edward of York (the future King Edward VIII, Duke of Windsor) in 1894

The Prince and Princess of Wales visited *King George V and Queen Mary in their*
Cornwall in 1910, shortly before the death *coronation robes, 1911*
of Edward VII

prestige was based on the political and commercial importance of her
colonies. Thus, in March 1901, the Duke and Duchess were dispatched on
a world-tour that was to take in India and a visit to the Antipodes where
George was to open the first Parliament of the Australian Federation. No
heir to the throne – and certainly no heir's wife – had travelled so far, and
India, at least, was to see George and May again and again in future years as
they strove to bind their distant subjects closer to the home centre of
government. It was an investment which paid dividends in the loyalty
and service accorded to the mother-country and the Crown in the two
World Wars of the first half of the 20th century.

Eight days after George and May's return to England, in November
1901, the King bestowed the title of Prince of Wales on his son, and it was
as 'Victoria Mary, Princess of Wales' that May was known for the rest of
the decade.

Though the Prince had increasing concern with state business and
politics, and though the Princess made every effort to assist him, she never
sought to meddle, interfere or influence: her role, as she saw it, was to

help her husband elevate the prestige of the monarchy (though George loved his father deeply, both he and May deplored the excesses and vagaries of the King which had brought him so much disrepute), and her time in these years was divided between her children, her charities and the ceremonial duties which she shared with her husband. And the round of family visits, formal and informal, was still kept up, in this last era of peace before the First World War divided the network of international royal families beyond repair. The Kaiser and the young Tsar of Russia, Nicholas II, were first cousins of the Prince of Wales, and he was on intimate terms with both (Nicholas, in fact, was so like George in facial features and build that they were regularly mistaken for each other as young men). Though Edward and Alexandra continued to look warily on the Kaiser, especially in the difficult years of the Boer War, George and May had no prejudice against him – indeed, May was flattered by his smooth attentions to her. And still the family, descendants from Queen Victoria, was being enlarged. Its blood, if not its influence, was sent into the royal House of Spain, in 1906, with the wedding of George's cousin Princess Victoria Eugenie ('Ena') of Battenberg to King Alfonso. George and May, like so many other members of the family attending that wedding, were near to death in the anarchists' bombing of the royal procession in the streets of Madrid.

Princess Mary Adelaide had died in the autumn of 1897 and the Duke of Teck in 1900. Not content with seeing her daughter on the path to the throne, it had been Mary Adelaide's fervent wish to have her second son, 'Frank', marry George's sister Maud. Though Maud herself was reputedly in love with the dashing young officer (all May's brothers were in the British army), the Prince could work up no enthusiasm for her – fortunately, as it transpired, for so large did his gambling debts become in the 1890s that it was found necessary to send him off to India, out of harm's way – with a firm warning to his commanding officer not to treat him too 'regally'. Frank never married, since he was enamoured of a married woman who would never be acceptable to his family, and for years he was on bad terms with his sister. All three Teck brothers fought in – and survived – the Boer War and, though Frank died in 1910, both 'Alge' and 'Dolly' lived to see their sister Queen. Adolphus, second Duke of Teck, married Lady Margaret Grosvenor, daughter of the Duke of Westminster (whose dowry was a welcome addition to the Teck family funds), and Alexander married the Prince of Wales's cousin Princess Alice of Albany.

I have lost my best friend and the best of fathers [wrote George in his diary in May 1910, when he succeeded Edward VII on the throne].

. . . I am heart-broken and overwhelmed with grief but God will help me in my great responsibilities, and darling May will be my comfort as she has always been.[6]

In the quarter-century of King George V's reign, both God and 'darling May' fulfilled those hopes. Scarcely had the King weathered a constitutional crisis than he was plunged into the trials of the First World War. Perhaps that war was more terrible to the King than to any of his subjects, for his own close relations were numbered among his major enemies. And, in 1918, his Russian cousins were massacred in the aftermath of revolution.

May, too, had her sorrows. While she worked tirelessly throughout the war, encouraging and comforting her husband and undertaking innumerable public duties, she had the heartache of knowing that her beloved aunt Augusta, Grand Duchess of Mecklenburg-Strelitz, was in Germany, dying, aged ninety-four, even in the midst of the war, in 1916: the old lady contrived to have a message sent home that it was a stout 'English heart' which had ceased to beat among the enemy.

In 1917, overwhelmed by the nation's vehement hatred of all things German, the King decreed that his House should no longer bear the name 'Saxe-Coburg-Gotha' (which his grandmother Victoria's marriage to Prince Albert had given it) but that of 'Windsor', requesting his relations in England to discard their foreign names and titles too. Thus the Duke of Teck became Marquess of Cambridge and his brother Alexander Earl of Athlone. There was never any doubt but that they, and their sister Queen Mary, totally identified with Britain in the war, despite their close ties with Germany. Nevertheless, for all the bitterness engendered by the dividing loyalties of the war, the King and Queen were later among the most generous providers of aid and comfort to cousins driven from thrones and homes by defeat and revolution.

Mary of Teck made a supreme success of her marriage and career. The royal Silver Jubilee of 1935 was a triumph of national affection for the monarchy, rivalled only by widespread scenes of grief the following year at the death of George V.

There was no consolation of retirement for Queen Mary such as Queen Victoria had demanded for years after the death of her husband. Within just a few months of King George's death, their son David, the new King Edward VIII, plunged the monarchy into crisis. By seeking to marry an American divorcée, Mrs Simpson, he was openly flouting the Anglican Church – of which, he, as King, was Head – by opposing its ruling against the sanctified remarriage of divorcés. To Queen Mary, with her un-

A Victorian figure in the modern age: Queen Mary in the last years of her life

qualified and unquestioning respect for monarchy and Church, there seemed only one resolution to the dilemma: the King must renounce Mrs Simpson. Mary, whose head rather than her heart had governed her own decision to marry, understood her eldest son's unhappiness but could not condone his determination to continue on a course which, it seemed to her, could bring the monarchy into disrepute – even, some said, to ruin. While statesmen and clergy debated the problem, while the nation

Queen Mary 'wooding' at Badminton during the Second World War, assisted by her dispatch-riders

wrangled the case for and against the King's marriage, Queen Mary remained aloof and silent. When Edward VIII abdicated and went into self-imposed exile with his bride, with his brother Albert taking his place on the throne, as King George VI, their mother presented a calm exterior to the world whatever her inward feelings. Indeed, she has often been criticised for her lack of sympathy towards her son – though, in his memoirs, the Duke of Windsor (as Edward VIII became after abdicating) said no word against her stance of 1936; even after the crisis situation had subsided, it was many years before the Queen and her son met again, and never, to the end of her life, would she consent to receive his Duchess. But Mary of Teck's moral code was not that of the 'enlightened' 20th century: she was a Victorian through to her ramrod backbone, herself a lifelong devotee to duty who expected similar high standards from her family.

She could have no complaints of dereliction against her son George VI and his consort (the former Lady Elizabeth Bowes-Lyon). They brought patient submission and uncomplaining self-sacrifice to their new, supremely trying, way of life, and rapidly restored the prestige of the royal House. The Second World War crowned their efforts, with their tireless travelling through the country at great risk to their lives. Queen Mary was by then in her seventies, though still active and alert. Part of the war she spent in the country, at Badminton, but for the rest she took an appreciable share in the family's arduous round, a majestic figure trampling through bomb-sites, touring factories and reviewing troops.

By the time of her death, on 24 March 1953, Queen Mary was 'an institution', the *doyenne* of the royal family, for she had seen six reigns and had played her part in the life of the royal family and the nation in all of them. And Queen Victoria's trust in that insignificant Princess of Teck had been well justified by 'May's' years of service to crown, kingdom and empire.

REFERENCES

1 JOAN OF KENT

1 Henry Knighton, *Chronicon*, ed. J. R. Lumby (1889–95), vol. II, pp. 57–8.
2 Froissart, *Oeuvres*, ed. K. de Lettenhove (1870–7), vol. II, p. 243.
3 *Chronique des quatre premiers Valois*, ed. S. Luce (1862), p. 123.
4 Ibid., pp. 123–5.
5 L. Babinet, *Jeanne de Kent* (1894), pp. 12–13.
6 *Life of the Black Prince*, ed. and trans. M. K. Lodge and E. C. Pope (Clarendon Press, 1910), p. 152.
7 M. Collis, *The Hurling Time* (Faber & Faber, 1958), p. 134.
8 Ibid., p. 279.

2 ANNE NEVILLE

1 'Rous Roll', ed. W. Pickering (1859), text for plate 62.
2 Ibid., text for plate 56.
3 *Lettres de Louis XI . . .*, ed. J. Vaesen et al. (1883–1910), vol. IV, p. 113.
4 *Original Letters Illustrative of English History*, ed. H. Ellis (1827), second series, vol. I, p. 134.
5 *State Papers and Manuscripts . . . Milan*, ed. A. B. Hinds (1912), vol. I, pp. 117–18.
6 *The History of Commines Englished by Thomas Danett* (1897), vol. I, p. 183.
7 *Ingulphus Chronicle of the Abbey of Croyland*, ed. H. T. Riley (1854), pp. 469–70.
8 Ibid., pp. 496–7.
9 Ibid., pp. 571–3.

3 CATHERINE OF ARAGON

1 M. A. E. Wood, *Letters of Royal and Illustrious Ladies* (1852), vol. I, pp. 121–2.
2 *Calendar of State Papers: Spanish* (State Paper Commission, 1886–1947), vol. I, p. 468.
3 F. A. Mumby, *The Youth of Henry VIII* (Constable, 1913), p. 41.
4 A. Strickland, *Lives of the Queens of England* (1861), vol. II, pp. 478–9.
5 Ibid., p. 483.
6 Mumby, op. cit., p. 73.
7 Strickland, op. cit., p. 553.

4 CAROLINE OF ANSPACH

1 R. L. Arkell, *Caroline of Anspach* (Oxford University Press, 1939), p. 7.
2 A. D. Greenwood, *Lives of the Hanoverian Queens of England* (George Bell & Sons, 1909), p. 18.
3 W. H. Wilkins, *Caroline the Illustrious* (Longmans Green, 1901), vol. I, pp. 29–30.
4 Lord Hervey, *Some Materials Towards Memoirs of the Reign of George II* (Eyre & Spottiswoode, 1931), vol. I, p. 43.
5 *A Selection from Papers of the Earls of Marchmont* (1831), vol. II, p. 409.
6 Dr Doran, *Lives of the Queens of England of the House of Hanover* (1855), vol. I, p. 229.
7 H. Walpole, *Memoirs and Portraits*, ed. M. Hodgart (Batsford, 1963), p. 23.

5 AUGUSTA OF SAXE-GOTHA

1 *The Misfortunate Margravine*, ed. N. Rosenthal (Macmillan, 1970), p. 92.
2 *The Diary of the First Earl of Egmont* (Historical Manuscripts Commission, 1923), vol. II, pp. 263–4.
3 *Lord Hervey's Memoirs*, ed. R. Sedgwick (William Kimber, 1952), p. 172.
4 R. L. Arkell, *Caroline of Anspach* (Oxford University Press, 1939), p. 270.
5 *Gentleman's Magazine* (17 April 1736), p. 231.
6 Arkell, op. cit., p. 270.
7 Ibid., p. 270.
8 Ibid., p. 270.
9 Ibid., p. 270.
10 Sedgwick, op. cit., p. 186.
11 Ibid., p. 186.
12 Ibid., p 275.
13 Ibid., p. 276.
14 Ibid., p. 280.
15 H. Walpole, *Memoirs and Portraits*, ed. M. Hodgart (Batsford, 1963), p. 8.
16 *Memoirs and Correspondence of George, First Lord Lyttelton* (1845), vol. I, p. 440.
17 J. Brooke, *King George III* (Constable, 1972), p. 30.
18 Ibid., p. 26.
19 *Letters of George III to Lord Bute*, ed. R. Sedgwick (Macmillan, 1939), pp. 2–3.

6 CAROLINE OF BRUNSWICK-WOLFENBUTTEL

1 James Harris, Earl of Malmesbury, *Diaries and Correspondence* (1844), vol. III, pp. 169–70.
2 Ibid., p. 211.
3 Ibid., p. 218.
4 *The Diary of a Lady-in-Waiting . . .*, ed. A. F. Steuart (The Bodley Head, 1908), p. 37.

5 *The Correspondence and Diaries of . . . J. W. Croker . . .*, ed. L. J. Jennings (1885), vol. I, p. 232.

6 *Letters of the Princess Charlotte, 1811–17*, ed. A. Aspinall (Home & van Thal, 1949), pp. 137–8.

7   ALEXANDRA OF DENMARK

1 *Dearest Child*, ed. R. Fulford (Evans Brothers, 1964), p. 223.

2 Ibid., p. 293.

3 Ibid., p. 313.

4 Ibid., p. 313.

5 Ibid., p. 294.

6 Ibid., p. 294.

7 Ibid., pp. 223–4.

8 G. Battiscombe, *Queen Alexandra* (Constable, 1969), p. 5.

9 Ibid., p. 152.

8   MARY OF TECK

1 *My Dear Duchess*, ed. A. L. Kennedy (John Murray, 1956), p. 116.

2 *Your Dear Letter*, ed. R. Fulford (Evans Brothers, 1971), p. 69.

3 J. Pope-Hennessy, *Queen Mary, 1867–1953* (George Allen & Unwin, 1959), p. 165.

4 Ibid., p. 228.

5 Ibid., p. 280.

6 Ibid., p. 417.

FURTHER READING

I JOAN OF KENT

Short (and not wholly adequate) biographies of Joan are *Jeanne de Kent* by L. Babinet (1894) and *The Fair Maid of Kent* by F. Chambers (1877). They may be supplemented by tentative identifications of Joan in A. Gransden, 'The alleged rape by Edward III of the Countess of Salisbury' (*English Historical Review*, 1972, vol. LXXXVII) and M. Galway, 'Joan of Kent and the Order of the Garter' (*University of Birmingham Historical Journal*, 1947, vol. I).

The life of the Black Prince is well covered in R. P. Dunn Pattison, *The Black Prince* (Methuen, 1910); H. D. Sedgwick, *The Life of the Black Prince* (Bobbs-Merrill, USA, 1932); B. Emerson, *The Black Prince* (Weidenfeld & Nicolson, 1976); and H. Cole, *The Black Prince* (Granada, 1976).

Joan's and Edward's wills may be found in J. Nichols, *A Collection of all the Wills . . . of Kings and Queens of England . . .* (1780).

The best biography of Richard II is still that by A. Steel (Cambridge University Press, 1941), but H. F. Hutchinson, *The Hollow Crown* (Eyre & Spottiswoode, 1961), is also worth reading, and G. Mathew, *The Court of Richard II* (John Murray, 1968) provides a valuable picture of the social life of the nobility.

S. Armitage-Smith's *John of Gaunt* (Constable, 1904) and G. Kay's biography of Alice Perrers, *Lady of the Sun* (Frederick Muller, 1966) are also useful.

Of the many chronicles of the period, the most relevant are *The Life of the Black Prince by the herald of Sir John Chandos*, edited and translated by M. K. Pope and E. C. Lodge (Clarendon Press, 1910); *Chronique de Jean le Bel*, edited by J. Viard and E. Deprez (Société de l'histoire de France, 1904–5); *Chroniques des quatre premiers Valois*, edited by S. Luce (1862); and the three main editions of Froissart's Chronicles by S. Luce et al. (1869–99), K. de Lettenhove (1867–77) and Lord Berners (Tudor Translations, 1901–3).

M. McKisack's *The Fourteenth Century* (Oxford University Press, 1959) provides the mainstream background of the period, and M. Collis, *The Hurling Time* (Faber & Faber, 1958) deals with the French war and the Peasants' Revolt.

2 ANNE NEVILLE

There is no biography of Anne Neville apart from the chapter in Agnes Strickland's *Lives of the Queens of England* (1855), vol. II. This work is of very dubious merit, combining inaccuracy of fact with a good deal of unwarranted speculation, and treating contemporary sources uncritically.

Various chronicles of the time deal with the main events of Anne's life. The most important are the edition of the 'Rous Roll' by W. Pickering (1859), of the Croyland Chronicle by H. T. Riley (1854) and of the memoirs of Philippe de Commines by T. Danett (1897). To these the letters of Louis XI may be added, edited by J. Vaesen et al. (1883–1910).

Secondary sources on Anne's family and contemporaries are more numerous. There are two excellent biographies of her father, the Earl of Warwick, both entitled *Warwick the Kingmaker*, by C. W. Oman (1891) and P. Murray Kendall (George Allen & Unwin, 1957). Margaret of Anjou's biographers are P. Erlanger, translated by E. Hyams (Elek Books, 1970) and J. J. Bagley (Herbert Jenkins, 1948). Numerous books have been written on Edward IV and Richard III: the best of the former are by C. L. Scofield (Longmans Green, 1923) and C. Ross (Eyre Methuen, 1974), and of the latter by P. Murray Kendall (George Allen & Unwin, 1955). There is also a life of Louis XI by P. Murray Kendall (George Allen & Unwin, 1971).

Of the many books suitable for background reading, the most useful is E. F. Jacob's *The Fifteenth Century* (Oxford University Press, 1961). Of the many books on the Wars of the Roses, those by J. R. Lander (Secker & Warburg, 1965) and H. Cole (Hart-Davis MacGibbon, 1973) bring clarity to a complex situation. A more personal view is taken in R. L. Storey's *The End of the House of Lancaster* (Barrie & Rockliff, 1966).

3 CATHERINE OF ARAGON

There are several excellent biographies of Catherine of Aragon, of which the most important are by Francesca Claremont (Robert Hale, 1939) and Garrett Mattingly (Jonathan Cape, 1942), with M. M. Luke's *Catherine the Queen* (Frederick Muller, 1968), besides her life in Agnes Strickland's *Lives of the Queens of England* (1851, reprinted by Portway, 1973), vol. II.

Letters written by Catherine were printed in M. A. E. Wood's *Letters of Royal and Illustrious Ladies* (1852).

A useful work on the Princess's Spanish background is *Ferdinand and Isabella* by F. Fernandez-Armesto (Weidenfeld & Nicolson, 1975).

Of the many biographies of Henry VIII, that by A. F. Pollard (Goupil, 1902) is still valuable, as is F. A. Mumby's *The Youth of Henry VIII* (Constable, 1913), with more recent works by John Bowle (George Allen & Unwin, 1964) and J. J. Bagley (Batsford, 1962).

Henry VIII and his Court (Weidenfeld & Nicolson, 1971) provides fine background material, while J. E. Paul's *Catherine of Aragon and her Friends* (Burns & Oates, 1966) fills in, in more detail, the Queen's own circle.

For the principles and policies which comprised Tudor government in these years and which bore so heavily on Catherine's life, three books give a clear overall picture: J. D. Mackie, *The Early Tudors, 1485–1558* (Oxford University Press, 1952); H. A. L. Fisher, *The Political History of England from the Accession of Henry VII to the Death of Henry VIII* (Longmans Green, 1928); and G. R. Elton, *England under the Tudors* (Methuen, 1955).

4   CAROLINE OF ANSPACH

There are three excellent biographies of Caroline of Anspach: that by R. L. Arkell (Oxford University Press, 1939); *Caroline the Illustrious* by W. H. Wilkins (Longmans Green, 1901); and *Caroline of England* by P. Quennell (Collins, 1939). Her life is outlined in Dr Doran's *Lives of the Queens of England of the House of Hanover* (1855) and A. D. Greenwood's *Lives of the Hanoverian Queens of England* (George Bell & Sons, 1909).

The best biography of Caroline's husband is *George II* by Charles Chevenix Trench (Allen Lane, 1973) and of her friend Robert Walpole the book by J. H. Plumb (Cresset Press, 1956).

The House of Hanover by Alvin Redman (Redman, 1960) provides a useful background to the problems and personalities of the family, which may be filled out by the biography of Sophia of Hanover by M. Kroll (Gollancz, 1973) and the Electress's memoirs (1888). There is a recent biography of George I by J. Marlowe (Weidenfeld & Nicolson, 1974).

From primary sources fascinating background material may be found in Horace Walpole's *Memoirs of the reign of George II*, edited by Lord Holland (1847), his letters, edited by Mrs Paget Toynbee (Clarendon Press, 1903–5), his *Reminiscences . . .* (Clarendon Press, 1924) and his *Memoirs and Portraits*, edited by M. Hodgart (Batsford, 1963); and in *Some Materials towards Memoirs of the Reign of George II*, by Caroline's prejudiced, waspish confidant Lord Hervey, or the shorter *Lord Hervey's Memoirs*, both edited by R. Sedgwick (Eyre & Spottiswoode, 1931 and William Kimber, 1952, respectively). *Letters to and from Henrietta Howard, Countess of Suffolk*, edited by J. W. Croker (1824); *The Memoirs of Viscountess Sundon* (Mrs Clay), edited by K. Thompson (1847); and *The Diary of Mary, Countess Cowper, 1714–20* (1864) give lively sketches of Caroline's Court.

The best introduction to the political, social and economic history of the early Hanoverian years is *The Whig Supremacy* by Basil Williams (Oxford University Press, 1965).

5   AUGUSTA OF SAXE-GOTHA

Unfortunately there is no biography of Augusta of Saxe-Gotha, and the details of her life must be gleaned from biographies of other members of the royal family and from the diaries and memoirs of contemporaries. The dearth of information on the Gotha family is partly rectified by the comments of James Boswell, who visited the duchy in 1764, *Boswell on the Grand Tour: Germany and Switzerland, 1764*, edited by F. A. Pottle (Heinemann, 1953).

There have been several biographies written of Frederick, Prince of Wales, of which the most valuable are *Poor Fred, the People's Prince*, by Sir George Young (Oxford University Press, 1937); A. Edwards, *Frederick Louis, Prince of Wales* (Staples Press, 1947); and M. Marples, *Poor Fred and the Butcher* (Michael Joseph, 1970). His relations with his parents are also traced in books listed for the previous chapter.

Of the many biographies of George III, that by John Brooke (Constable, 1972) is the best of the most recent. N. Pain's *George III at Home* (Eyre Methuen, 1975) provides interesting personal details. The King's correspondence with Lord Bute was edited by R. Sedgwick (Macmillan, 1939), and there is a biography of that Prime Minister by J. A. Lovat-Fraser (Cambridge University Press, 1912).

Numerous diaries and memoirs of the 18th century have been published, the most relevant here being *Hervey's Memoirs of the Reign of George II*, edited by R. Sedgwick (Eyre & Spottiswoode, 1931 and William Kimber, 1952), and Walpole's work of the same title (1847) – though these biased sources must be treated with caution. Less controversial are *The Political Journal of George Bubb Dodington*, edited by J. Carswell and L. A. Dralle (Oxford University Press, 1965) and *The Diary of the First Earl of Egmont* (Historical Manuscripts Commission, 1923).

The 'Oxford Histories of England' *The Whig Supremacy* by B. Williams and *The Reign of George III*, by S. Watson (Oxford University Press, 1962 and 1960 respectively) still provide the basic background material, but *The Wickedest Age* by A. Lloyd (David & Charles, 1971) is a livelier study.

6   CAROLINE OF BRUNSWICK-WOLFENBUTTEL

Besides the two works on the Hanoverian queens of England by Doran and Greenwood cited in previous chapters, the main biographies of Caroline are those by Sir Edward Parry (Ernest Benn, 1930) and J. Richardson – *The Disastrous Marriage* (Jonathan Cape, 1960).

Of the innumerable books on the life of George IV, the following are the best: C. Hibbert, *George IV: Prince of Wales* and *George IV: Regent and King* (Longman, 1972 and 1975 respectively); J. Richardson, *George IV: A Portrait* (Sidgwick & Jackson, 1966); R. Fulford, *George IV* (Duckworth, 1949). There is a biography of Mrs Fitzherbert by A. Leslie (Hutchinson, 1960) and a study of the marriage in *Mrs Fitzherbert and George IV* by W. H. Wilkins (Longmans Green, 1905).

The most useful biography of Princess Charlotte is by D. Creston, *The Regent and his Daughter* (Thornton Butterworth, 1932) and her letters, 1811–17, have been edited by A. Aspinall (Home & van Thal, 1949).

A great many memoirs, diaries and selections of correspondence for the period have been published, but the most useful here are: *The Life and Times of Henry, Lord Brougham, written by himself* (1871); *The Diary of a Lady-in-Waiting . . . Lady Charlotte Bury . . .*, edited by A. F. Steuart (The Bodley Head, 1908); and the Earl of Malmesbury's *Diaries and Correspondence* (1844).

7   ALEXANDRA OF DENMARK

An excellent recent biography of Queen Alexandra is that by Georgina Battiscombe (Constable, 1969); of the rest, the best are *Queen Alexandra* by Sir Arthur George (Chapman & Hall, 1934) and *The Private Life of Queen Alexandra* by H. Madol (Hutchinson, 1940).

The biographies of Edward VII by Sir Sidney Lee (Macmillan, 1925–7) and Sir Philip Magnus (John Murray, 1964) are the accepted 'standard' works, but details are filled in by V. Cowles's *Edward VII and his Circle* (Hamish Hamilton, 1956) and G. Brook-Shepherd's *Uncle of Europe* (Collins, 1974).

The biography of Queen Victoria by Elizabeth Longford provides background material for the Queen's relationship with her daughter-in-law, as do the volumes of her published letters, edited by Viscount Esher et al., and the series *Dearest Child, Dearest Mamma* and *Your Dear Letter*, edited by Roger Fulford (Evans Brothers, 1964–71).

There is a biography of Alexandra's father, Christian IX of Denmark, by H. Madol (Collins, 1939) and one of her brother, King George I of Greece, by W. Christmas (Eveleigh Nash, 1914).

8   MARY OF TECK

The main biography of Mary of Teck is that by James Pope-Hennessy, *Queen Mary* (George Allen & Unwin, 1959), though there are other, quite valuable works by K. Woodward (Hutchinson, 1954) and C. Cavendish (A. E. Marriott, 1930) also.

Of the many biographies of King George V, the 'official' text is that by Sir Harold Nicolson, *George V: His Life and Reign* (Constable, 1952), which can well be read with biographies written by J. Gore (John Murray, 1941) and W. J. Makin (George Newnes, 1936).

For the early part of 'May's' life, works cited for the previous chapter are useful, as are *My Memories of Six Reigns*, by Princess Marie Louise (Evans Brothers, 1956); *For My Grandchildren*, by Princess Alice, Countess of Athlone (Evans Brothers, 1966); the *Memoir* of Princess Mary Adelaide, Duchess of Teck by C. Kinloch Cooke (1900); and *Clarence* by M. Harrison (W. H. Allen, 1972). The later life of Queen Mary by the biographers named above may be supplemented by lives of her two elder sons, especially Edward VIII's (the Duke of Windsor's) auto-biography *A King's Story* (Cassell, 1951) and *The Life and Reign of King George VI* by Sir John Wheeler-Bennett (Macmillan, 1958).

INDEX